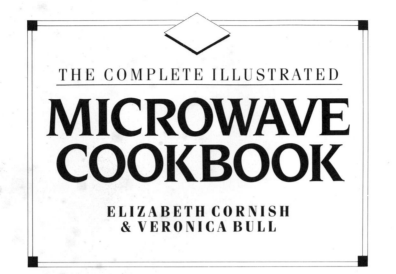

THE COMPLETE ILLUSTRATED

MICROWAVE COOKBOOK

**ELIZABETH CORNISH
& VERONICA BULL**

THE COMPLETE ILLUSTRATED

MICROWAVE COOKBOOK

ELIZABETH CORNISH
& VERONICA BULL

VIKING O'NEIL

Viking O'Neil
Penguin Books Australia Ltd
487 Maroondah Highway, PO Box 257
Ringwood, Victoria 3134, Australia

This Australian edition published by Penguin
Books Australia Ltd 1988

ISBN 0-670-90065-6

This book was designed and produced by
Quintet Publishing Limited
6 Blundell Street
London N7 9BH

Art Director: Peter Bridgewater
Editor: Judith Simons
Photographers: Trevor Wood, Michael Bull
Home Economist: Veronica Bull

Typeset in Great Britain by
Central Southern Typesetters, Eastbourne
Manufactured in Hong Kong by Regent
Publishing Services Limited
Printed in Hong Kong by Leefung-Asco
Printers Limited

CONTENTS

A selection of cookware suitable for use in the microwave oven. Plain plastic dishes, specially designed for microwaving, are available in many different shapes and sizes. Plain glass ovenware and most ceramic dishes may also be used safely.

ABOUT THE MICROWAVE OVEN

IF YOU are new to cooking with the microwave, the first thing to do is to read the instruction booklet supplied with your model. This will tell you all you need to know about how your cooker works and how to operate it.

Microwave cookers work by emitting concentrated infra red radiation that penetrates and therefore heats food much faster than conventional cookers. They consequently save considerably on cooking time.

The microwave is like any other kitchen appliance that makes life easier for the cook. Once you are used to it, which takes remarkably little time for such a sophisticated gadget, experience will tell you how long it will take to cook or reheat a given dish. If in doubt, always undercook – you can easily add on another minute or so.

To familiarize yourself with the cooker try baking a potato. Scrub the potato and prick the skin a few times with a fork. Lay it on a piece of absorbent kitchen paper and cook on full power for about 6 minutes for a 185 g/6 oz potato. Stop cooking half-way through to turn the potato over. A successfully baked potato will demonstrate how easy microwave cooking is.

Remember to stir or rearrange items during cooking or the food may not be evenly cooked, and

always cover a dish with a lid or plastic wrap which you have pierced in two or three places with a knife to make vents through which the steam can escape.

Don't use anything metallic in the microwave, and this includes china decorated with silver or gold leaf. If you want to test if a dish is microwave-proof, put it in the oven next to a cup of water and cook on full for a minute. If the water is hot and the dish stays cool, it is safe to use. If the dish is hotter than the water, avoid using it.

Always prick the skins of vegetables and fish to prevent them from bursting. Eggs should always be pricked for the same reason. Never put an egg in its shell in the microwave – it will explode.

All the recipes in this book are timed for a 700-watt oven, and where the recipe times are not specific, this is to avoid errors. A microwave may be a scientific instrument, but even identical ovens may cook at slightly different rates, and neither cooks nor food can be standardized – no two carrots are the same shape and no two cooks cut them in the same way.

However, the following can be taken as a general guide for ovens with a different power rating from that of the model used in the book. For every minute of cooking time specified in these recipes, add 5 seconds for a 650-watt oven, 10 seconds for a 600-watt oven and 30 seconds for a 500-watt oven. But remember, it is *always* safer to undercook and test.

Crockery, cutlery, glassware and cookware with metal parts such as that shown above must NOT be used in a microwave oven.

COOKING WITH

Soups

AND HORS D'OEUVRES

ELIZABETH CORNISH

SOUPS AND HORS D'OEUVRES

SOUPS and hors d'oeuvres can be prepared ahead of time for reheating, which in a microwave will not spoil either their good looks or taste. Some soups and starters can be assembled and cooked at the last minute, others can be eaten cold.

When you are cooking with a microwave, it is particularly easy to plan a menu as much to please the eye as the palate, because foods keep their natural shapes and colours. This is important when you are entertaining, as there is nothing more pleasing to guests than having something really appetizing placed before them, and nothing more pleasing to a host than an expression of delighted anticipation – and clean plates at the end of the meal.

When you're not entertaining, a soup or a starter, or a soup *and* a starter, can make a whole meal, especially when served with bread and salad.

Home-made soups, like home-made bread, are a simple luxury that until recently many cooks could not spare the time to make. With a microwave, you can enjoy the satisfying flavour and natural goodness of a soup made from fresh ingredients in only a little more time than it takes to heat up a tin, or reconstitute a packet.

There is a soup in this book to suit every occasion and taste, from delicate cool numbers for summer dinner parties to a thick fish soup that will leave you wanting only a siesta to follow.

As for starters – there is a wide and interesting range of appetizers both hot and cold, light and substantial, so that you will have several choices to complement your main course. For an elegant late-night supper you could opt simply to serve a selection of starters, with perhaps fruit and coffee to follow.

CONTENTS

SPINACH AND RICOTTA PANCAKES

S E R V E S   4   /   S E T :   H I G H

Ingredients

185 g/6 oz flour
a pinch of salt
2 eggs
475 ml/¾ pt milk
1 tablespoon melted butter or oil
SPINACH AND RICOTTA FILLING
1 kg/2 lb fresh spinach
30 g/1 oz butter
250 g/8 oz ricotta cheese
salt and freshly ground black pepper
a pinch of nutmeg

Although pancakes can't themselves be made in the microwave, there is no better way of heating up stuffed pancakes so that each one tastes as if it had been freshly made and the edges aren't dry and leathery.

◆ First make the pancakes. Sift the flour with the salt into a bowl, make a well in the middle and break in the eggs. Add the milk slowly, beating to incorporate the flour.

◆ When half the milk has been added, stir in the melted butter or oil and beat until smooth. Add the remaining milk. The batter should be the consistency of thin cream. Leave it to stand for at least 30 minutes.

◆ For the filling, wash the spinach and discard any tough stalks and discoloured leaves.

◆ Put the butter in a large dish and cook for 1 minute until melted. Cram in the spinach, cover and cook for 6 minutes, turning the dish once, until the spinach is soft but still bright emerald green.

◆ Chop the spinach with the ricotta, mixing well, and season with salt, pepper and nutmeg.

◆ Make the pancakes on the burner. Pour a little oil into a heavy based pan and heat until very hot. Stir the batter well and spoon in enough to coat the bottom of the pan. Tilt and jiggle the pan over the heat until the pancake has set, then toss or turn it over with a spatula and cook the other side.

◆ Discard your first pancake as it will be too oily.

◆ Pile the pancakes on a plate as you make them, but don't attempt to keep them hot, or they will dry out.

◆ Divide the filling between the pancakes and roll up. Pack them into an oblong dish, cover with vented plastic wrap and cook for 2–3 minutes until hot through.

◆ Serve with tomato sauce (see recipe for Stuffed Cabbage Leaves).

BORLOTTI BEAN SOUP

SERVES 4 / SET: HIGH

Ingredients

250 g/8 oz soup macaroni

oil

625 ml/1 pt boiling meat stock

1½ tbsp tomato paste

440 g/14 oz canned borlotti beans, drained

salt and freshly ground black pepper

◆ Put the macaroni in a large dish with a little oil and pour over half the stock. Cover and cook for 8 minutes.

◆ Add the tomato paste, diluted in the rest of the stock, and the borlotti beans, cover and cook for 4 minutes.

◆ Season to taste and serve, with grated cheese if liked.

Borlotti Bean Soup

MUSSEL AND POTATO SOUP

SERVES 4 / SET: HIGH

Ingredients

750 g/1½ lb mussels

2 tbsp oil

1 small glass dry white wine

1 small onion, chopped

1 clove garlic, crushed

2 rashers bacon, chopped

625 ml/1 pt boiling fish stock (see recipe for Fish Soup).

250 g/8 oz cooked potato, diced

90 g/3 oz rice

salt and freshly ground black pepper

◆ Scrub the mussels thoroughly under cold running water and scrape away their beards. Discard any that are broken or damaged.

◆ Put half the oil in a large dish with the wine and cook for 2 minutes, until very hot. Add the mussels. Cover and cook for about 3 minutes, stirring halfway through, until the shells open. Discard any mussels that remain closed.

◆ Remove the mussels from their shells, keeping some shells for decoration. Put mussels and cooking liquor to one side.

◆ Put the remaining oil in the dish with the onion, garlic and bacon, cover and cook for 3 minutes. Add half the fish stock, stir in the cooked potato and rice. Cover and cook for 10 minutes, until the rice is tender.

◆ Stir in the remaining fish stock, add the mussels and their cooking liquor and season to taste.

◆ Serve, decorated with a couple of mussels in their shells if liked.

FISH SOUP

SERVES 4 / SET: HIGH

Ingredients

1 tbsp olive oil
1 onion, chopped
1 clove garlic, crushed
½ fennel bulb, chopped
2 large or 4 small tomatoes, skinned and chopped
1 kg/2 lb mixed white fish, cleaned and skinned
2 tsp turmeric
625 ml/1 pt boiling water or fish stock (see below)
salt and freshly ground black pepper
Parmesan cheese

NOTE *To make a fish stock, put the fish trimmings in a large dish, add a bay leaf, a piece each of carrot, celery and onion and pour over 625 ml/1 pt boiling water. Cover and cook in the microwave for 7 minutes, then strain off the stock.*

◆ Put the oil in a large dish and cook for 30 seconds. Stir in the onion, garlic and fennel, cover and cook for 5 minutes.

◆ Add the tomatoes and fish, stir in the turmeric, then pour over the water or stock. Cover and cook for 8–10 minutes, until the fish is done.

◆ Season to taste and serve with plenty of Parmesan cheese.

CHESTNUT SOUP

SERVES 4 / SET: HIGH

Ingredients

30 g/1 oz butter
1 large onion, chopped
1 carrot, chopped
1 stick celery, chopped
440 g/14 oz canned chestnut purée
940 ml/1½ pt very hot milk and stock, mixed
salt and freshly ground black pepper

NOTE *If making this soup with fresh chestnuts, peel them according to the instructions in the recipe for Savoury Stuffed Vine Leaves and cook them in the stock and milk for 10–12 minutes until soft, then blend the soup in a liquidizer.*

◆ Put the butter in a large dish and cook for one minute until melted. Stir in the onion, carrot and celery. Cover and cook for 5 minutes.

◆ Stir in the chestnut purée and pour over the hot milk and stock. Cover and cook for 6 minutes.

◆ Season and serve.

Chestnut Soup

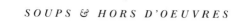

MINESTRONE ALLA MILANESE

S E R V E S   6   /   S E T :   H I G H

Ingredients

4 rashers bacon

30 g/1 oz butter

1 onion, chopped

1 clove garlic, crushed

1 carrot, chopped

1 stick celery, chopped

2 zucchini, sliced

90 g/3 oz rice

940 ml/1 1/2 pt boiling chicken stock

1/4 white cabbage, shredded

500 g/1 lb peas

220 g/7 oz canned tomatoes, mashed, with juice

a small handful of parsley, chopped

a few leaves each of basil and sage

salt and freshly ground black pepper

Parmesan cheese

◆ Put the bacon on a plate or bacon rack covered with absorbent kitchen paper and microwave for 4 minutes, turning once. Cut into pieces and set aside.

◆ Put the butter in a large bowl and cook for 1 minute until melted. Stir in the onion, garlic, carrot and celery, cover with vented plastic wrap and cook for 4 minutes.

◆ Add the zucchini and rice, pour over half the stock, cover and cook for 10 minutes.

◆ Add the cabbage, peas, tomatoes and herbs, pour on the rest of the stock, cover and cook for 5 minutes.

◆ Season to taste and serve with Parmesan cheese.

PASTA AND PEA SOUP

SERVES 4 / SET: HIGH

Ingredients

30 g/1 oz butter
1 onion, chopped
1 clove garlic, crushed
1 stick celery, finely chopped
1 carrot, finely chopped
1 tbsp tomato paste
625 ml/1 pt boiling beef stock
125 g/4 oz pasta shapes
220 g/7 oz peas
salt and freshly ground black pepper
a handful of parsley, chopped (optional)
Parmesan cheese (optional)

◆ Put the butter in a large dish and cook for 1 minute until melted. Stir in the onion, garlic, celery and carrot. Cover with vented plastic wrap and cook for 4 minutes.

◆ Stir in the tomato paste, pour over the boiling stock and add the pasta. Cover and cook for 8 minutes.

◆ Add the peas 6 minutes before the end of cooking time if fresh, 4 minutes if canned or defrosted.

◆ Season to taste and serve sprinkled with parsley or Parmesan cheese if liked.

GARLIC MUSHROOMS

SERVES 4 / SET: HIGH

Ingredients

16 mushrooms, about 3 cm/1½ in across
1 tablespoon oil
2 cloves garlic, crushed
3 tbsp chopped fresh herbs
2 slices wholemeal bread, soaked in milk and squeezed
salt and freshly ground black pepper

◆ Peel the mushrooms or wipe them. Cut off the stalks and chop finely.
◆ Put the oil in a small bowl and cook for 30 seconds. Add the garlic and cook for 1 minute.
◆ Mix the garlic with the mushroom stalks, herbs and bread, mashing it to a paste.
◆ Divide the filling between the mushroom caps, put them in a lightly oiled dish, covered with vented plastic wrap and cook for 5 minutes, turning once.
◆ Serve hot.

CREAMED TOMATO SOUP

SERVES 4 / SET: HIGH

Ingredients

2 kg/4 lb ripe tomatoes
1 onion
60 g/2 oz chopped ham
½ cucumber, diced
1 tsp Worcestershire sauce
a squeeze of lemon juice
150 ml/5 fl oz cream
chopped basil or parsley

This is a luxurious soup to make if you have a glut of fresh tomatoes. The finished soup will be lukewarm – the ideal temperature at which to serve it.

◆ Plunge the tomatoes into boiling water for 1 minute until the skins split. Peel them and chop them, discarding the seeds and the cores.
◆ Put them in a large dish, cover with vented plastic wrap and cook for 5 minutes, stirring once, until thick and pulpy. Blend in a food processor or blender until smooth.
◆ Put the onion in a cloth (cheesecloth) and squeeze it hard over the tomatoes to get as much juice out as you can.
◆ Stir all the ingredients together in a large bowl and serve, sprinkled with basil or parsley.

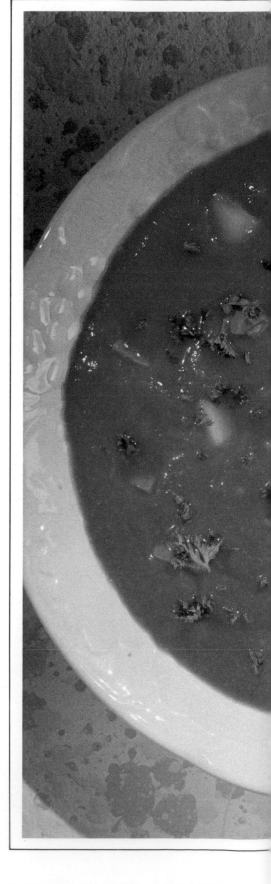

Creamed Tomato Soup

SHRIMP-STUFFED TOMATOES

SERVES 4 / SET: HIGH

Ingredients

4 large tomatoes
salt
30 g/1 oz butter
1 onion, finely chopped
1 clove garlic, crushed
185 g/6 oz shrimp
90 g/3 oz fresh white breadcrumbs
2 tbsp chopped parsley
1½ tbsp tomato paste
cayenne pepper
lemon wedges

◆ Cut the tops off the tomatoes, scoop out the pulp and reserve. Sprinkle the insides of the tomatoes with salt and leave upside down to drain.

◆ Meanwhile, make the filling. Put the butter in a bowl and cook for 1 minute. Stir in onion and garlic. Cover with vented plastic wrap and cook for 2 minutes.

◆ Stir in tomato pulp and remaining ingredients, except lemon wedges. Mix well and season with cayenne pepper to taste.

◆ Stuff the tomatoes and put them upright in a dish they just fit. Cook, covered with vented plastic wrap, for 5 minutes, then allow to stand for 1–2 minutes.

◆ Serve hot with lemon wedges.

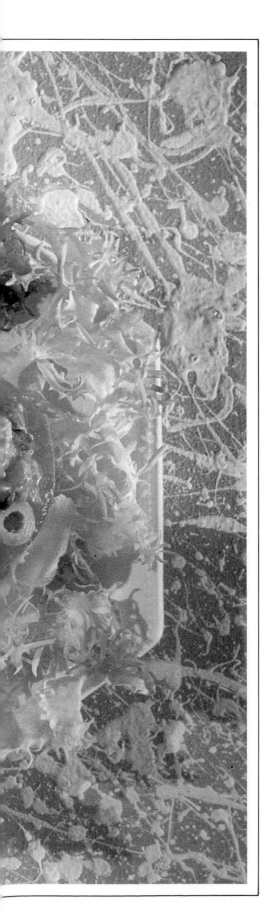

ANCHOVY-STUFFED TOMATOES

SERVES 4 / SET: HIGH

Ingredients

4 large tomatoes
salt
30 g/1 oz butter
1 onion, chopped
8 anchovy fillets, soaked in water and drained
1 bunch of parsley, chopped
approx 30 capers
2 tbsp fresh breadcrumbs
10 olives, stoned and chopped
freshly ground black pepper

◆ Cut the tops off the tomatoes, scoop out the pulp and reserve. Sprinkle the insides of the tomatoes with salt and leave upside down to drain.

◆ Meanwhile, make the filling. Put the butter in a bowl and cook for 1 minute until melted. Stir in the onion and cook for 2 minutes.

◆ Pound the anchovy fillets and stir into the onion with the remaining ingredients. Season with pepper, and salt if necessary. (The salt in the anchovies may be enough, so make sure you taste the mixture first.) Fill the tomatoes with the mixture.

◆ Put the tomatoes upright in a dish they just fit and cook, covered with vented plastic wrap, for 5 minutes.

◆ Allow to stand for 1–2 minutes and serve hot.

Anchovy-Stuffed Tomatoes

SAVOURY STUFFED VINE LEAVES

SERVES 4 / SET: HIGH

Ingredients

250 g/8 oz chestnuts
olive oil
1 small onion, chopped
2 cloves garlic, crushed
250 g/8 oz brown rice
625 ml/1 pt boiling water
15 g/1/2 oz butter
125 g/4 oz mushrooms, chopped
2 tomatoes, peeled and chopped
1 1/2 tbsp chopped fresh mixed herbs
salt and freshly ground black pepper
20 vine leaves

◆ To prepare chestnuts, pierce the skins with a sharp knife and heat them in the microwave in 3 batches for 1 1/2 minutes per batch. Peel off the skins.

◆ Put 1 tbsp oil in a large dish and cook for 30 seconds. Add the onion and garlic, cover with vented plastic wrap and cook for 2 minutes.

◆ Stir in the rice and pour on the boiling water. Cover with vented plastic wrap and cook for 12 minutes. Drop in the chestnuts and cook for a further 10 minutes. Let the dish stand for 5–10 minutes.

◆ Put the butter in a dish and cook for 1 minute until melted. Add the mushrooms, tomatoes and herbs and sprinkle with pepper. Stir to coat in the butter, cover with vented plastic wrap and cook for 3 minutes.

◆ Chop the chestnuts and mix them into the rice with the mushrooms and tomatoes. Place a spoonful of the stuffing on each vine leaf, roll them up and pack them, join down, into an oblong dish.

◆ Brush the tops of the vine leaves with olive oil and cook for 1 1/2 minutes.

◆ Serve hot.

ARTICHOKES WITH MELTED BUTTER

SERVES 4 / SET: HIGH

Ingredients

4 globe artichokes
lemon juice
150 ml/¼ pt boiling water
125 g/4 oz butter, diced

◆ Soak the artichokes for an hour in a bowl of water acidulated with a little lemon juice to clean them of earth and insects.

◆ Trim away the tough outer leaves and cut the stalks off neatly so that the artichokes stand up on their bases. Rub any cut edges with lemon juice to stop them discolouring. There is no need to cut the points off the leaves – this only spoils the look of the vegetable.

◆ Put the artichokes in a large dish with the boiling water and cook, covered, for 15–20 minutes, rearranging the artichokes twice.

◆ To test if they are done, tug gently at one of the lower leaves on the largest artichoke. If it will come away easily, they are ready. Drain the artichokes upside down in a colander.

◆ Put the butter in a small jug and cook for 1½ minutes until melted.

◆ Stand the artichokes on individual plates and pass the butter round. Provide your guests with finger bowls and generous napkins.

GARLIC PRAWNS WITH EGGS

SERVES 4 / SET: HIGH AND MEDIUM

Ingredients

1½ tbsp olive oil
1 fat clove garlic, crushed
250 g/8 oz shelled prawns
4 eggs

A starter with a distinctively Spanish flavour.

◆ Divide the oil and garlic equally between 4 individual ramekin dishes. Cover with vented plastic wrap and cook on high for 1 minute.

◆ Divide the prawns between the dishes and stir to coat in the oil. Push the prawns to one side of the dish and break an egg into the other.

◆ Pierce each yolk carefully with a toothpick to prevent them bursting, cover the dishes with vented plastic wrap and cook on medium power for 3½ minutes, turning the dishes once.

◆ Let the dishes rest for 1 minute, then serve with crusty bread to mop up the garlic juices.

Garlic Prawns with Egg

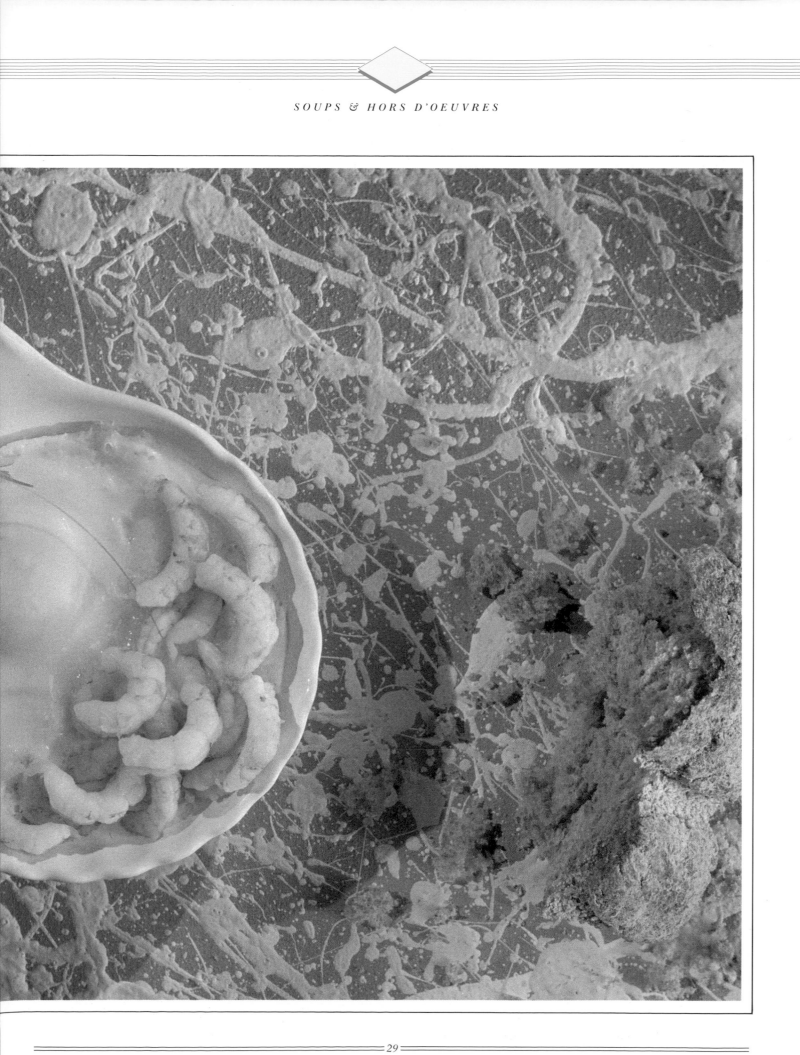

CHEESE AND ONION SOUP

SERVES 4 / SET: HIGH

Ingredients

45 g/1½ oz butter
2 medium onions, sliced
30 g/1 oz flour
625 ml/1 pt boiling chicken stock
185 g/6 oz strong Cheddar cheese, finely grated
salt
Worcestershire sauce

A very tasty and nourishing thick soup to serve with wholemeal bread on a cold winter's day.

◆ Put the butter in a large dish and cook for 1 minute until melted. Add the onions, stirring to coat, cover and cook for 4 minutes. Stir in the flour and cook for 1 minute. Stir again.

◆ Pour on the stock and cook for 5 minutes, stirring every minute, until thickened.

◆ Stir in the cheese, a little at a time, until it has melted. Season with salt and Worcestershire sauce.

◆ Return to the microwave for a further 1½ minutes to reheat, then serve.

PIPERADE

SERVES 2—4
SET: FULL AND DEFROST

Ingredients

2 tbsp olive oil
1/2 onion, finely sliced
1 clove garlic, chopped
1/2 green pepper, cut into julienne strips
1/2 red pepper, cut into julienne strips
1 large tomato, peeled and finely sliced
5 eggs
1 tablespoon chopped fresh basil
salt and freshly ground black pepper
sprigs of watercress

This makes an interesting first course before plainly cooked fish or meat, rather like the French might eat an omelette before a steak.

◆ Pour olive oil into a shallow oval dish and cook for 1 minute. Stir in onion, garlic and peppers and cook for 3 minutes. Add the tomatoes and cook for a further 2 minutes, or until vegetables are done.
◆ Beat the eggs with the chopped basil and season. Stir egg mixture into vegetables. Cook for about 3 minutes on defrost power, or until nearly cooked, stirring every minute to scramble the eggs.
◆ Allow to stand for 1 minute, then garnish with watercress and serve.

Piperade

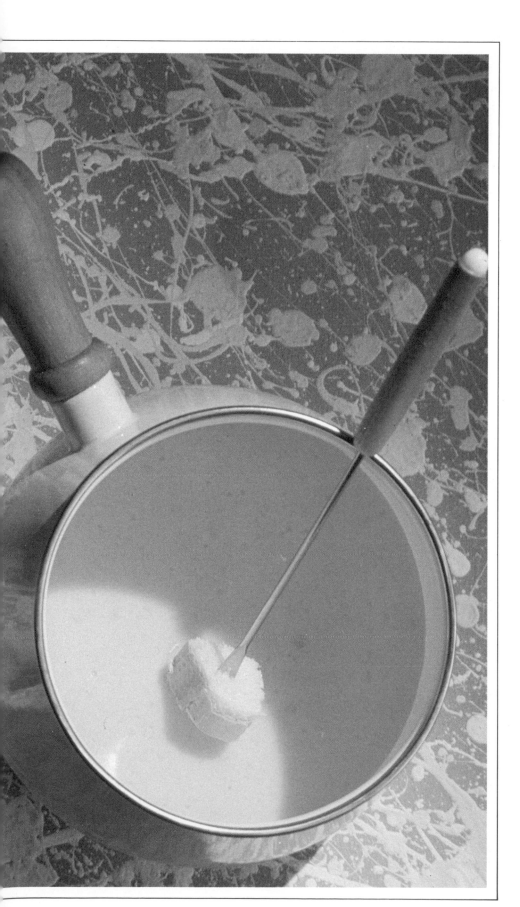

CHEESE FONDUE

SERVES 4 / SET: HIGH

Ingredients
1 clove garlic, crushed
200 ml/⅓ pt dry white wine
250 g/8 oz Gruyère cheese, finely grated
2 tsp cornflour
2 tbsp brandy
freshly ground black pepper
nutmeg

◆ Put garlic and wine in a bowl and cook for 2 minutes.
◆ Add cheese. Cook for 4 minutes, stirring 3 times, until cheese has melted.
◆ Mix together cornflour, brandy, pepper and nutmeg. Stir into cheese. Cook for 4 minutes.
◆ Serve with French bread cut into bite-sized pieces and accompany with a crisp salad. Provide each guest with a fondue fork or kebab stick for spearing the bread.

WELSH RAREBIT

SERVES 4
SET: HIGH AND MEDIUM

Ingredients

4 slices wholemeal toast

4 slices ham

250 g/8 oz grated cheddar cheese

15 g/¹/₂ oz butter

salt and freshly ground black pepper

¹/₂ tsp Worcestershire sauce

¹/₂ tsp paprika

2 tbsp light cream

tomato wedges

sprigs of watercress

This can also be served instead of a dessert, if you prefer to end your meal on a savoury note.

◆ Top each slice of toast with a slice of ham and keep warm.
◆ Put the cheese and butter in a bowl and cook on high, stirring every minute, for 3 minutes until cheese has melted.
◆ Season, stir in the Worcestershire sauce, paprika and cream and cook on medium for 8 minutes, stirring every minute, until smooth and creamy.
◆ Top the toast and ham with the cheese mixture and serve garnished with tomato wedges and sprigs of watercress.

Welsh Rarebit

CHICK PEA SOUP

SERVES 4 / SET: HIGH

Ingredients

30 g/1 oz butter

1 small onion, chopped

1 clove garlic, crushed

220 g/7 oz canned tomatoes, mashed, with juice

440 g/14 oz canned chick peas, drained

a pinch of marjoram, or 1 tsp chopped fresh marjoram

625 ml/1 pt boiling beef stock

salt and freshly ground black pepper

4 slices crusty white bread, toasted

Parmesan cheese

If using dried chick peas, soak them overnight, drain and boil vigorously in fresh water on the burner for 10 minutes. Turn down the heat and simmer until cooked. This may take up to 5 hours, depending on the age of the chick peas. How much simpler and cheaper to use the canned variety!

◆ Put the butter in a large dish and cook for 1 minute, until melted. Add the onion and garlic, cover and cook for 2 minutes.
◆ Add the tomatoes, chick peas and marjoram. Pour on the beef stock, cover and cook for 6 minutes. Season to taste.
◆ Lay a slice of toasted bread in each of 4 soup plates. Pour over the hot soup and serve with Parmesan cheese.

VEGETABLE SOUP WITH PESTO

SERVES 4 / SET: HIGH

Ingredients

250 g/8 oz spinach
45 g/1 ½ oz butter
2 cooked potatoes, diced
125 g/4 oz green beans, cut into pieces
½ white cabbage, shredded
1 leek, sliced
1 onion, sliced
625 ml/1 pt boiling chicken stock
PESTO
4 cloves garlic
3 tbsp grated Parmesan cheese
1 ½ tbsp pine nuts
a large bunch of basil
2–3 tbsp olive oil

Stir a tablespoonful of pesto sauce into a tureen of soup for a lovely garlicky flavour. Make up a small jar of the sauce and keep it in the fridge for use on pasta too.

◆ First make the pesto by blending all the ingredients, except the oil, in a food processor or blender or, alternatively, pounding them in a mortar with a pestle.

◆ Add enough olive oil to make a thick, smooth paste. Store the sauce in a jar in the fridge and use as required.

◆ For the soup, wash the spinach and discard any tough stalks and discoloured leaves. Cram it into a big dish with half the butter, cover with vented plastic wrap and cook for 6 minutes, turning once, until soft. Chop finely and set aside.

◆ Put the rest of the butter in the dish and cook for 30 seconds until melted. Add the remaining vegetables, stirring to coat them with the butter. Cover with vented plastic wrap and cook for 5 minutes.

◆ Pour over the chicken stock, stir in the spinach and cook for a further 6 minutes, stirring twice.

◆ Serve with pesto sauce.

MOULES A LA MARINIERE

SERVES 2 / SET: HIGH

Ingredients

1.25 l/2 pt mussels
60 g/2 oz butter
1 onion, chopped
1 clove garlic, crushed
a handful of fresh parsley, chopped
freshly ground black pepper
1 glass dry white wine

◆ Scrub the mussels thoroughly under cold running water, scraping away the beards. Discard any mussels that are open or broken.

◆ Put the butter in a large bowl and cook for 1 minute. Add the onion, garlic, parsley, pepper and wine. Cover and cook for 2 minutes.

◆ Add the mussels, cover and cook for about 3 minutes until shells are open, giving the dish a good stir halfway through. Discard any mussels that remain closed.

◆ Serve in deep soup plates with French bread to mop up the juices and provide a dish for the discarded shells.

Moules à la Marinière

SMOKED SALMON SCRAMBLED EGGS

SERVES 2 / SET: HIGH

Ingredients

6 medium eggs

1 tbsp milk

freshly ground black pepper

125 g/4 oz smoked salmon, cut into
1 cm/½ in squares

30 g/1 oz butter

a pinch of cayenne pepper

This most luxurious starter makes a good prelude to a main dish of vegetables. Serve it with chilled champagne or Buck's Fizz. Have thin triangles of wholemeal toast buttered and kept hot on warmed plates so that all that remains to be done once the eggs are cooked is to pop the cork.

◆ Beat the eggs with the milk and season with black pepper. Stir in the salmon.

◆ Put the butter in a shallow oval dish and cook for 1 minute until melted.

◆ Stir in the eggs and smoked salmon. Cook for about 3 minutes, or until nearly done, stirring every minute.

◆ When the eggs are thick and creamy, pile them onto the hot toast. Add a sprinkling of cayenne pepper, allow to stand for 1 minute, then serve.

RISOTTO

SERVES 4 / SET: HIGH

Ingredients

125 g/4 oz butter
1 large onion, chopped
2 small zucchini, diced
1 carrot, diced
1 large tomato, peeled and chopped
60 g/2 oz mushrooms, wiped and sliced
440 g/14 oz long-grain rice
1 l/1¾ pt boiling chicken stock
1 tbsp tomato paste
salt and freshly ground black pepper
Parmesan cheese

This makes a substantial starter when there is plainly cooked meat or fish to follow. A risotto should be moist and succulent, not dry and fluffy.

◆ Put half the butter in a large bowl and cook for 1 minute. Stir in the vegetables, cover and cook for 8 minutes, stirring once.

◆ Stir in the rice, pour over the stock and add the tomato paste. Season with a little salt, cover and cook for 15 minutes, stirring once.

◆ Allow to stand, covered, for 7 minutes. Stir in the remaining butter, plenty of black pepper and some Parmesan cheese.

◆ Serve, with more Parmesan cheese separately.

Risotto

SMOKED FISH PATE

SERVES 4 / SET: MEDIUM

Ingredients

4 frozen smoked fish fillets
1 onion, finely chopped
30 g/1 oz butter
3 tsp lemon juice
90 g/3 oz full fat cream cheese
3 tsp sherry
salt and freshly ground black pepper
parsley
lemon twists

◆ Put the smoked fish, onion, butter and lemon juice in a dish, cover and cook on medium for 8–10 minutes, turning once.

◆ Purée the smoked fish and onions with the sherry and cream cheese in a blender or food processor, or mash with a fork, and season to taste.

◆ Fill 4 individual ramekin dishes with the pâté and garnish with sprigs of parsley and lemon twists.

◆ Chill and serve with hot toast.

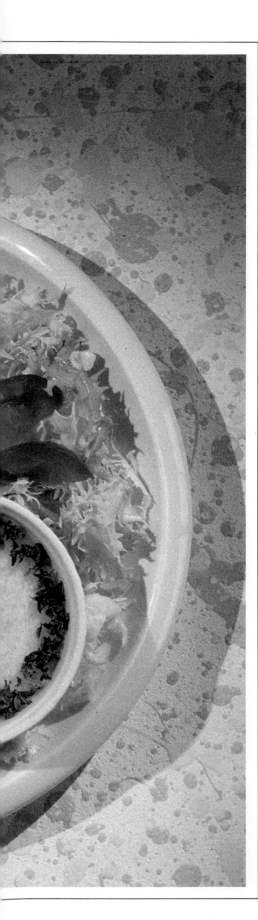

CHICKEN LIVER PATE

SERVES 4 / SET: HIGH

Ingredients
250 g/8 oz chicken livers
1 small onion, finely chopped
2 cloves garlic, crushed
155 g/5 oz butter
the leaves from 2 sprigs of fresh thyme, chopped
3 tsp port
3 tsp cream
salt and freshly ground black pepper
sprigs of fresh thyme
juniper berries

◆ Put the livers, onion, garlic, half the butter and the thyme in a bowl. Cover with vented plastic wrap and cook for 5 minutes, stirring once.
◆ Put the mixture in a blender or food processor, with the port and cream and blend until smooth. Season and divide between 4 individual ramekin dishes.
◆ Put the remaining butter in a bowl and cook for 30 seconds, or until melted. Pour over the pâté and chill.
◆ Garnish with fresh thyme and juniper berries and serve with crusty bread or triangles of wholemeal toast.

Chicken Liver Pâté

THICK TOMATO SOUP

SERVES 4 / SET: HIGH

Ingredients
1½ tbsp olive oil
1 or 2 cloves garlic, crushed
1 kg/2 lb ripe tomatoes, skinned and chopped
625 ml/1 pt boiling meat stock
salt and freshly ground black pepper
4 slices stale, crusty, white bread
a few leaves of sage and basil, chopped

This is a favourite supper time soup with children in Italy.

◆ Put the olive oil in a large dish and cook for 2 minutes. Add the garlic, stirring well to coat. Cook for 1 minute. Stir in the tomatoes, cover and cook for 8 minutes, stirring once or twice.
◆ Pour on the meat stock, stir well and cook for a further 3 minutes. Season to taste.
◆ Lay a slice of bread in each of 4 soup plates. Pour the soup over and sprinkle sage and basil leaves on top.
◆ Serve with grated cheese if liked.

CABBAGE SOUP

SERVES 4 / SET: HIGH

Ingredients
1 savoy cabbage
625 ml/1 pt boiling chicken stock
salt and freshly ground black pepper
4 slices crusty white bread
Parmesan cheese

◆ Wash the cabbage, discard any discoloured or tough leaves, quarter it and cut out the stalk.

◆ Put the leaves in a roasting or boiling bag with a generous spoonful of water and tie the top loosely. Microwave for 6 minutes. Remove and chop the cabbage.

◆ Put the cabbage in a large dish, pour over the boiling stock and cook, covered, for 3 minutes. Season to taste.

◆ Lay a slice of bread in the bottom of each of 4 soup plates. Pour over the soup and serve with plenty of Parmesan cheese.

MUSHROOM SOUP

SERVES 4 / SET: HIGH

Ingredients
45 g/1½ oz butter
1 small onion, chopped
1 clove garlic
750 g/1½ lb mushrooms, peeled or wiped,
and sliced
625 ml/1 pt boiling chicken stock
125 g/4 oz tomatoes, peeled and chopped
salt and freshly ground black pepper
a pinch of nutmeg

◆ Put the butter in a large dish and cook for 1 minute. Add the onion and garlic, whole, cover with vented plastic wrap and cook for 1 minute.
◆ Stir in the mushrooms, add a few spoonfuls of the chicken stock, cover and cook for 4 minutes, stirring once.
◆ Remove the garlic, add the tomatoes and pour on the rest of the chicken stock. Cover and cook for 4 minutes.
◆ Season to taste, add the nutmeg and serve.

BROAD BEAN AND HAM SOUP

SERVES 4 / SET: HIGH

Ingredients

30 g/1 oz butter
1 onion, chopped
1 clove garlic, crushed
60 g/2 oz diced ham, off the bone
1.25 kg/2½ lb broad beans
1.25 l/2 pt boiling chicken stock
salt and freshly ground black pepper
2 tbsp cream

This soup is best made with the first young broad beans of the season. Later in the summer, as the beans get tougher, remove the inner skins by lifting the beans from the soup with a slotted ladle when they are cooked, and pressing them out of the skins between your thumb and forefinger. Out of season, use canned or frozen beans.

◆ Put the butter in a large dish and cook for 1 minute until melted. Stir in the onion and garlic and cook, covered, for 2 minutes.

◆ Add the ham and beans and pour over the stock. Cover and cook for 6 minutes, or until the beans are tender. Season to taste.

◆ Pour into soup plates and add a swirl of cream.

Broad Bean and Ham Soup

CURRIED PARSNIP SOUP

SERVES 4 / SET: HIGH

Ingredients

15 g/¹/₂ oz butter
¹/₂ tsp fennel seeds
1 slice fresh root ginger
1 very large parsnip, finely sliced, weighing about 500 g/1 lb
315 ml/¹/₂ pt boiling chicken stock
315 ml/¹/₂ pt hot milk
salt and freshly ground black pepper
a pinch of garam masala

The curry spices bring out the delicious natural sweetness of the parsnip. Parsnips are even sweeter after the first frost, which causes their sugar content to rise.

◆ Put the butter in a bowl and cook for 1 minute until very hot. Add the fennel seeds and ginger, cover and cook for 45 seconds. Add the parsnip and 1–2 tbsp water.

◆ Cover and cook for 8 minutes, turning once, until the parsnip is really tender.

◆ Add the boiling chicken stock and cook for 3 minutes. Remove the ginger and purée the soup in a blender or food processor.

◆ Add enough hot milk to reach the desired consistency, season to taste with salt and pepper and stir in a pinch of garam masala.

◆ Heat through in the microwave for a couple of minutes if necessary and serve.

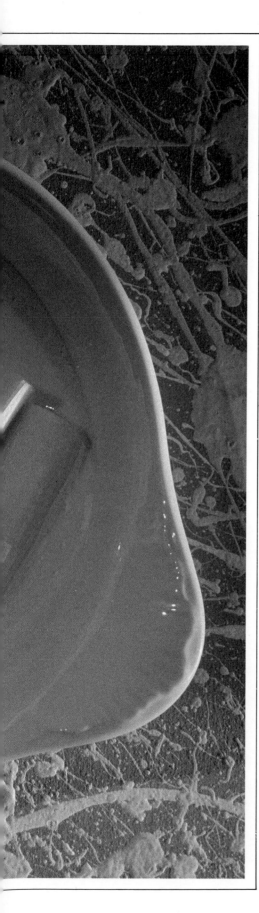

YOUNG LEEKS WITH HOLLANDAISE SAUCE

SERVES 4 / SET: HIGH AND MEDIUM OR DEFROST

Ingredients

500 g/1 lb young leeks
2 tbsp water
HOLLANDAISE SAUCE
125 g/4 oz butter, diced
1½ tbsp lemon juice
3 egg yolks
salt and white pepper

◆ Trim the leeks, slit them and wash thoroughly. Lay them in a dish, add the water, cover and cook on high power for 6–8 minutes, rearranging once, until tender.

◆ Let the dish stand for a few minutes, then drain and arrange the leeks on a heated serving dish or individual plates.

◆ Meanwhile, make the sauce. Put the butter in a bowl and cook for 2 minutes on medium or defrost until melted. Add the lemon juice and the egg yolks and whisk lightly.

◆ Cook on medium or defrost for 1 minute, whisk again and season with salt and white pepper (black pepper would spoil the appearance of the sauce).

◆ Transfer the sauce to a heated jug and serve with the leeks.

STUFFED ZUCCHINI

SERVES 4
SET: HIGH AND DEFROST

Ingredients

1 tbsp oil
1 small onion, chopped
1 clove of garlic, chopped
1½ tbsp chopped parsley
1½ tbsp Parmesan cheese, grated
2 slices of bread, soaked in milk, squeezed out and crumbled
salt and freshly ground black pepper
4 fat zucchini
150 ml/¼ pt Tomato Sauce (see recipe for Stuffed Cabbage Leaves)

◆ Put the oil in a small bowl and cook for 30 seconds. Stir in the onion and garlic, cover with vented plastic wrap and cook for 2 minutes.

◆ Mix in the parsley, Parmesan cheese and crumbled bread and season to taste.

◆ Cut the ends off the zucchini and hollow out the centres with an apple corer. Stuff the zucchini with the onion and bread mixture and arrange them in an oblong dish.

◆ Cover with vented plastic wrap and cook on defrost power for 6 minutes, until tender, rearranging once.

◆ Serve the zucchini with the hot Tomato Sauce.

Young Leeks with Hollandaise Sauce

COUNTRY PATE

SERVES 6—8 / SET: HIGH

Ingredients

125 g/4 oz butter
2 onions, chopped
2 cloves garlic, crushed
315 g/10 oz pigs' liver, chopped
315 g/10 oz belly pork, trimmed and chopped
3 tsp chopped fresh sage leaves
3 tbsp sherry
3 tbsp heavy cream
salt and freshly ground black pepper
bay leaves
juniper berries

◆ Put half the butter in a large bowl and cook for 1 minute. Stir in the onion and garlic, cover with vented plastic wrap and cook for 4 minutes, until soft.

◆ Stir in the pigs' liver and belly pork, cover and cook for 8–10 minutes, stirring once or twice, until cooked through.

◆ Put the mixture in a blender or food processor with the sage, sherry, cream and seasoning and blend until smooth. Fill a terrine with the pâté and smooth over the top.

◆ Dice the remaining butter and put it in a bowl and cook for 4 minutes until melted but not brown. Strain through a piece of muslin (cheese-cloth) and pour over the top of the pâté. Decorate with bay leaves and juniper berries and chill.

◆ Serve with hot toast.

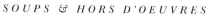

HOT PASTA AND EGG SALAD

SERVES 4 / SET: HIGH

Ingredients

250 g/8 oz pasta shells
315 ml/½ pt boiling water
1½ tbsp olive oil
125 g/4 oz cooked or canned green beans
1 red pepper, cut into julienne strips
60 g/2 oz black olives
2 hardboiled eggs, quartered
salt and freshly ground black pepper

◆ Put the pasta shells in a dish with the boiling water, a little salt and a few drops of the oil. Cover and cook for 10 minutes.

◆ Leave to stand for 3 minutes, then drain and toss in the remaining oil.

◆ Mix in the beans, pepper and olives, season and divide the mixture between 4 individual dishes. Arrange the eggs on top.

◆ Serve and eat while the pasta is still warm – it makes an interesting contrast with the cold salad.

Hot Pasta and Egg Salad

LENTIL SOUP

SERVES 4 / SET: HIGH

Ingredients

30 g/1 oz butter
a squeeze of lemon juice
1 onion, finely sliced
1 clove garlic, crushed
1/2 fresh green chilli, minced
1 carrot, chopped
1 stick celery, finely sliced
185 g/6 oz lentils
625 ml/1 pt boiling chicken stock
salt and freshly ground black pepper
a handful of fresh parsley, roughly chopped

Brown and green lentils should be soaked overnight before use. The small red lentils can be used immediately.

◆ Put the butter in a large dish and cook for 1 minute until melted. Add the lemon juice, onion, garlic, chilli, carrot and celery, cover with vented plastic wrap and cook for 3 minutes.
◆ Stir in the lentils and pour over the boiling stock. Cover with vented plastic wrap and cook until the lentils are soft: 15 minutes if using red lentils and 20 minutes if using green or brown.
◆ Blend half the soup, return to the dish and season to taste.
◆ Serve strewn with parsley.

CORN ON THE COB WITH HERB BUTTER

SERVES 4 / SET: HIGH

Ingredients

125 g/4 oz butter
4 corn on the cob, fresh or frozen
2 tbsp chopped mixed fresh herbs

The herb butter can be made in advance, allowed to cool, then chilled and served in pats if required.

◆ Cut up the butter and place in a small dish. Cook for 1 minute.
◆ Brush the corn with some of the melted butter and wrap individually in waxed paper. Pack into a shallow dish.
◆ Cover and cook until grains are tender when pierced: 10 minutes if fresh or 12 if frozen.
◆ Transfer corn to serving dishes.
◆ Stir herbs into remaining butter and cook for 30 seconds.
◆ Pour herb butter over corn to serve.

Corn on the Cob with Herb Butter

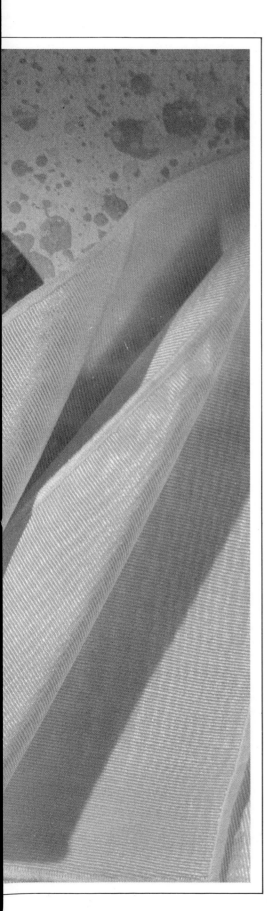

TOMATO, CARROT AND ORANGE SOUP

SERVES 4 / SET: HIGH

Ingredients

440 g/14 oz canned tomatoes, mashed, with juice

250 g/8 oz carrots, chopped

juice of 1 orange

1 bay leaf

625 ml/1 pt hot chicken stock

rind of half an orange, finely grated

salt and freshly ground black pepper

light cream

Carrots cook more quickly and evenly if they are chopped or chipped than they do when thickly sliced.

◆ Put tomatoes, carrots, orange juice and bay leaf in a bowl. Cover with vented plastic wrap and cook for 10–15 minutes, stirring once or twice, until carrots are cooked.

◆ Remove the bay leaf and purée the mixture in a blender or food processor. Return to the bowl and add the stock and orange rind. Season to taste.

◆ Cook for 4 minutes and serve hot or cold with a swirl of cream.

VARIATION You can make this soup with lemon instead of orange, using the juice of only half the fruit.

RICE AND TURNIP SOUP

SERVES 4 / SET: HIGH

Ingredients

30 g/1 oz butter

1 onion, chopped

2 turnips, peeled and diced

90 g/3 oz rice

625 ml/1 pt boiling chicken stock

60 g/2 oz ham, chopped

salt and freshly ground black pepper

a handful of parsley, chopped

Parmesan cheese

◆ Put the butter in a large dish and cook for 1 minute until melted. Stir in the onion and cook for 2 minutes.

◆ Stir in the turnips and rice, pour over enough chicken stock to cover, add the ham and cook, covered, for 12 minutes.

◆ Add the rest of the chicken stock, season to taste and add the parsley.

◆ Serve with plenty of Parmesan cheese.

Tomato, Carrot and Orange Soup

CHERRY SOUP

SERVES 4 / SET: HIGH

Ingredients

1 kg/2 lb ripe black cherries

juice of half a lemon

ground cinnamon

honey to taste

water

sour cream

mint leaves (optional)

This is a lovely fruit soup from Hungary, where it might be eaten to sharpen the palate before a rich main course of duck or game. Serve it with black bread if you have a hearty appetite.

◆ Wash and pick over the cherries. Take out the stones. Put the cherries in a bowl with the lemon juice, cover with vented plastic wrap and cook for 3–5 minutes until the fruit is very soft.

◆ Transfer the cherries to a blender or food processor and blend with a little honey and a small pinch of cinnamon to taste. Add enough water to thin the soup to the desired consistency.

◆ Allow to cool, then chill in the fridge.

◆ Serve with a swirl of sour cream and decorate with mint leaves if liked.

TUSCAN VEGETABLE SOUP

SERVES 4 / SET: HIGH

Ingredients

30 g/1 oz butter

125 g/4 oz potatoes, peeled and diced

125 g/4 oz carrots, scraped and thinly sliced

125 g/4 oz onions, sliced

1–2 cloves garlic, crushed

125 g/4 oz cabbage, roughly shredded

440 g/14 oz canned butter beans, drained

440 g/14 oz canned tomatoes, mashed, with juice

625 ml/1 pt hot beef stock

salt and freshly ground black pepper

4 slices crusty bread

Parmesan cheese

In Tuscany soup is often poured over a thick slice of bread in the bottom of the soup plate. It is a good way of using up the last slices of the loaf. You can toast the bread and rub it with a cut clove of garlic.

◆ Put the butter in a large dish and cook for 1 minute. Add the potatoes, carrots, onion and garlic, cover with vented plastic wrap and cook for 8 minutes, stirring once.

◆ Add the remaining vegetables and pour on the beef stock. Cover and cook for 6 minutes, stirring once, until the potato and carrot are cooked. Season to taste.

◆ Lay a slice of crusty bread in each of 4 soup bowls. Pour on the soup and serve sprinkled liberally with Parmesan cheese.

VICHYSSOISE

SERVES 4 / SET: HIGH

Ingredients

375 g/12 oz potatoes, peeled and diced
1 onion, sliced
¾ cucumber
3 leeks, trimmed, washed and sliced
60 g/2 oz butter
3 tbsp water
625 ml/1 pt boiling chicken stock
salt and freshly ground black pepper
150 ml/¼ pt light cream

This soup is best served chilled on a hot summer's day.

◆ Put the potatoes in a bowl with the onion, two-thirds of the cucumber, peeled and diced, the leeks, butter and water. Cover and cook for 10 minutes, stirring once.

◆ Pour on the boiling stock, cover and cook for 7 minutes, until the potatoes are soft, then purée in a blender or food processor. Season, allow to cool and chill well.

◆ Serve cold with a swirl of cream and decorated with the remaining cucumber, thinly sliced.

Vichyssoise

POACHED EGGS ON SPINACH WITH HOLLANDAISE SAUCE

SERVES 4
SET: HIGH AND DEFROST

Ingredients

250 g/8 oz frozen spinach, thawed and thoroughly drained

salt and freshly ground black pepper

4 eggs

Hollandaise Sauce (see recipe for Young Leeks with Hollandaise Sauce)

◆ Divide the spinach between 4 individual buttered ramekin dishes and cook on high for 1½ minutes. Stir and season with salt and pepper.

◆ Break the eggs onto the spinach and prick the yolks gently with a toothpick to prevent them bursting. Cover the dishes with plastic wrap and cook for 3 minutes on defrost power.

◆ Serve the Hollandaise sauce separately or pour over the eggs to serve.

THANKSGIVING SOUP

SERVES 4 / SET: HIGH

Ingredients

1 tablespoon oil
1 onion, chopped
375 g/12 oz pumpkin, peeled, pips removed and diced
250 g/8 oz carrots, chopped
2 potatoes, peeled and chopped
625 ml/1 pt boiling chicken stock
2 small zucchini, thinly sliced
salt and freshly ground black pepper
parsley

◆ Put the oil in a dish and cook for 30 seconds. Add the onion, cover with vented plastic wrap and cook for 2 minutes.

◆ Add the pumpkin, carrots and potatoes and pour over the boiling stock. Cover and cook for 15 minutes, until the vegetables are soft, adding the zucchini 5 minutes before the end of cooking time.

◆ Keeping back most of the zucchini blend or partially blend the soup. Season to taste.

◆ Float the reserved zucchini on top and serve sprinkled with parsley.

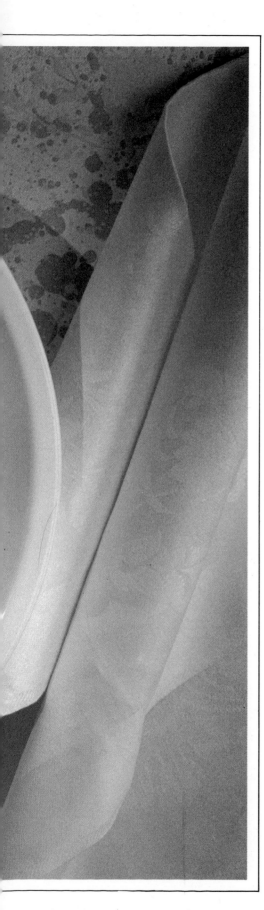

STUFFED CABBAGE LEAVES

SERVES 4
SET: HIGH AND DEFROST

Ingredients

8 Savoy cabbage leaves

2 tablespoons water

30 g/1 oz butter

1 onion, chopped

185 g/6 oz cooked chicken or veal, chopped

185 g/6 oz salami, derinded and chopped

1½ tbsp chopped fresh herbs

4 slices bread, crusts removed, soaked in milk, squeezed out and crumbled

salt and freshly ground black pepper

a little olive oil

TOMATO SAUCE

½ tbsp oil

½ large onion, chopped

½ clove garlic, crushed

1 small carrot, chopped

½ stick celery, chopped

220 g/7 oz canned tomatoes, with juice

½ tbsp tomato paste

a few sprigs of basil

salt and freshly ground black pepper

◆ Choose even-sized cabbage leaves. Wash them well and trim off each stalk at its base. Put them in a boiling or roasting bag with the water, fasten the top loosely and cook for 4 minutes. Lay the leaves flat on a kitchen towel to absorb the excess water.

◆ Meanwhile make the sauce. Put the oil in a dish and cook for 30 seconds. Add the onion, garlic, carrot and celery and cook, covered with vented plastic wrap for 4 minutes.

◆ Stir in the tomatoes and their juice, tomato paste and basil. Cover and cook for 8 minutes, stirring twice.

◆ Put the sauce in a blender or food processor and blend until smooth, then season to taste.

◆ To make the filling for the cabbage leaves, put the butter in a dish and cook for 1 minute until melted. Stir in the onion, cover and cook for 3 minutes, until soft.

◆ Stir in the cooked chicken or veal, salami, herbs and breadcrumbs and season well, then divide the mixture between the cabbage leaves and roll up into parcels.

◆ Pack the cabbage parcels, join down, into a dish they just fit. Brush the tops with a little olive oil, cover the dish with vented plastic wrap and cook on defrost setting for 8 minutes until hot through.

◆ Serve with the reheated tomato sauce.

CELERY SOUP

S E R V E S 4 / S E T : H I G H

Ingredients

45 g/1¹/₂ oz butter
1 onion, chopped
¹/₂ bunch celery, finely chopped
45 g/1¹/₂ oz flour
315 ml/¹/₂ pt milk
315 ml/¹/₂ pt boiling chicken stock
salt and freshly ground black pepper
1¹/₂ tbsp cream
crispy bacon pieces

◆ Put the butter in a large dish and cook for 1 minute. Stir in the onion and celery, cover and cook for 4 minutes, until soft.

◆ Stir in the flour and cook for 1 minute. Stir in the milk and cook for 3 minutes, stirring every minute, until thick. Stir in the chicken stock and cook for a further 3 minutes. Season to taste.

◆ Pour into individual soup bowls, add a swirl of cream and sprinkle with crispy bacon pieces to serve.

SPINACH SOUP

S E R V E S 4 / S E T : H I G H

Ingredients

1 kg/2 lb spinach
90 g/3 oz butter
1 small onion, chopped
45 g/1¹/₂ oz flour
315 ml/¹/₂ pt milk
315 ml/¹/₂ pt chicken stock
salt and freshly ground black pepper
2 egg yolks
1¹/₂ tbsp cream
2 slices white bread, cut into 1 cm/ ¹/₃ in dice

◆ Wash the spinach, discarding discoloured leaves and tough stalks. Pack it into a large dish, cover and cook for 6 minutes, turning once, until tender. Purée the spinach in a blender or food processor.

◆ Put half the butter in the dish and cook for 1 minute until melted. Add the onion and cook for 1 minute. Stir in the flour and cook for 1 minute.

◆ Whisk in the milk and cook for 3 minutes, whisking every minute. Whisk again until the sauce is smooth.

◆ Stir in the spinach, pour on the chicken stock and stir well. Cook to heat through for 4 minutes. Season to taste.

◆ Whisk the egg yolks with the cream, stir into the soup and heat for 30 seconds.

◆ Ladle the soup into individual soup bowls and serve garnished with croûtons made by frying the diced bread on the burner in the remaining butter until golden.

VARIATION This soup can also be made with sorrel or young nettles, picked before the plants flower.

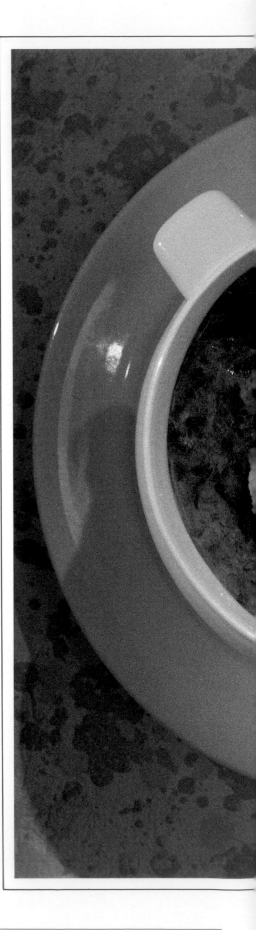

Spinach Soup

COOKING WITH

Pasta

ELIZABETH CORNISH

PASTA

THE Italians claim to have as many types of pasta as there are days of the year, and when it comes to sauces their imagination never flags. Apart from the meat ragù traditionally served in Bologna, there are sauces of prawns, spinach, clams, chicken livers, herbs, tuna, beans, asparagus, cheese, squid, garlic, cream, mushrooms and even chillies, nuts and raisins. Cooking with a microwave brings all these delicious flavours of Italy to your table with less fuss than ever before. If you have had problems with overcooked pasta sticking together in a lump, a kitchen full of steam and a saucepan that needs soaking for a week, relax: your microwave will come to the rescue. You can cook and serve pasta in the same dish, heating up the sauce while the pasta rests until it is just perfectly *al dente*.

Pasta is traditionally served in Italy as a starter, which is probably why it has unfairly been called fattening. A pasta dish from this book followed by a meat or fish dish with vegetables, then cheese and fruit would certainly be a very calorific meal. But the same pasta dish with a crisp salad and a glass of wine is a healthy balanced meal, and won't make you fat. Many of the sauces in this book are low-calorie anyway, because microwave cooking needs little or no fat.

Pasta should always have a little bit of a bite left in it (*al dente* = 'to the tooth') and it should always be served very hot in hot soup plates; offer extra black pepper and Parmesan cheese at the table. Cheese is not served on fish dishes in Italy.

When you are making an olive oil dressing for pasta (or for a salad too, for that matter), use the best olive oil you can afford. *Extra vergine* is the golden green oil from the first cold pressing, and it is both pungent and delicious.

CONTENTS

TAGLIATELLE WITH VEGETABLES AND HAM

SERVES 4 / SET: HIGH

Ingredients

1 tablespoon olive oil
1 clove garlic, crushed
1 small onion, chopped
2 zucchini, chopped
1 small red pepper, diced
125 g/4 oz mushrooms, wiped and sliced
60 g/2 oz ham, chopped
220 g/7 oz canned tomatoes, drained and mashed
salt and freshly ground black pepper
440 g/14 oz tagliatelle
boiling water
chopped parsley
Parmesan cheese

◆ Put the oil in a bowl and cook for 30 seconds. Add the garlic and onion and cook for 2 minutes. Add the zucchini, red pepper and mushrooms, cover with vented plastic wrap and cook for 3 minutes. Add the ham and tomatoes, cover and cook for 2 minutes. Season to taste. Keep warm.

◆ Put the tagliatelle in a deep dish, just cover with boiling water and add a pinch of salt and a few drops of oil. Cover and cook for 6 minutes. Let the dish stand, covered, while you reheat the sauce if necessary.

◆ Drain the pasta, pour on the sauce, sprinkle with parsley and serve with plenty of Parmesan cheese.

PASTA WITH EARLY SUMMER VEGETABLES

SERVES 4 / SET: HIGH

Ingredients

440 g/14 oz tagliatelle
boiling water
salt
oil
125 g/4 oz broad beans, shelled
125 g/4 oz peas
125 g/4 oz green beans, topped and tailed and cut into pieces
150 ml/¼ pt light cream
chopped fresh herbs
Parmesan cheese
freshly ground black pepper

◆ Put the tagliatelle in a deep dish and just cover with boiling water. Add a pinch of salt and a few drops of oil, cover and cook for 6 minutes. Set aside, covered.

◆ Put the broad beans, peas and green beans in a bowl with the cream. Cover with vented plastic wrap and cook for 3 minutes.

◆ Drain the pasta, pour over the vegetable mixture and sprinkle with chopped fresh herbs.

◆ Serve hot with Parmesan cheese and offer black pepper at the table.

PENNE WITH SULTANAS AND PINE NUTS

SERVES 4 / SET: HIGH

Ingredients

440 g/14 oz penne (pasta quills)
boiling water
salt
2 tbsp olive oil
1 clove garlic, chopped
45 g/1½ oz sultanas plumped up in a little marsala
45 g/1½ oz pine nuts
2 tbsp fennel leaves, finely chopped
grated Parmesan cheese
freshly ground black pepper

◆ Put the penne in a bowl and pour on enough boiling water to cover. Add a pinch of salt and a few drops of oil, cover and cook for 9 minutes. Set aside, covered, while you prepare the sauce.

◆ Put the olive oil in a dish and cook for 30 seconds. Add the garlic and cook for 1 minute. Stir in the sultanas and pine nuts and cook for 2 minutes, stirring once.

◆ Drain the pasta, pour on the sauce, add the fennel and toss well.

◆ Serve with plenty of freshly grated Parmesan cheese and offer black pepper at the table.

RIGATONI WITH BORLOTTI BEANS

S E R V E S 4 / S E T : H I G H

Ingredients

440 g/14 oz rigatoni (or macaroni)
boiling water
salt
1½ tbsp olive oil
30 g/1 oz butter
1 clove garlic, crushed
440 g/14 oz canned borlotti beans, drained
185 g/6 oz mozzarella cheese, diced
chopped parsley
freshly ground black pepper

◆ Put the pasta in a deep dish and pour over enough boiling water to just cover. Add a pinch of salt and a few drops of the oil, cover and cook for 10 minutes. Leave covered.

◆ Put the remaining oil in a bowl with the butter and cook for 1 minute. Add the garlic and cook for 1 minute. Stir in the borlotti beans and cook for 2 minutes.

◆ Drain the pasta and stir in the bean mixture and cheese. Cover and cook for 1½ minutes, until the mozzarella begins to melt.

◆ Sprinkle with chopped parsley and serve. Offer black pepper at the table.

Rigatoni with Borlotti Beans

SPAGHETTI WITH RICOTTA AND ALMONDS

SERVES 4 / SET: HIGH AND MEDIUM

Ingredients

440 g/14 oz spaghetti
1 l/1¾ pt boiling water
salt
oil
90 g/3 oz ground almonds
125 g/4 oz ricotta cheese
150 ml/¼ pt single cream
a pinch of mixed spice
flaked, toasted almonds
Parmesan cheese

A delicious and very unusual combination of tastes.

◆ Hold the spaghetti in a deep dish and pour the water over it. As it softens, push the spaghetti under the water. Add a pinch of salt and a few drops of oil, cover and cook on high for 12 minutes. Let the pot stand, covered, while you make the sauce.

◆ Blend together the ground almonds, ricotta cheese and cream. Stir in the mixed spice to taste. Cover and heat through on medium for 3 minutes.

◆ Drain the pasta and stir in the sauce.

◆ Sprinkle with flaked toasted almonds and serve hot with plenty of Parmesan cheese.

PENNE WITH ZUCCHINI AND PISTACHIO NUTS

SERVES 4 / SET: HIGH

Ingredients

440 g/14 oz penne (pasta quills)
salt
1½–2 tbsp olive oil
315 g/10 oz baby zucchini, sliced
1½ tbsp water
1 clove garlic, crushed
60 g/2 oz pistachio nuts, shelled
freshly ground black pepper
Parmesan cheese (optional)

◆ Put the penne in a deep dish and just cover with boiling water. Add a pinch of salt and a few drops of the oil, cover and cook for 9 minutes. Set aside, covered.

◆ Put the zucchini in a dish with the water, cover with vented plastic wrap and cook for 3 minutes.

◆ Put the olive oil in a dish and cook for 30 seconds. Add the garlic and cook for 1 minute. Drain the zucchini and add them with the pistachio nuts. Stir well to coat in the oil. Cover and cook for 1–2 minutes.

◆ Drain the pasta, pour over the sauce and season with black pepper. Offer Parmesan cheese at the table, if liked.

Penne with Zucchini and Pistachio Nuts

SPAGHETTI WITH EGGPLANT AND GARLIC

SERVES 4 / SET: HIGH

Ingredients

440 g/14 oz spaghetti
1 l/1¾ pt boiling water
1 large eggplant
1½–2 tbsp olive oil
1–2 cloves garlic, crushed
Parmesan cheese (optional)

◆ Hold the spaghetti in a dish and pour on the boiling water. Push the spaghetti into it, add a few drops of oil and a little salt. Cover and cook for 12 minutes.

◆ Meanwhile, top and tail the eggplant and cut into thick matchsticks.

◆ Remove the spaghetti from the microwave when it is ready and leave to stand, covered.

◆ Put the olive oil in a dish and add the garlic and eggplant. Cover and cook for 5 minutes, stirring once.

◆ Drain the spaghetti and toss in the eggplant and garlic.

◆ Serve with Parmesan cheese if liked.

SPAGHETTI WITH GARLIC AND OIL

SERVES 4 / SET: HIGH

Ingredients
440 g/14 oz spaghetti
1 l/1³/₄ pt boiling water
salt
2 tbsp olive oil
2 cloves of garlic, crushed
freshly ground black pepper

◆ Hold the spaghetti in a dish and pour on the boiling water. Push the spaghetti down into the water, add a pinch of salt and a few drops of oil, cover and cook for 12 minutes. Leave to stand, covered, while you prepare the sauce.

◆ Put the oil in a bowl and cook for 45 seconds. Add the garlic and cook for 2–3 minutes.

◆ Drain the spaghetti, pour over the hot garlic oil, add pepper, toss well and serve immediately.

MACARONI WITH TUNA

SERVES 4 / SET: HIGH

Ingredients
45 g/1¹/₂ oz butter
45 g/1¹/₂ oz flour
315 ml/¹/₂ pt milk
45 g/1¹/₂ oz Parmesan cheese
salt and pepper
440 g/14 oz macaroni
boiling water
oil
220 g/7 oz canned tuna in brine, drained and flaked
pepper slices to garnish

◆ First make the sauce. Put the butter in a bowl and cook for 1 minute. Stir in the flour and cook for 1 minute. Stir in the milk and cook for 3 minutes, whisking after each minute. Stir in the cheese and cook for 1 minute. Whisk again and season to taste. Keep warm.

◆ Put the macaroni in a deep dish and just cover with boiling water. Add a pinch of salt and a few drops of oil. Cover and cook for 10 minutes. Let the dish stand, covered, for 3 minutes.

◆ Drain the pasta, stir in the sauce and tuna and heat through for 2–3 minutes. Garnish with pepper slices and serve hot.

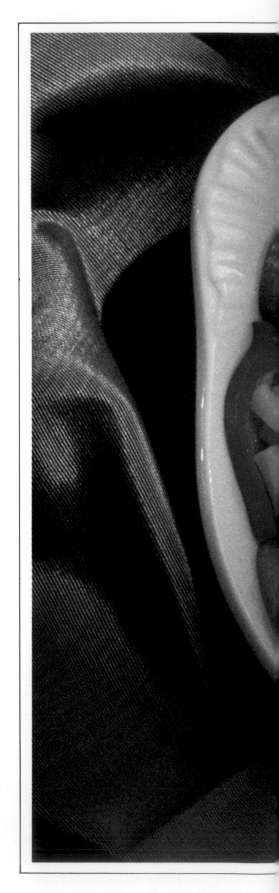

Macaroni with Tuna Fish

LASAGNE WITH SPINACH

SERVES 4 / SET: HIGH AND MEDIUM

Ingredients
10–12 sheets lasagne
boiling water
salt
1 kg/2 lb fresh spinach
200 ml/⅓ pt cream
250 g/8 oz ricotta cheese
freshly ground black pepper
nutmeg
1 tablespoon oil
1 clove garlic, crushed
1 small onion, finely chopped
220 g/7 oz canned tomatoes, sieved

◆ Put the lasagne sheets in a deep oblong dish and cover with boiling water. Add a pinch of salt and a few drops of oil, cover and cook on full power for 10 minutes. Allow to stand, covered, while you make the sauces.

◆ Wash the spinach and discard any tough stalks and discoloured leaves. Put it in a boiling or roasting bag, with only the water clinging to it, tie loosely and cook on high for 6 minutes. Drain and chop roughly.

◆ Mix together the cream and ricotta cheese until well blended. Stir in the spinach and season with salt, pepper and nutmeg to taste.

◆ Assemble the lasagne in an oiled oblong dish. Layer the pasta and the spinach sauce until all are used up. Begin with a layer of pasta and end with a layer of sauce.

◆ Make the tomato sauce. Put the oil in a bowl, add the onion and garlic and cook on high for 2 minutes. Add the sieved tomatoes and cook on high for 2 minutes. Season to taste.

◆ Pour the tomato sauce over the lasagne and heat through on medium for 4 minutes. Serve hot.

Lasagne with Spinach

PAPPARDELLE WITH CHICKEN LIVERS

SERVES 4 / SET: HIGH

Ingredients
440 g/14 oz pappardelle
boiling water
salt
a few drops of oil
1 tablespoon oil
1½ tbsp marsala
2 shallots, finely chopped
1 clove garlic, crushed
250 g/8 oz chicken livers, trimmed and chopped
chopped parsley
lemon wedges

◆ Put the pappardelle in a deep dish and pour over enough boiling water to cover. Add a pinch of salt and a few drops of oil, cover and cook for 9 minutes. Leave to stand, covered, while you prepare the sauce.

◆ Put the oil and marsala in a dish with the shallots and garlic. Cover and cook for 2 minutes. Stir in the chicken livers, and cook for 2–3 minutes, stirring once, until just done.

◆ Drain the pasta and top with the sauce. Sprinkle with chopped parsley and serve with lemon wedges.

TAGLIATELLE WITH ASPARAGUS SPEARS

SERVES 4 / SET: HIGH

Ingredients

440 g/14 oz tagliatelle
boiling water
salt
oil
150 ml/¼ pt light cream
440 g/14 oz freshly cooked or canned asparagus spears
Parmesan cheese

◆ Put the tagliatelle in a deep dish and just cover with boiling water. Add a pinch of salt and a few drops of oil, cover and cook for 6 minutes. Set aside, covered.

◆ Put the cream in a bowl and stir in the asparagus spears. Cook for 2 minutes.

◆ Drain the pasta, pour over the sauce and serve with plenty of Parmesan cheese.

Tagliatelle with Asparagus

LINGUINE WITH BACON AND CHICKEN

S E R V E S   4 / S E T :   H I G H

Ingredients

440 g/14 oz linguine
boiling water
salt
a few drops of oil
45 g/1½ oz butter
1 shallot, chopped
2 large tomatoes, peeled, seeded and chopped
155 g/5 oz cooked chicken, chopped
2 rashers bacon, cooked and chopped
freshly ground black pepper

◆ Put the linguine in a dish and pour over enough boiling water to cover. Add a pinch of salt and a few drops of oil, cover and cook for 9 minutes. Leave to stand, covered, while you prepare the sauce.

◆ Put the butter in a dish and cook for 45 seconds. Add the shallot and cook for 2 minutes. Add the tomatoes, chicken and bacon and cook for 3 minutes, stirring once, until hot. Season to taste.

◆ Drain the linguine, top with the sauce and serve at once.

HAY AND STRAW

SERVES 4 / SET: HIGH

Ingredients

220 g/7 oz yellow tagliatelle
220 g/7 oz green tagliatelle
boiling water
salt
oil
125 g/4 oz Parma ham, chopped
150 ml/¼ pt light cream
freshly ground black pepper
Parmesan cheese

The Italian name of this dish is paglia e
fieno. *'Hay and straw' refers to the two
colours of tagliatelle used. It is very quick
to make.*

◆ Put the yellow and green
tagliatelle together in a deep dish and
pour on enough boiling water to just
cover. Add a pinch of salt and a few
drops of oil. Cover and cook for
6 minutes. Let the dish stand,
covered, while you make the sauce.
◆ Stir the ham and cream together
in a bowl and season with black
pepper. Cook for 2 minutes.
◆ Drain the pasta, stir in the sauce
and serve with plenty of Parmesan
cheese.

Hay and Straw

SPAGHETTI WITH FETA CHEESE AND BLACK OLIVES

SERVES 4 / SET: HIGH

Ingredients

440 g/14 oz spaghetti
1 l/1¾ pt boiling water
salt
2 tbsp olive oil
1 clove garlic, crushed
12 black olives, stoned and chopped
155 g/5 oz feta cheese, crumbled
4 sage leaves, chopped
freshly ground black pepper

◆ Hold the spaghetti in a dish and pour on the boiling water. Push the spaghetti down into the water and add a pinch of salt and a few drops of oil. Cover and cook for 12 minutes. Leave the dish to stand, covered, while you make the sauce.

◆ Put the oil in a dish and cook for 45 seconds. Add the garlic and cook for 1 minute. Add the olives and cook for 30 seconds.

◆ Add the feta cheese to the hot oil, with the chopped sage. Grind on a little black pepper and mix the sauce well.

◆ Drain the spaghetti and stir in the sauce.

◆ Serve at once.

PASTA BOWS WITH CHICKEN LIVERS

SERVES 4 / SET: HIGH

Ingredients

440 g/14 oz farfalle (pasta bows)
boiling water
salt
oil
250 g/8 oz chicken livers, chopped
1½ tbsp marsala
1 clove garlic, crushed
cayenne pepper
Parmesan cheese

◆ Put the pasta into a deep dish and just cover with boiling water. Add a pinch of salt and a few drops of oil and cook, covered, for 9 minutes. Let the dish stand, covered, while you make the sauce.

◆ Put the chicken livers, marsala and garlic in a bowl and cook, covered, for 3 minutes.

◆ Drain the pasta, pour on the sauce, sprinkle with cayenne pepper and serve with Parmesan cheese.

TAGLIATELLE WITH ANCHOVIES AND TUNA

SERVES 4 / SET: HIGH

Ingredients

1½ tbsp olive oil
1 clove garlic, crushed
4 anchovy fillets, drained, soaked in milk, rinsed and chopped
125 g/4 oz canned tuna, drained
1½ tbsp capers
60 g/2 oz black olives, stoned
440 g/14 oz tagliatelle
boiling water
salt
chopped parsley

◆ Put the oil in a bowl and add the garlic. Cook for 1 minute. Stir in the anchovies, tuna, capers and olives, cover and cook for 3 minutes.

◆ Put the tagliatelle in a deep dish and just cover with boiling water. Add a pinch of salt and a few drops of oil, cover and cook for 6 minutes. Let the dish stand for 3 minutes and reheat the sauce for 2 minutes while it is waiting.

◆ Drain the pasta, pour over the sauce and garnish with chopped parsley.

Tagliatelle with Anchovies and Tuna

LASAGNE WITH LEEKS AND SAUSAGE

SERVES 4 / SET: HIGH

Ingredients

2 large leeks, sliced
250 g/8 oz spicy sausage, sliced
220 g/7 oz canned tomatoes, sieved
a pinch dried mixed herbs
salt
6 sheets spinach lasagne
boiling water
a few drops of oil
45 g/1½ oz butter
45 g/1½ oz flour
315 ml/½ pt milk
60 g/2 oz grated cheese
salt and freshly ground black pepper
3 tbsp fresh breadcrumbs

◆ Put the leeks and sausage in a deep oblong dish with 4 tbsp of the sieved tomatoes. Cover with vented plastic wrap and cook for 6 minutes, stirring once. Add the rest of the tomato and the herbs, season, and set aside.

◆ Put the lasagne in a deep dish and pour over enough boiling water to cover. Add a pinch of salt and a few drops of oil, cover and cook for 15 minutes. Drain and rinse thoroughly under cold running water. Lay the pasta on a tea towel to dry. (Do not use kitchen paper – it will stick.)

◆ Make the cheese sauce. Put the butter in a dish and cook for 1 minute. Stir in the flour. Pour on the milk. Cook for 3 minutes, whisking after each minute. Stir in the cheese. Cook for a further minute and whisk again. Season to taste.

◆ Assemble the dish in layers until all the ingredients are used up, finishing with a layer of cheese sauce.

◆ Top with breadcrumbs and heat through in the microwave or, if you would like the dish to brown, in a conventional oven or under the grill.

◆ Serve hot.

CHICKEN LASAGNE

SERVES 4 / SET: HIGH AND MEDIUM

Ingredients

10–12 sheets lasagne

boiling water

salt

oil

45 g/1½ oz butter

1 onion, chopped

1 clove garlic, crushed

125 g/4 oz mushrooms, sliced

1 tsp dried oregano

45 g/1½ oz flour

475 ml/¾ pt milk

1 chicken stock cube

315 g/10 oz cooked chicken, chopped

45 g/1½ oz grated Parmesan cheese, plus extra for the topping

◆ Put the lasagne sheets in a deep oblong dish and cover with boiling water. Add a pinch of salt and a few drops of oil, cover and cook on high for 10 minutes. Allow to stand, covered, while you make the sauce.

◆ Put the butter in a bowl and cook on high for 1 minute. Stir in the onion and garlic and cook on high for 2 minutes. Stir in the mushrooms and oregano and cook on high for 2 minutes.

◆ Stir in the flour and gradually add the milk, stirring. Crumble on the stock cube. Cook on high for 3 minutes, stirring after each minute. Stir in the chicken and cheese and cook on high for 1 minute. Keep warm.

◆ Drain the lasagne and lay the sheets out on a tea towel.

◆ Assemble. In an oiled oblong dish, layer the pasta and sauce until both are used up. Start with a layer of pasta and end with a layer of sauce. Sprinkle more Parmesan cheese on the top and cook on medium power for 5 minutes, turning the dish once.

◆ Serve hot.

TAGLIATELLE WITH MUSSELS AND SHRIMP

SERVES 4 / SET: HIGH

Ingredients

1 tbsp olive oil
1 clove garlic, crushed
220 g/7 oz canned tomatoes, drained and mashed
½ tsp dried basil, or fresh basil to taste, chopped
freshly ground black pepper
250 g/8 oz shrimp, plus a few unpeeled ones for garnish
440 g/14 oz tagliatelle
boiling water
salt
625 ml/1 pt mussels, scrubbed clean
1 glass dry white wine
chopped parsley

◆ Put the oil in a bowl and cook for 30 seconds. Add the garlic and cook for 1 minute. Add the tomatoes, basil, pepper and peeled shrimp and cook for 4 minutes. Season with salt to taste, set aside and keep warm.

◆ Put the tagliatelle in a deep dish and pour over enough boiling water to just cover. Add a pinch of salt and a few drops of oil, cover and cook for 6 minutes. Set aside, covered.

◆ Discard any broken or open mussels and put the rest in a deep dish. Pour over the white wine. Add parsley to taste. Cover and cook for 3 minutes, or until the mussels open.

◆ Remove some mussels from their shells and stir into the sauce. Drain the pasta, pour over the sauce and garnish with the remaining mussels and the unpeeled shrimp.

TAGLIATELLE BOLOGNESE

SERVES 4 / SET: HIGH

Ingredients

1 tbsp oil
1 clove garlic, crushed
1 onion, finely chopped
1 carrot, finely chopped
1 stick celery, finely chopped
220 g/7 oz canned tomatoes, drained and mashed
220 g/7 oz minced beef
60 g/2 oz ham
2 tbsp red wine
1 bay leaf
3 chicken livers, chopped
salt and freshly ground black pepper
440 g/14 oz tagliatelle
boiling water
Parmesan cheese

◆ Put the oil in a bowl and cook for 30 seconds. Add the garlic, onion, carrot and celery and cook for 2 minutes. Stir in the tomatoes, beef and ham and add the red wine to moisten. Tuck the bay leaf into the mixture. Cook for 5 minutes, stirring once.

◆ Add the chicken livers and cook for 2 minutes. Season, set aside and keep warm.

◆ Put the tagliatelle in a deep dish and pour over enough boiling water to just cover. Add a pinch of salt and a few drops of oil, cover and cook for 6 minutes. Leave to stand, covered, for 3 minutes while you reheat the sauce if necessary.

◆ Drain the pasta, pour over the sauce and serve with plenty of Parmesan cheese.

BUCATINI WITH RED LENTIL SAUCE

SERVES 4 / SET: HIGH

Ingredients

1 tbsp oil
1 onion, chopped
1 clove garlic, crushed
220 g/7 oz canned tomatoes, drained and mashed
salt and freshly ground black pepper
155 g/5 oz red lentils
315 ml/½ pt boiling water
440 g/14 oz bucatini
Parmesan cheese

◆ Put the oil in a dish and cook for 30 seconds. Add the onion and garlic, cover and cook for 2 minutes. Add the tomatoes and seasoning. Set aside.

◆ Put the lentils in a dish and pour over the boiling water. Cover and cook for 12 minutes. Stir in the tomato sauce and set aside.

◆ Put the bucatini in a deep dish. Cover with boiling water and add a few drops of oil. Cover and cook for 9 minutes. Set aside.

◆ Reheat the sauce.

◆ Drain the bucatini, stir in the sauce and serve topped with plenty of Parmesan cheese.

Tagliatelle Bolognese

STUFFED CANNELLONI

SERVES 4 / SET: HIGH

Ingredients

1 tbsp oil
1 onion, finely chopped
1 carrot, finely chopped
1 stick celery, finely chopped
2 tbsp red wine
1 tbsp tomato paste
220 g/7 oz lean, minced beef
220 g/7 oz lean, minced veal
125 g/4 oz ham, chopped
250 g/8 oz cannelloni
boiling water
45 g/1 1/2 oz butter
45 g/1 1/2 oz flour
315 ml/1/2 pt milk
freshly ground black pepper
nutmeg
45 g/1 1/2 oz Parmesan cheese, grated
1 egg yolk

◆ First make the stuffing. Put the oil in a bowl and cook for 30 seconds. Stir in the onion, carrot and celery and cook for 2 minutes. Stir in the wine mixed with the tomato paste. Add the beef, veal and ham and combine well. Cover and cook for 5 minutes, until done. Season with salt and pepper.

◆ Put the cannelloni in a deep oblong dish and just cover with boiling water. Add a pinch of salt and a few drops of oil. Cover and cook for 9 minutes. Leave for 3 minutes, covered, then drain and stuff with the meat mixture.

◆ Meanwhile, make the sauce. Put the butter in a bowl and cook for 1 minute. Stir in the flour and cook for 1 minute. Pour on the milk and cook for 3 minutes, whisking after every minute. Add salt and pepper and a little nutmeg to taste. Stir in the Parmesan cheese and cook for a further minute. Whisk again, then stir in the egg yolk.

◆ Lay the stuffed cannelloni in a greased dish, in a single layer if possible. Pour over the sauce. Cover with vented plastic wrap and cook for 1–2 minutes to heat through.

◆ Serve hot.

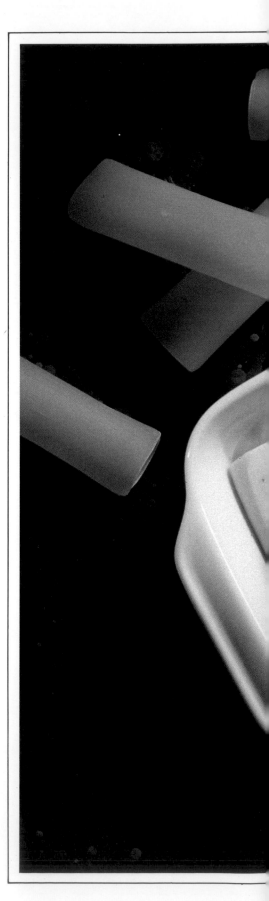

LINGUINE WITH MUSHROOM SAUCE

SERVES 4 / SET: HIGH

Ingredients

250 g/8 oz mushrooms, wiped and sliced
1½ tbsp milk
440 g/14 oz green linguine
boiling water
salt
oil
150 ml/5 fl oz light cream
chopped parsley

◆ Put the mushrooms in a dish and add the milk. Cover and cook for 3 minutes, stirring once. Set aside.

◆ Put the linguine in a deep dish and pour over enough boiling water to cover. Add a pinch of salt and a few drops of oil. Cover and cook for 9 minutes. Set aside.

◆ Stir the cream into the mushrooms. Reheat for 1 minute.

◆ Drain the pasta, pour on the mushrooms, garnish with parsley and serve.

TAGLIATELLE WITH PEAS AND CREAM

SERVES 4 / SET: HIGH

Ingredients

440 g/14 oz tagliatelle
boiling water
salt
oil
150 ml/¼ pt heavy cream
440 g/14 oz cooked or canned peas
60 g/2 oz Emmenthal cheese, grated
60 g/2 oz Parmesan cheese, grated
strips of green pepper

◆ Put the tagliatelle in a dish and pour over enough boiling water to just cover. Add a pinch of salt and a few drops of oil, cover and cook for 6 minutes. Leave to stand, covered.

◆ Pour the cream into a bowl and stir in the peas. Cook for 1½ minutes. Stir in both cheeses and cook for 1½ minutes, stirring twice, until melted.

◆ Drain the tagliatelle, stir in the sauce and serve at once garnished with strips of pepper.

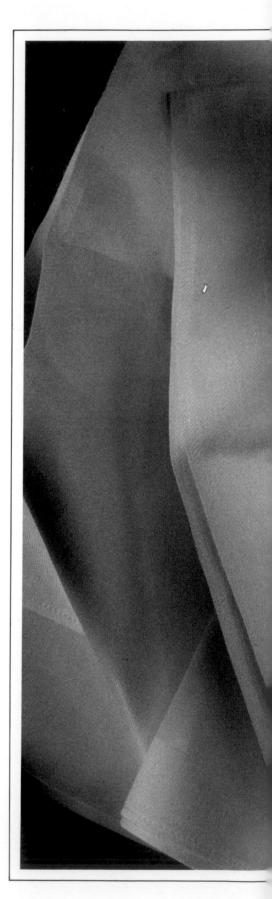

Tagliatelle with Peas and Cream

LINGUINE WITH GREEN BEANS, TOMATOES AND PUMPKIN SEEDS

SERVES 4 / SET: HIGH

Ingredients

250 g/8 oz green beans, topped and tailed and cut into bite size pieces
2 tbsp water
250 g/8 oz tomatoes, peeled, seeded and cut into strips
60 g/2 oz pumpkin seeds
440 g/14 oz green linguine
boiling water
salt
1–2 tbsp oil
Parmesan cheese (optional)

◆ Put the beans in a dish with the water, cover with vented plastic wrap and cook for 4 minutes.

◆ Add the tomatoes and cook for a further 4 minutes. Add the pumpkin seeds. Keep covered and keep warm.

◆ Put the linguine in a deep dish with enough boiling water to cover. Add a pinch of salt and a few drops of oil. Cover and cook for 8 minutes. Set aside, covered.

◆ Drain the vegetables and dress with the oil. Reheat, covered, for 1 minute.

◆ Drain the pasta and mix in the vegetables.

◆ Serve with Parmesan cheese if liked.

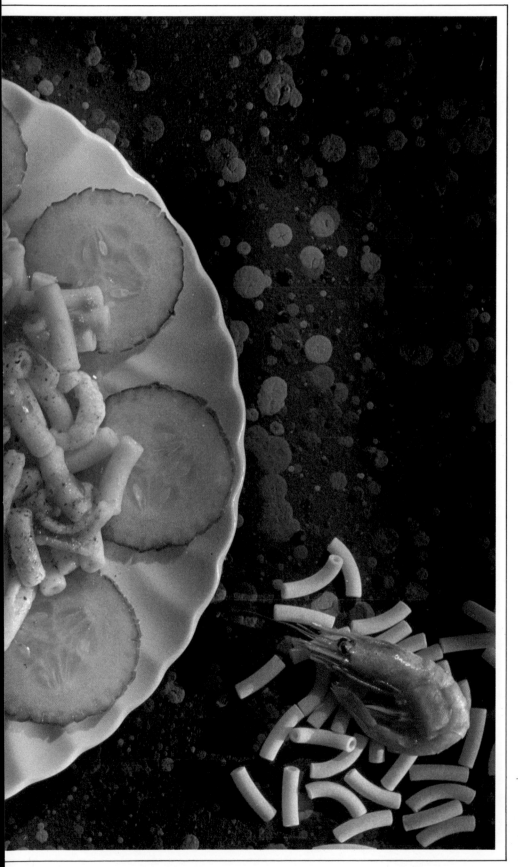

MACARONI WITH PRAWNS

S E R V E S   4 / S E T :   H I G H

Ingredients

1 tbsp oil
2 cloves garlic, crushed
1 red chilli, seeded and chopped
440 g/14 oz canned tomatoes, drained and mashed
375 g/12 oz shelled prawns
1 tbsp lemon juice
freshly ground black pepper
a sprig of thyme
1 bay leaf
a few sprigs of parsley
440 g/14 oz macaroni
boiling water
salt
cucumber slices

◆ Put the oil in a bowl and cook for 30 seconds. Add the garlic and chilli and cook for 1 minute. Stir in the tomatoes and cook for 3 minutes. Stir in the prawns and lemon juice, sprinkle with black pepper and add the herbs. Cover and cook for 2 minutes.

◆ Put the macaroni in a bowl and just cover with boiling water. Add a pinch of salt and a few drops of oil, cover and cook for 10 minutes. Leave to stand for 3 minutes. Reheat the sauce if necessary.

◆ Drain the pasta and mix in the sauce.

◆ Garnish with cucumber slices and serve hot.

Macaroni with Prawns

BUCATINI ALL'AMATRICIANA

S E R V E S   4 / S E T :   H I G H

Ingredients

90 g/3 oz bacon, derinded and chopped

30 g/1 oz butter

1 onion, finely chopped

440 g/14 oz canned tomatoes, drained and mashed

220 g/7 oz canned peas, drained

salt

440 g/14 oz bucatini

boiling water

salt

oil

grated pecorino cheese

◆ Put the bacon on a plate covered with absorbent kitchen paper. Cook for 2 minutes. Set aside.

◆ Put the butter in a bowl and cook for 1 minute. Add the onion and cook for 2 minutes. Stir in the tomatoes and cook for 2 minutes. Stir in the peas and bacon and cook for 2 minutes.

◆ Put the bucatini in a dish and just cover with boiling water. Add a pinch of salt and a few drops of oil, cover and cook for 10 minutes. Set aside, covered. Reheat the sauce if necessary during standing time.

◆ Drain the pasta, top with the sauce and serve with grated pecorino cheese.

SPAGHETTI WITH SNOW PEAS

SERVES 4 / SET: HIGH

Ingredients

1 tbsp oil
30 g/1 oz butter
1 clove garlic, crushed
125 g/4 oz snow peas
125 g/4 oz button mushrooms, wiped and sliced
125 g/4 oz fresh tomatoes, skinned and chopped
salt and freshly ground black pepper
440 g/14 oz spaghetti
1 l/1¾ pt boiling water
chopped fresh herbs
Parmesan cheese

◆ Put the oil in a bowl with the butter and cook for 1 minute. Add the garlic and cook for 1 minute. Stir in the snow peas, mushrooms and tomatoes. Cover with vented plastic wrap and cook for 3 minutes. Season and set aside.

◆ Hold the spaghetti in a deep dish. Pour over the boiling water and push the spaghetti down into the dish. Add a pinch of salt and a few drops of oil, cover and cook for 12 minutes. Leave to stand, covered, for 5 minutes. Reheat the sauce during standing time if necessary.

◆ Drain the pasta and top with the sauce. Sprinkle with fresh herbs and offer Parmesan cheese at the table.

FARFALLE AL GORGONZOLA

SERVES 4 / SET: HIGH

Ingredients

185–250 g/6–8 oz ripe gorgonzola cheese
150 ml/¼ pt cream
440 g/14 oz farfalle (bow-shaped pasta)
boiling water
salt
oil
freshly ground black pepper

This is a luxurious dish that can be prepared very quickly.

◆ If necessary, soften the cheese by putting it, wrapped, in the microwave for a few seconds on defrost power. Cream the cheese with the cream in a blender or food processor. Put the mixture in a bowl and cook for 2 minutes to warm through.

◆ Put the pasta in a deep dish and just cover with boiling water. Add a pinch of salt and a few drops of oil, cover and cook for 10 minutes. Leave to stand for 3 minutes.

◆ Heat the sauce through again if necessary during the standing time. It should be warm, not hot.

◆ Drain the pasta and stir in the sauce. Offer black pepper at the table.

Farfalle al Gorgonzola

BEAN-STUFFED CANNELLONI

SERVES 4 / SET: HIGH

Ingredients

440 g/14 oz canned cannellini beans, drained
125 g/4 oz ricotta cheese
1 bunch parsley, chopped
1 onion, chopped
250 g/8 oz tomatoes, skinned, peeled and chopped
salt and freshly ground black pepper
8 cannelloni
boiling water
a few drops of oil
150 ml/¼ pt light cream

When cooked like this, the onion and tomato in the stuffing will still be crisp and firm respectively, which makes a refreshing change.

◆ Make the stuffing by mixing together the beans, ricotta, parsley, onion and tomatoes, and season well with salt and pepper.

◆ Put the cannelloni in a deep oblong dish and cover with boiling water. Add a few drops of oil and a pinch of salt. Cover and cook for 12 minutes. Drain and rinse under cold running water.

◆ Stuff the cannelloni with the bean mixture and arrange in the dish. Pour the cream over and reheat for 2 minutes.

◆ Serve at once.

GREEN TAGLIATELLE WITH PEPPERS

SERVES 4 / SET: HIGH

Ingredients

1 tbsp olive oil
1 small onion, chopped
1 clove garlic, crushed
440 g/14 oz canned tomatoes, drained
salt and freshly ground black pepper
½ red pepper, cut into strips about 2.5 cm/ 1 in long
½ green pepper, cut into strips about 2.5 cm/1 in long
½ yellow pepper, cut into strips about 2.5 cm/1 in long
2 tbsp water
440 g/14 oz spinach tagliatelle
boiling water
salt
Parmesan cheese

◆ Put the oil in a bowl and cook for 30 seconds. Add the onion and garlic and cook for 2 minutes. Add the tomatoes and cook for 2 minutes. Purée in a blender or food processor and season to taste.

◆ Put the pepper strips in a bowl and add the water. Cover with vented plastic wrap and cook for 4 minutes, until tender. Set aside.

◆ Put the tagliatelle in a deep dish and just cover with boiling water. Add a pinch of salt and a few drops of oil, cover and cook for 6 minutes. Leave to stand for 3 minutes. Reheat the sauce if necessary during standing time.

◆ Drain the pasta, pour over the sauce and garnish with the strips of pepper.

◆ Serve with Parmesan cheese.

TAGLIATELLE WITH SPINACH AND WALNUT SAUCE

SERVES 4 / SET: HIGH

Ingredients

500 g/1 lb fresh spinach
4 rashers bacon, derinded and chopped
15 g/½ oz butter
1 clove garlic, crushed
150 ml/5 fl oz light cream
60 g/2 oz walnut pieces
440 g/14 oz tagliatelle
boiling water
salt
oil
Parmesan cheese

◆ Wash the spinach and discard any tough leaves and stalks. Put it into a roasting or boiling bag with only the water clinging to it, tie loosely and cook for 6 minutes, until the leaves have collapsed. Purée the spinach in a blender or food processor.

◆ Put the bacon on a plate covered with absorbent kitchen paper and cook for 2 minutes until done.

◆ Put the butter in a small bowl with the garlic, add the bacon and cook for 2 minutes.

◆ Stir the spinach into the cream, add the walnuts and cook for 4 minutes. Set aside, covered.

◆ Put the tagliatelle in a deep bowl and just cover with boiling water. Add a pinch of salt and a few drops of oil and cook for 6 minutes. Let the bowl stand, covered, while you reheat the spinach cream sauce if necessary.

◆ Drain the pasta and stir in the cream sauce. Top with the garlic and bacon.

◆ Serve hot with Parmesan cheese.

LASAGNE WITH FISH

SERVES 4 / SET: HIGH

Ingredients

6 sheets lasagne
boiling water
salt
oil
250 g/8 oz cooked white fish, flaked
220 g/7 oz canned corn kernels, drained
220 g/7 oz canned tomatoes, strained
chopped parsley
freshly ground black pepper
45 g/1½ oz butter
45 g/1½ oz flour
315 ml/½ pt milk
60 g/2 oz Edam cheese, grated
1½ tbsp Parmesan cheese

◆ Put the lasagne in a dish and pour over enough boiling water to cover. Add a pinch of salt and a few drops of oil. Cover and cook for 15 minutes. Drain and rinse well under cold running water. Lay the sheets on a tea towel to dry. (Do not use kitchen paper – it will stick.)

◆ Mix the fish, corn kernels, tomatoes and parsley together and season with salt and pepper.

◆ Put the butter in a bowl and cook for 1 minute. Stir in the flour. Pour on the milk and cook for 3 minutes, whisking after each minute. Stir in the Edam cheese and cook for a further minute. Whisk again. Season with salt and pepper.

◆ Assemble. Begin with a layer of fish and tomato, then cover with lasagne and top with cheese sauce. Continue until all the ingredients have been used up, ending with the cheese sauce. Sprinkle with Parmesan cheese.

◆ Heat through in the microwave, or under the grill, or in a conventional oven if you want the top to brown.

PENNE AL PESTO

SERVES 4 / SET: HIGH

Ingredients

1 large bunch fresh basil
1 tbsp pine nuts
4 cloves garlic
2 tbsp Parmesan cheese, grated
virgin olive oil
salt and freshly ground black pepper
440 g/14 oz penne (pasta quills)
boiling water

This dish is a speciality of Genoa, on the Ligurian coast of Italy. Pesto sauce can be served equally well with rice.

◆ To make the pesto sauce chop the basil leaves into a mortar. Add the pine nuts and garlic and crush with the pestle. Add Parmesan cheese and olive oil, pounding all the while, until you have a thick paste. Season with salt and pepper. You can make the sauce by combining all the ingredients in a blender or food processor, but it is more satisfying by hand.

◆ Put the penne in a large dish and just cover with boiling water. Add a pinch of salt and a few drops of oil, cover and cook for 10 minutes. Leave to stand for a couple of minutes, then drain and stir in the sauce.

◆ Serve hot.

Penne al Pesto

RIGATONI COUNTRY-STYLE

SERVES 4 / SET: HIGH

Ingredients

440 g/14 oz rigatoni (or macaroni)

boiling water

salt

oil

185 g/6 oz spicy sausage, cut into chunks or sliced

125 g/4 oz cauliflower florets

1 tbsp water

125 g/4 oz green beans, topped and tailed and cut into bite size pieces

1–2 tbsp olive oil

cayenne pepper

1 whole mozzarella cheese, diced

Use the long spicy sausages sold in coils for this dish. If you can't find these, use diced salami.

◆ Put the rigatoni in a deep dish and just cover with boiling water. Add a pinch of salt and a few drops of oil. Cover and cook for 10 minutes. Leave to stand, covered, while you make the sauce.

◆ Put the sausage pieces on a plate covered with absorbent kitchen paper and cook for 1½ minutes. Cover and keep warm.

◆ Put the cauliflower in a bowl with the water. Cover and cook for 1 minute. Add the beans, cover and cook for 3 minutes.

◆ Drain the pasta and vegetables. Pour the olive oil over the pasta and season with cayenne pepper. Stir in the cauliflower, beans, sausage and diced mozzarella cheese, cover and heat through for 1 minute.

◆ Serve hot.

Rigatoni Country-Style

LASAGNE AND HAM ROLLS

SERVES 4 / SET: HIGH

Ingredients

4 sheets spinach lasagne

boiling water

salt

oil

4 slices ham, the same size as the lasagne sheets

This makes a tasty and attractive appetizer and it is also an unusual accompaniment to drinks. It is simple to prepare, but looks elegant.

◆ Put the lasagne in a deep dish with enough boiling water to cover. Add a pinch of salt and a few drops of oil. Cover and cook for 10 minutes. Leave to stand for 3 minutes. Drain and rinse well under cold running water.

◆ Lay the lasagne sheets out on a tea towel to dry. Do not use kitchen paper – it will stick to the pasta.

◆ When the lasagne has cooled, lay a slice of ham on top of each sheet and roll up tightly.

◆ Cut each roll into slices and serve cold.

SPAGHETTI WITH CLAMS

SERVES 4 / SET: HIGH

Ingredients

750 g/1½ lb clams (or other small shellfish)
2 tbsp olive oil
1 clove garlic, crushed
500 g/1 lb ripe tomatoes, peeled and chopped
salt and freshly ground black pepper
440 g/14 oz spaghetti
1 l/1¾ pt boiling water
a small glass of dry white wine
chopped parsley

This dish is one of the specialities of Naples.

◆ Clean the clams thoroughly under running water.

◆ Put the olive oil in a bowl and cook for 30 seconds. Add the garlic and cook for 1 minute. Add the tomatoes, cover with vented plastic wrap and cook for 4 minutes, until soft. Season with salt and pepper and keep warm.

◆ Hold the spaghetti in a large dish and pour the boiling water over it. Push the spaghetti down into the water, add a pinch of salt and a few drops of oil, cover and cook for 2 minutes. Set aside, covered.

◆ Put the clams in a dish with the white wine, cover and cook for 2–3 minutes, until the shells open. Set aside.

◆ Drain the spaghetti and stir in the tomato sauce. Drain the clams and pile on top of the pasta.

◆ Sprinkle with parsley and serve hot.

VARIATION The clams may be removed from their shells before serving if you prefer.

Spaghetti with Clams

MACARONI WITH BROCCOLI AND ALMONDS

SERVES 4 / SET: HIGH

Ingredients

440 g/14 oz macaroni
boiling water
oil
salt
60 g/2 oz butter
250 g/8 oz broccoli florets
60 g/2 oz flaked, toasted almonds
3 tbsp grated pecorino cheese

◆ Put the macaroni in a deep dish and pour over enough boiling water to cover. Add a few drops of oil and a pinch of salt, cover and cook for 9 minutes. Allow to stand.

◆ Put half the butter in a dish and cook for 1 minute. Add the broccoli and almonds and cook for 6 minutes, stirring twice, until the broccoli is tender, but still crisp.

◆ Drain the pasta, add the rest of the butter and the broccoli and almonds, toss and sprinkle with grated cheese before serving.

SPAGHETTI ALLA PUTANESCA

SERVES 4 / SET: HIGH

Ingredients

440 g/14 oz spaghetti
1 l/1¾ pt boiling water
salt
oil
2 cloves garlic, crushed
60 g/2 oz black olives, stoned and roughly chopped
3 tsp capers, roughly chopped
5 anchovies, soaked in milk, rinsed, dried and chopped
1 red chilli, seeded and chopped
1½ tbsp olive oil
220 g/7 oz canned tomatoes, drained and chopped
chopped parsley

Legend has it that this dish was prepared by the whores of Rome. It is hot and fiery.

◆ Hold the spaghetti in a dish and pour the boiling water over it. Push the spaghetti down into the dish, add a pinch of salt and a few drops of oil, cover and cook for 12 minutes. Set aside, covered.

◆ Put the garlic, olives, capers, anchovies, chilli and olive oil in a bowl. Stir well, cover and cook for 2 minutes. Stir in the tomatoes, cover and cook for 3 minutes.

◆ Drain the spaghetti, stir in the sauce and top with chopped parsley to serve.

Spaghetti alla Putanesca

PASTA AND FISH SALAD

SERVES 4 / SET: HIGH

Ingredients

440 g/14 oz farfalle (bow-shaped pasta)
boiling water
salt
2 tbsp oil
220 g/7 oz canned tuna in brine, drained and flaked
2 pink onions, chopped
220 g/7 oz canned kidney beans, drained
freshly ground black pepper
chopped parsley
lemon wedges

◆ Put the farfalle in a dish and pour on enough boiling water to cover. Add a pinch of salt and a few drops of oil, cover and cook for 9 minutes. Drain and rinse thoroughly under cold running water. Drain thoroughly.

◆ Toss the pasta in the oil, add the tuna, onions and kidney beans and mix well.

◆ Season with salt and pepper, sprinkle with parsley and serve with lemon wedges.

PASTA AND HAM SALAD

SERVES 4 / SET: HIGH

Ingredients

440 g/14 oz shell pasta
boiling water
salt
a few drops of oil
125 g/4 oz diced ham
220 g/7 oz cooked broad beans (or use canned beans, drained)
150 ml/5 fl oz sour cream
freshly ground black pepper
mint leaves

◆ Put the pasta in a dish and pour over enough boiling water to cover. Add a pinch of salt and a few drops of oil, cover and cook for 9 minutes. Drain and rinse thoroughly under cold running water. Drain thoroughly.

◆ Toss the pasta with the ham and broad beans in sour cream. Season with salt and pepper and garnish with mint leaves.

PASTA WITH CHICK PEAS

SERVES 4 / SET: HIGH

Ingredients

440 g/14 oz multi-coloured pasta
boiling water
salt
1 tbsp oil
30 g/1 oz butter
1 clove garlic, crushed
440 g/14 oz canned chick peas, drained
60–90 g/2–3 oz freshly grated Parmesan cheese
freshly ground black pepper

This is a very simple dish called 'thunder and lightning' in Italy. Make it with canned chick peas to save time.

◆ Put the pasta in a bowl and just cover with boiling water. Add a pinch of salt and a few drops of oil, cover and cook for 10 minutes. Allow to stand, covered.

◆ Put the butter in a bowl and cook for 1 minute. Stir in the garlic and chick peas, cover and cook for 2 minutes.

◆ Drain the pasta. Pour over the oil and the garlic chick peas and add the Parmesan cheese.

◆ Stir and serve at once. Offer black pepper at the table.

Pasta with Chick Peas

SPAGHETTI WITH SQUID

SERVES 4 / SET: HIGH

Ingredients

440 g/14 oz small squid
2 tbsp olive oil
1 onion, finely chopped
1 clove garlic, crushed
1 stick celery, finely sliced
1 carrot, finely chopped
15 ml/1 tbsp lemon juice
chopped parsley
salt and freshly ground black pepper
440 g/14 oz spaghetti
1 l/1¾ pt boiling water

◆ Remove the eyes and mouth of the squid, take out the cuttlefish bone and wash the squid thoroughly, peeling off the outer skin as you do so. Cut the body and tentacles into slices.

◆ Put the oil in a dish and cook for 30 seconds. Add the onion, garlic, celery, carrot and squid, sprinkle with lemon juice, cover and cook for 5 minutes. Stir in the parsley and season with salt and pepper.

◆ Hold the spaghetti in a dish and pour the water over it. As the spaghetti softens, push it down into the water. Add a pinch of salt and a few drops of oil, cover and cook for 12 minutes. Leave to stand for 5 minutes while you reheat the squid mixture.

◆ Drain the spaghetti and stir in the sauce. Serve at once.

Spaghetti with Squid

SPINACH AND RICOTTA ROLLS

SERVES 4 / SET: HIGH

Ingredients

1 kg/2 lb fresh spinach
250 g/8 oz ricotta cheese
salt and freshly ground black pepper
freshly grated nutmeg
8 sheets lasagne
boiling water
15 ml/1 tbsp oil
1 clove garlic, crushed
1 small onion, chopped
440 g/14 oz canned tomatoes, sieved

◆ Wash the spinach and remove tough stalks and discoloured leaves. Put it in a roasting or boiling bag, tie loosely and cook for 6 minutes, shaking the bag once. Allow to cool.

◆ Chop the spinach, draining away excess moisture. Mix it well with the ricotta and season with salt, pepper and nutmeg.

◆ Put the lasagne in a dish and pour over enough boiling water to cover. Add a pinch of salt and a few drops of oil. Cover and cook for 15 minutes. Drain and rinse thoroughly under cold running water. Lay the lasagne sheets out on a tea towel to dry.

◆ Meanwhile, make the sauce. Put the oil in a bowl and cook for 30 seconds. Add the garlic and onion and cook for 3 minutes. Stir in the sieved tomato and cook for 4 minutes. Season to taste with salt and pepper.

◆ To assemble, divide the spinach and ricotta mixture between the lasagne sheets. Spread it out to cover the lasagne and roll each sheet up. Pack them in a dish they just fit and pour over the hot tomato sauce.

◆ Heat through in the microwave for a couple of minutes and serve hot.

SPAGHETTI ALLA CARBONARA

SERVES 4 / SET: HIGH AND MEDIUM

Ingredients

440 g/14 oz spaghetti
1 l/1¾ pt boiling water
salt
oil
150 ml/5 fl oz heavy cream
30 g/1 oz butter
4 eggs
3 tbsp grated Parmesan cheese
90 g/3 oz diced ham
freshly ground black pepper

This favourite Roman dish is named after the charcoal burners who are said to have invented it.

◆ Put the spaghetti in a dish and pour on the boiling water. Push the spaghetti down into the dish. Add a pinch of salt and a few drops of oil. Cover the dish and cook on high for 12 minutes. Leave to stand, covered.
◆ Put the cream in a bowl with the butter and heat through on medium for 1½ minutes. Break in the eggs and beat well. Stir in the Parmesan and ham and season with black pepper. Cook on medium for 2–3 minutes, until the eggs are almost cooked and lightly scrambled in the cream, stirring twice.
◆ Drain the spaghetti, stir in the hot sauce and serve at once.

Spaghetti alla Carbonara

SPAGHETTI MASCARPONE

SERVES 4 / SET: HIGH

Ingredients

440 g/14 oz spaghetti
1 l/1¾ pt boiling water
salt
a few drops of oil
2 egg yolks
125 g/4 oz mascarpone cheese
freshly ground black pepper
3 tbsp grated Parmesan cheese

Mascarpone is an Italian cheese sold in muslin (cheesecloth) bags. You can substitute cream cheese if you can't get the real thing.

◆ Hold the spaghetti in a deep dish and pour over the boiling water. Push the spaghetti down into the water. Add more to cover if necessary. Add a pinch of salt and a few drops of oil, cover and cook for 12 minutes. Leave to stand.
◆ Stir the egg yolks into the mascarpone.
◆ Drain the pasta, top with the mascarpone and sprinkle with black pepper and Parmesan.
◆ Heat through for 1 minute, then serve.

PASTA SHELLS WITH CRAB MEAT

SERVES 4 / SET: HIGH

Ingredients

440 g/14 oz pasta shells
boiling water
salt
oil
220 g/7 oz canned or fresh crab meat, flaked
150 ml/¼ pt light cream
1 tbsp marsala
cayenne pepper
chopped parsley

◆ Put the pasta shells in a deep dish, just cover with boiling water, add a pinch of salt and a few drops of oil, cover and cook for 9 minutes. Allow to stand, covered, while you make the sauce.

◆ Stir the crab meat into the cream, add the marsala and cook for 3 minutes.

◆ Drain the pasta, stir in the sauce, sprinkle with cayenne pepper and garnish with chopped parsley.

Pasta Shells with Crab Meat

RIGATONI WITH SARDINES

SERVES 4 / SET: HIGH

Ingredients

440 g/14 oz rigatoni

boiling water

salt

1 tbsp oil

1 clove garlic, crushed

155 g/5 oz canned sardines in tomato sauce

4 leaves fresh sage, chopped

freshly ground black pepper

◆ Put the rigatoni in a dish and cover with boiling water. Add a pinch of salt and a few drops of the oil, cover and cook for 9 minutes. Leave to stand, covered, while you prepare the sauce.

◆ Put the remaining oil in a bowl and cook for 30 seconds. Add the garlic and cook for 1½ minutes.

◆ Mash the sardines in their tomato sauce and add to the bowl. Cover and cook for 2–3 minutes, stirring once, until hot through.

◆ Drain the pasta, pour the sauce over it, sprinkle with fresh sage and pepper and serve.

COOKING WITH

Fish

ELIZABETH CORNISH

FISH

ANYONE who has ever tasted fish cooked in a microwave will agree that there is no better way of retaining its succulence, freshness, delicacy of flavour and fineness of texture.
Fish is so moist that it can be cooked in little or no liquid or fat, so none of its flavour is lost or changed. It can also be cooked very fast, so it won't go dry or rubbery.
Fish is an excellent source of protein, vitamins and minerals and is becoming increasingly popular, particularly in comparison with meat, because it is less fat.

As people eat more and more fish, so the selection available grows and unusual varieties begin to appear. There are at least 50 types of edible fish, so most of us have many more to look forward to.
This book features a selection of fish, among them salmon, trout, flounder, whiting, and schnapper, all types of seafood and molluscs, and even eel and squid. If you find a fish that you haven't tried before which isn't in the book, ask for advice on its preparation when you buy it. You will certainly be able to adapt several recipes to suit different fish because most of them, soft- or firm-fleshed are cooked in the same way.
Perhaps in the past the plainness of traditional fish cooking has put some people off eating it more than once a week. It's just as easy to be adventurous with fish as with any other food, and as the photographs in this book demonstrate, you can create something that looks spectacular and tastes exciting with very little effort.
Fish is such a clean and simple food and it lends itself perfectly to dishes that are bright and elegant with combinations of tastes that surprise and delight. As these dishes take such little time to prepare, you will be able to cook something good enough for a dinner party every night of the week.

CONTENTS

PAELLA

SERVES 4 / SET: HIGH

Ingredients

1 tbsp olive oil
1 onion, finely sliced
1 clove garlic, crushed
250 g/8 oz long-grain rice
a few strands of saffron
625 ml/1 pt boiling chicken stock
salt and freshly ground black pepper
220 g/7 oz peas
185 g/6 oz shrimp, plus a few for garnish
125 g/4 oz cooked chicken, chopped
125 g/4 oz cooked ham, chopped
625 g/1 lb 4 oz mussels, scrubbed and rinsed
315 g/10 oz clams (or other small shellfish), thoroughly rinsed
small glass of dry white wine

It is important to scrub the mussels thoroughly under running water to remove their beards and any grit. Discard any shells that are open or broken.

◆ Put the oil in a large dish and cook for 30 seconds. Stir in the onion and garlic and cook for 2 minutes. Stir in the rice and saffron, pour over the boiling stock, add seasoning, cover and cook for 8 minutes.

◆ Stir in the peas, shrimp, chicken and ham, cover and cook for 4 minutes. Leave the dish to stand, covered, while you cook the mussels and clams.

◆ Put the mussels and clams in a large dish and pour over the wine. Cook for about 3 minutes, until the shells have opened. Discard any shells that remain closed.

◆ Arrange the paella on a heated serving plate. Take some of the mussels and clams out of their shells and add to the rice. Garnish the dish with the remaining mussels, clams and shrimp.

SALMON STEAKS WITH HOLLANDAISE SAUCE

SERVES 4 / SET: DEFROST AND HIGH

Ingredients

125 g/4 oz butter, diced
1 1/2 tbsp lemon juice
3 egg yolks
salt and white pepper
4 salmon steaks, about 185 g/6 oz each

Serve this dish on a special occasion with new peas and new potatoes. Salmon is so succulent that it will cook perfectly without the addition of any water or fat.

◆ First make the sauce. Put the butter in a bowl and cook for 2 minutes on medium or defrost until melted. Add the lemon juice and the egg yolks and whisk lightly.

◆ Cook on medium or defrost for 1 minute, whisk again and season with salt and white pepper (black pepper would spoil the appearance of the sauce). Transfer the sauce to a heated jug and keep warm while you cook the salmon.

◆ Rinse the salmon steaks, pat dry and lay in a shallow dish: Cover with vented plastic wrap and cook on high for 3 1/2–4 minutes, turning the dish once.

◆ Serve the salmon steaks with the Hollandaise sauce.

◆ This dish is equally good served cold, but not chilled.

FISHERMAN'S PIE

SERVES 4 / SET: HIGH

Ingredients

750 g/1½ lb smoked cod or haddock fillets, skinned
125 g/4 oz mushrooms
4 small leeks, sliced
300 ml/½ pt milk
45 g/1½ oz butter
45 g/1½ oz flour
45 g/1½ oz Gruyère cheese, grated
45 g/1½ oz Parmesan cheese, grated
salt and freshly ground black pepper
2 hardboiled eggs, sliced
250 g/8 oz shrimp, peeled
750 g/1½ lb potatoes, cooked and mashed with plenty of butter and a little milk

◆ Put the fish fillets in a deep pie dish with the mushrooms and leeks and add about 4 tbsp of the milk. Cover and cook for 3–4 minutes until fish is tender. Pour off the milk and reserve. Flake the fish with a fork.

◆ Put the butter in a jug or bowl and cook for 1 minute, until melted. Stir in the flour. Cook for 1 minute. Pour on the milk the fish was cooked in and the remaining milk. Cook for 3 minutes, whisking the sauce after each minute. Add the cheeses and season. Cook for a further minute and whisk again.

◆ Combine the fish, mushrooms, leeks, eggs and shrimp in the pie dish and stir in the sauce. Top with the mashed potato and heat through for about 4 minutes.

◆ Brown the top under the grill if liked before serving.

Fisherman's Pie

FRIED FISH ROE

SERVES 1 / SET: HIGH

Ingredients

a little flour
1 fish roe
a little beaten egg
60 g/2 oz fresh breadcrumbs
15 g/½ oz butter
lemon wedges

The fish roe that you buy will have already been cooked. Fried fish roe makes a very nourishing lunch for one with a crisp salad.

◆ Sprinkle flour over the roe to coat it evenly. Dust off the excess. Roll it in egg, then in breadcrumbs, pushing them on with your fingers.

◆ Heat a browning dish to maximum according to the manufacturer's instructions. Put the butter on the dish and, wearing oven gloves, tilt it so that it is covered in hot fat.

◆ Put the roe on the dish and cook for 30–45 seconds on each side.

◆ Let it stand for 1 minute, then serve with lemon wedges.

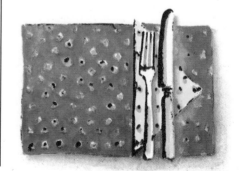

HOMEMADE FISH CAKES IN TOMATO SAUCE

S E R V E S   4 – 6 / S E T :   H I G H

Ingredients

500 g/1 lb firm, white fish fillets
2 tbsp water
500 g/1 lb even size potatoes
45 g/1½ oz butter
45 g/1½ oz flour
315 ml/½ pt milk
chopped parsley
salt and freshly ground black pepper
dried breadcrumbs
TOMATO SAUCE
1 tbsp oil
1 onion, chopped
1 clove garlic, crushed
440 g/14 oz canned tomatoes, drained
1 tbsp tomato paste

◆ Put the fish fillets in a dish with the water. Cover with vented plastic wrap and cook for 4 minutes, until done. Drain and flake the fish with a fork.

◆ Put the potatoes in the oven and cook for 4–7 minutes, depending on their size, rearranging once. When they are done, remove and allow them to cool. Remove the skins and mash the potato well.

◆ Put the butter in a bowl and cook for 1 minute. Stir in the flour and cook for 1 minute. Stir in the milk and cook for 3 minutes, whisking after each minute.

◆ Mix the fish and potatoes together and bind with the sauce. Add enough sauce so that you have a very stiff mixture. Mix in the parsley and seasoning.

◆ Form the mixture into cakes. Roll them in dried breadcrumbs and set aside while you make the tomato sauce.

◆ Put the oil in a bowl and mix in the onion and garlic. Cook for 2 minutes. Add the tomatoes, tomato paste and seasoning. Cook for 3 minutes. Mix until smooth in a food processor or blender. Return to the oven to heat through for 2 minutes.

◆ Cook the fish cakes. Heat a browning dish to maximum, according to the manufacturer's instructions, and cook the cakes in batches of 3 for 3 minutes each, turning them over half-way through. If you have no browning dish, they can be cooked on a greased plate, but they won't be crisp.

◆ Spoon a pool of sauce onto each plate and lay the fish cakes in it. Serve at once.

VARIATION This is an excellent way of serving bought fish fingers.

FILLETS OF FLOUNDER WITH GRAPES, ALMONDS AND PRAWNS

SERVES 4 / SET: HIGH

Ingredients

12 large green grapes
90 g/3 oz toasted flaked almonds
8 large prawns
150 ml/¼ pt canned consommé
1 tbsp sherry
4 flounder fillets, skinned
a little butter

◆ Halve the grapes and remove the pips. Put them in a dish with the flaked almonds, prawns, consommé and sherry and cook for 2–3 minutes, until hot through. Keep warm.
◆ Lay the flounder fillets in a buttered dish and dot with butter. Cover with vented plastic wrap and cook for 2–3 minutes, turning once, until cooked through.
◆ Put the fillets on 4 heated plates and spoon the sauce around them. Serve at once.

Fillets of Flounder with Grapes, Almonds and Prawns

FISH IN VERMOUTH SAUCE

SERVES 4 / SET: HIGH

Ingredients

1 tbsp oil
1 shallot, chopped
90 g/3 oz mushrooms, wiped and sliced
2 tbsp dry vermouth
150 ml/¼ pt light cream
salt
cayenne pepper
4 fillets white fish
a little butter

Use any white fish fillets for this recipe.

◆ First make the sauce. Put the oil in a dish and cook for 30 seconds. Add the shallot and cook for 2 minutes. Add the mushrooms and vermouth, cover with vented plastic wrap and cook for 3 minutes, stirring once.

◆ Stir in the cream and season to taste with salt and cayenne pepper. Set aside.

◆ Put the fish fillets in a dish and dot with butter. Cover with vented plastic wrap and cook for 3–4 minutes, until done, rearranging once.

◆ Heat the sauce through for 1 minute.

◆ Lay the fish fillets on heated plates, pour over the sauce and serve.

FISH IN SWEET AND SOUR SAUCE

SERVES 2—4 / SET: HIGH

Ingredients

1 tbsp minced onion
1 clove garlic, crushed
2 hot chillies, seeded and finely sliced
1 slice root ginger, grated
2 tbsp sherry
4 firm, white fish fillets, weighing about 500 g/1 lb in total
220 g/7 oz canned tomatoes, drained and sieved
1 tbsp tomato paste
a pinch of sugar
finely shredded spring onions (scallions)
tomato slices

Serve this dish with fluffy white rice.

◆ For the marinade, mix together in a dish the onion, garlic, chillies, ginger and sherry. Lay the fish in the marinade and leave for an hour, turning occasionally.

◆ Mix together the tomatoes, tomato paste and sugar and pour over the fish. Cover with vented plastic wrap and cook for about 5 minutes, until done, turning once.

◆ Serve garnished with finely shredded spring onions (scallions) and tomato slices.

FILLETS OF FISH WITH CRANBERRY SAUCE

SERVES 4 / SET: HIGH

Ingredients

2 medium-sized, dark-fleshed fish

250 g/8 oz cranberries

1½ tbsp lemon juice

1 tbsp port

salt and freshly ground black pepper

lettuce

A colourful and tasty winter dish.

◆ To fillet the fish, gut them, cut off the fins and carefully remove the bone from the head downwards. Cut off the heads. Remove the skin and the remaining bones.

◆ Make the sauce. Combine the cranberries, lemon juice and port in a bowl and season with salt and pepper. Cook for 4 minutes, until the berries are soft. Keep warm.

◆ Lay the fish in a shallow dish, cover with vented plastic wrap and cook for 4 minutes, turning once.

◆ Arrange the fish fillets on heated plates, on a bed of lettuce, pour over the sauce and serve.

VARIATION Try using gooseberries instead of cranberries.

TROUT WITH CUCUMBER AND MUSHROOM

SERVES 4 / SET: HIGH AND MEDIUM

Ingredients

¹/₄ cucumber, sliced
125 g/4 oz mushrooms, sliced
150 ml/¹/₄ pt canned consommé
4 small trout of even size
3 tbsp water
parsley
lemon wedges

◆ Put the cucumber and mushrooms in a dish and pour over the consommé. Cover with vented plastic wrap and cook for 4 minutes. Set aside.

◆ Put the trout in a dish, add the water, cover with vented plastic wrap and cook for 4 minutes, turning once, until cooked through.

◆ Put the trout on heated plates and pour the sauce over.

◆ Serve garnished with parsley and lemon wedges.

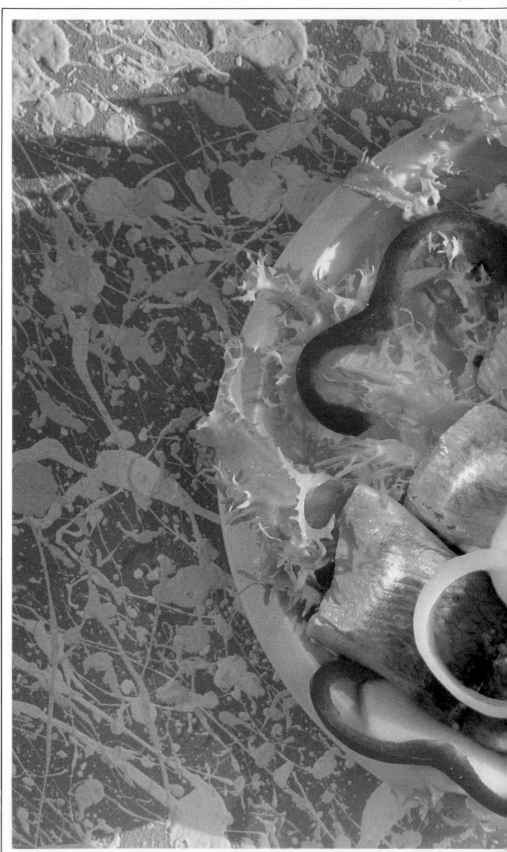

SOUSED FISH

SERVES 4 / SET: HIGH

Ingredients

1 tbsp oil
1 onion, cut into rings
1 large apple, peeled, cored and sliced
3 tsp pickling spices
1 bay leaf
150 ml/¼ pt cider vinegar
4 small, dark-fleshed fish, filleted

◆ Roll up the fish and secure with toothpicks.

◆ Put the oil in a dish and cook for 30 seconds. Add the onion and cook for 2 minutes.

◆ Mix the onion with the apple, add the pickling spices and bay leaf and pour over the cider vinegar. Lay the fish on top. Cover with vented plastic wrap. Cook until the vinegar boils and then for about 3 more minutes, until the fish are done. Leave to cool.

◆ Serve the fish cold with a spoonful of the cooking vinegar and apple and onion slices on top.

Soused Fish

FISH AND VEGETABLES ON A BED OF NOODLES

SERVES 4 / SET: HIGH

Ingredients

45 g/1½ oz butter
45 g/1½ oz flour
150 ml/¼ pt milk
150 ml/¼ pt light cream
45 g/1½ oz Parmesan cheese
1 egg yolk
4 firm, white fish fillets, about 185 g/6 oz each, skinned
2–3 tbsp milk
220 g/7 oz asparagus spears
220 g/7 oz broad beans, cooked or canned
250 g/8 oz fresh spinach tagliatelle
boiling water
salt
1 tsp oil
paprika

◆ First make the sauce. Put the butter in a bowl and cook for 1 minute. Stir in the flour and cook for 1 minute. Stir in the milk and cook for 2 minutes, whisking after each minute. Stir in the cream and cheese and cook for 2 minutes, whisking after each minute. Stir in the egg yolk. Keep the sauce warm.

◆ Put the fillets in a dish with the milk, asparagus spears and broad beans. Cover with vented plastic wrap and cook for 4 minutes, turning once, until the fish is done. Keep warm.

◆ Put the tagliatelle in a dish and pour over boiling water to just cover. Add a pinch of salt and the oil, cover and cook for 3–4 minutes, until *al dente* (firm to the bite).

◆ Pour pools of sauce onto 4 heated serving plates. Drain the noodles well and divide between the plates of sauce.

◆ Flake the fish on top of the noodles, dust with paprika and serve with the broad beans and asparagus spears.

FISH WITH CARROTS AND CELERY

SERVES 4 / SET: HIGH

Ingredients

1 bulb fennel, sliced
3 carrots, peeled and cut into strips lengthways
3 sticks celery, sliced
2 tbsp fish stock or milk
1 tbsp lemon juice
4 small, whole fish, cleaned
salt and freshly ground black pepper
chopped parsley or fennel fronds
lemon wedges

◆ Put the sliced fennel, carrots and celery in a large oblong dish and add the fish stock or milk and lemon juice. Cover with vented plastic wrap and cook for 8 minutes, stirring once, until the vegetables are tender.

◆ Lay the fish on top of the vegetables and cover again. Cook for 3 minutes, turning the dish once, until the fish are done.

◆ Lay the fish on warmed plates and spoon the vegetables beside them. Add a little of the cooking liquor, season and garnish with parsley or fennel fronds.

◆ Serve with lemon wedges.

FISH STEAKS WITH RED PEPPER SAUCE

SERVES 4 / SET: HIGH

Ingredients

1 zucchini, chopped
4 small tomatoes, skinned, seeded and chopped
1 tbsp water
1 large red pepper, seeded and chopped
½ clove of garlic, crushed
a little chopped onion
150 ml/¼ pt canned consommé
1 tbsp sherry
salt and white pepper
4 firm white fish steaks, about 185 g/6 oz each, skinned
a little butter
a lemon

◆ First make the garnish. Put the zucchini and tomatoes in a dish with the water. Cook for 2 minutes. Set aside.

◆ Make the sauce. Combine the pepper, garlic, onion, consommé and sherry in a small bowl and cook for 5 minutes, until the pepper is very soft. Blend in a food processor or blender, season and keep warm.

◆ Lay the fish steaks in a buttered dish and dot with butter. Cover with vented plastic wrap and cook for 3–4 minutes, turning once, until done.

◆ Put the fish on 4 heated plates. Add a spoonful of sauce and garnish with a little mound of the zucchini and tomato mixture and the lemon.

Fish Steaks with Red Pepper Sauce

PRAWNS AND ZUCCHINI IN TOMATO SAUCE

SERVES 4 / SET: HIGH

Ingredients

1 tbsp oil

2 shallots, chopped

4 baby zucchini, sliced

440 g/14 oz canned tomatoes, sieved

440 g/14 oz peeled prawns

freshly chopped basil

salt and freshly ground black pepper

◆ Put the oil in a bowl and cook for 30 seconds. Add the shallots and zucchini and cook for 3 minutes.

◆ Stir in the sieved tomatoes and the prawns and cook, covered with vented plastic wrap, for 5 minutes, until heated through.

◆ Sprinkle with plenty of basil and season to taste with salt and pepper.

◆ Serve with rice.

SQUID WITH BEETROOT

SERVES 4 / SET: HIGH

Ingredients

500 g/1 lb small squid
1 tbsp olive oil
1 small onion, chopped
1 clove garlic, crushed
1 stalk celery, finely chopped
2 cooked beetroot, chopped
½ glass dry white wine
1 tbsp tomato paste
salt and freshly ground black pepper
celery tips

◆ First clean the squid. Remove the eyes, mouth, ink sac and outer membrane. Take out the cuttlefish bone. Wash the squid well, then slice body and tentacles.

◆ Put the olive oil in a dish and cook for 30 seconds. Stir in the onion and garlic and cook for 2 minutes.

◆ Add the celery, beetroot and squid. Mix the white wine and tomato paste and pour over the squid. Cover and cook for 8 minutes, or until the squid is tender.

◆ Season with salt and pepper and serve garnished with celery tips.

Squid with Beetroot

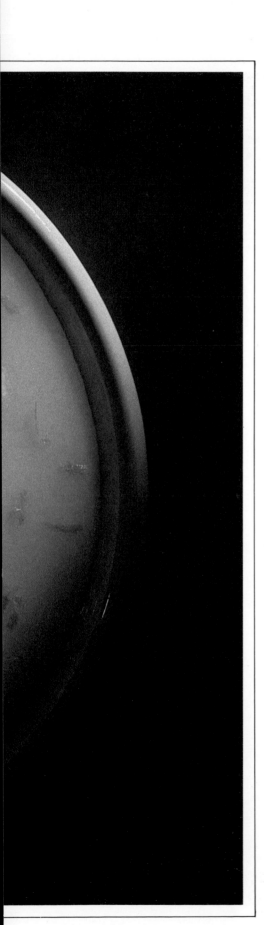

FISH STEAKS IN ORANGE SAUCE WITH BROCCOLI AND ALMONDS

SERVES 4 / SET: HIGH

Ingredients

30 g/1 oz butter

30 g/1 oz cornflour

315 ml/½ pt orange juice

grated rind of 1 orange

4 fish steaks, about 155 g/5 oz each

2 tbsp water

8 spears broccoli

60 g/2 oz flaked almonds

◆ Put the butter in a bowl and cook for 1 minute. Stir in the cornflour and cook for 1 minute. Stir in the orange juice and cook for 3 minutes, whisking after each minute. Stir in the orange rind. Keep the sauce warm.

◆ Put the fish steaks in a dish with the water. Add the broccoli and the almond slivers. Cover with vented plastic wrap and cook for 4 minutes, rearranging once, until the fish is done and the broccoli is tender.

◆ Pour the orange sauce over 4 heated plates, add the fish and garnish with the broccoli and almonds.

Fish Steaks in Orange Sauce with Broccoli and Almonds

FILLETS OF FISH IN CRAB SAUCE WITH RED PEPPERS

SERVES 4 / SET: HIGH

Ingredients

1 red pepper, seeded and cut into julienne strips

2 tbsp water

150 ml/¼ pt light cream

60 g/2 oz canned dressed crab meat

salt and white pepper

4 firm fish fillets

30 g/1 oz butter

◆ Put the strips of red pepper in a dish with the water. Cover with vented plastic wrap and cook for 4–5 minutes, until tender, stirring once. Set aside.

◆ Mash the cream into the crab meat until smooth. Season to taste with salt and white pepper.

◆ Put the fish fillets in a dish, dot with butter, cover with vented plastic wrap and cook for 4 minutes, rearranging once.

◆ Cook the crab sauce for 1–2 minutes to heat through.

◆ Spoon a pool of crab sauce onto 4 heated plates, put the fish on top and garnish with strips of red pepper.

FILLETS OF FLOUNDER WITH SPINACH SAUCE

SERVES 4 / SET: HIGH

Ingredients

75 g/2½ oz butter

45 g/1½ oz flour

315 ml/½ pt milk

1 egg yolk

125 g/4 oz frozen spinach, defrosted
and squeezed very thoroughly to drain

salt and freshly ground black pepper

4 flounder fillets

a squeeze of lemon juice

fine slices of carrot, cut into flower shapes

chives, chopped

*Serve this creamy dish with a crisp salad in
a contrasting colour – radicchio would go
very well.*

◆ First make the sauce. Put 45 g/
1½ oz of the butter in a bowl and cook
for 1 minute. Stir in the flour and
cook for 1 minute. Pour on the milk
and cook for 3 minutes, whisking after
every minute. Stir in the egg yolk and
spinach and season to taste. Cook for
1 minute, then keep warm.

◆ Lay the fillets in a dish, dot with
the remaining butter and sprinkle
with lemon juice. Cook for 3–4
minutes, rearranging once.

◆ Arrange the fish on heated plates,
pour the sauce over and garnish with
carrot slices and chives to look like
flowers and stalks.

◆ Serve at once.

Fillets of Flounder with Spinach Sauce

FISH STEAKS WITH TOMATOES AND BASIL

SERVES 4 / SET: HIGH

Ingredients

1 tbsp olive oil
1 tbsp onion, chopped
1 clove garlic, crushed
375 g/12 oz ripe tomatoes, peeled, seeded and chopped
a few leaves of basil or 1 tsp dried basil
4 firm, white fish steaks
a little butter
2 tbsp canned peas, drained
2 tbsp canned yellow or white beans, drained

◆ First make the sauce. Put the oil in a bowl and cook for 30 seconds. Stir in the onion and garlic and cook for 2 minutes. Stir in the tomatoes and basil, cover and cook for 4 minutes, or until soft, stirring twice.

◆ Put the fish in a buttered dish, cover with vented plastic wrap and cook for 4 minutes, until done, turning once.

◆ Put the peas and beans in a bowl and cook for 1 minute.

◆ Put a portion of mixed peas and beans onto 4 heated plates, lay the fish on top and pour the sauce over.

MUSSEL SALAD

SERVES 4 / SET: HIGH

Ingredients
15 g/½ oz butter
1 small onion, chopped
500 g/1 lb mussels, well scrubbed
2 tbsp lemon juice
2 tbsp dry white wine
4 sticks celery, sliced
125 g/4 oz cooked green beans, cut into bite-size pieces
1 red pepper, cut into julienne strips
250g/8 oz cooked potatoes, sliced
2 tbsp mayonnaise
chopped parsley
salt and freshly ground black pepper

◆ Put the butter in a deep dish and cook for 30 seconds. Add the onion and cook for 2 minutes.

◆ Put in the mussels (discarding any that are broken or open), pour in the lemon juice and white wine and cook, covered, for 3–4 minutes, until the mussels have opened.

◆ Discard any closed shells. Allow the mussels to cool, then remove them from their shells.

◆ Mix the mussels in a large bowl with the celery, green beans, red pepper and potatoes. Stir the mayonnaise into the cooking liquor and onion and pour over the salad.

◆ Add chopped parsley and seasoning, mix well and serve.

KEDGEREE

SERVES 4 / SET: HIGH

Ingredients
250 g/8 oz rice
625 ml/1 pt boiling fish or chicken stock
salt
4 smoked fish fillets
2 tbsp water
30 g/1 oz butter
2–4 hardboiled eggs, chopped or sliced
cayenne pepper
2 tomatoes, sliced or cut into wedges
sprigs of parsley
a few prawns (optional)

A traditional breakfast dish, kedgeree makes a good evening snack and can be put together easily from the store cupboard.

◆ Put the rice in a dish and pour over the boiling stock. Season with a pinch of salt, cover and cook for 12 minutes. Remove from the oven and leave covered while you prepare the smoked fish fillets.

◆ Lay the fillets in a dish with the water, cover and cook for 2 minutes. Flake the fish with a fork, discarding any bits of skin.

◆ Stir the fish, butter and eggs into the rice and season with cayenne pepper to taste. Garnish with tomatoes, parsley and a few prawns if liked.

◆ Serve hot.

Kedgeree

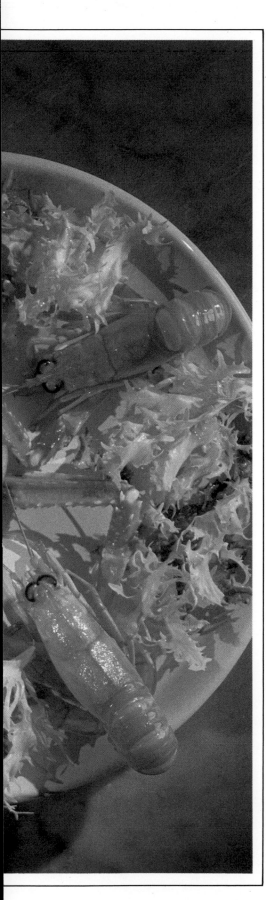

KING PRAWNS WITH MALTAISE SAUCE

SERVES 4 / SET: HIGH AND MEDIUM

Ingredients

125 g/4 oz butter, diced
grated rind and juice of 1 orange
3 egg yolks
salt and white pepper
12 king prawns
curly endive

◆ Put the butter in a bowl and heat on high for 1½ minutes until melted.

◆ Whisk the orange rind and juice with the egg yolks and whisk into the hot butter, blending well. Season to taste with salt and white pepper, then cook on medium power for 1 minute, watching to make sure that the sauce does not boil.

◆ Arrange the king prawns on curly endive on 4 plates and serve with the Maltaise sauce. Provide your guests with finger bowls and large napkins.

VARIATION This is an excellent way of serving crayfish.

King Prawns with Maltaise Sauce

RED SCHNAPPER WITH LEMON AND LIME

SERVES 4 / SET: HIGH

Ingredients

30 g/1 oz butter
½ fennel bulb, chopped
juice of ½ lemon
juice of 1 lime
4 small, red schnapper, cleaned
slices of lemon
slices of lime
fronds of fennel

◆ Put the butter in a dish and cook for 30 seconds. Add the chopped fennel, cover with vented plastic wrap and cook for 3 minutes, stirring once.

◆ Pour on the lemon and lime juice and lay the red schnapper on top of the fennel. Cover with vented plastic wrap and cook for 4 minutes, until done, turning the dish once.

◆ Arrange the fish and fennel on 4 heated plates and spoon over the juice. Garnish with slices of lemon and lime and fennel fronds.

WHITING, CAULIFLOWER AND SNOW PEAS

SERVES 4 / SET: HIGH

Ingredients

½ cauliflower
2 tbsp water
375 g/12 oz snow peas
375 g/12 oz whiting pieces (rockling, John Dory or other firm white fish)
2 tbsp dry sherry
2 tbsp soy sauce
1 clove garlic, crushed

This is a very popular dish in Singapore, where it is served with a bowl of rice.

◆ Break the cauliflower into florets, discarding tough stalks and leaves. Put it in a bowl with the water, cover and cook for 3–4 minutes, until you can pierce the stalks with the point of a sharp knife. Stir once during cooking.

◆ Cut the stalks from the snow peas. Put the cauliflower and peas in a bowl with the fish.

◆ Combine the sherry, soy sauce and garlic. Pour over the vegetables and fish, stirring well. Leave for 30 minutes to marinate, stirring occasionally.

◆ Cover the bowl with vented plastic wrap and cook for 3 minutes, stirring once.

◆ Serve immediately.

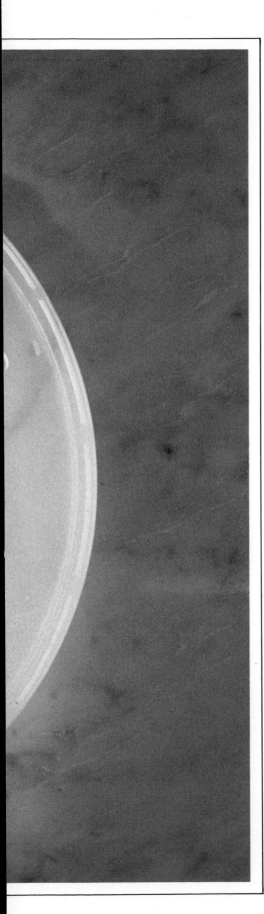

PRAWNS ST JACQUES

S E R V E S 4 / S E T : H I G H

Ingredients

45 g/1½ oz butter

45 g/1½ oz flour

150 ml/¼ pt milk

150 ml/¼ pt light cream

3 tbsp grated Parmesan cheese

salt and freshly ground black pepper

500 g/1 lb prawns, shelled weight

TOPPING

500 g/1 lb cooked mashed potato

45 g/1½ oz butter

salt

1½ tbsp grated Parmesan cheese

15 ml/1 tbsp dried breadcrumbs

chopped parsley

◆ Put the butter in a bowl and cook for 1½ minutes until melted. Stir in the flour and cook for 1 minute. Stir in the milk and cook for 1 minute. Stir or whisk in the cream and cook for 1 minute. Stir in the cheese and cook for 1 minute. Season the sauce to taste and whisk or stir until smooth.

◆ Reserve some prawns for the garnish. Stir the peeled prawns into the sauce.

◆ Mash the potato with the butter and season with salt.

◆ Divide the prawn mixture between 4 scallop shells, top with the mashed potato and sprinkle with Parmesan cheese, dried breadcrumbs and parsley. Heat through in the microwave for 1 minute, decorate with the unshelled prawns and serve hot.

Prawns St Jacques

WHITING AND BABY LEEKS IN CHEESE SAUCE

S E R V E S 4 / S E T : H I G H

Ingredients

440 g/14 oz whiting (flathead, rockling or any other firm white fish), skinned and cut into pieces

8 baby leeks, washed and trimmed

2–3 tbsp water

45 g/1½ oz butter

45 g/1½ oz flour

315 ml/½ pt milk

60 g/2 oz grated Parmesan cheese

salt and freshly ground black pepper

◆ Put the whiting (or equivalent) and leeks in a large oblong dish and add the water. Cover with vented plastic wrap and cook for 5 minutes, rearranging once, until the fish is done and the leeks are tender. Set aside while you make the sauce.

◆ Put the butter in a jug and cook for 45 seconds. Stir in the flour. Pour on the milk and cook for 3 minutes, whisking after each minute. Stir in the cheese and cook for a further minute. Whisk again. Season to taste.

◆ Pour the sauce over the leeks and fish and heat through before serving.

FISH STEAKS WITH TWO SAUCES

SERVES 4 / SET: HIGH AND MEDIUM

Ingredients

1 ripe avocado pear
315 ml/½ pt light cream
salt and white pepper
black pepper
250 g/8 oz strawberries
a squeeze of lemon juice
4 firm, white fish steaks
2 tbsp milk

Strawberries and avocados make a surprisingly good combination, and they look very pretty together too.

◆ First make the sauces. Cut the avocado in half with a sharp knife and remove the stone. Scoop out the flesh from one half and put in a blender or food processor with half the cream. Blend until smooth. Season with salt and white pepper and put in a jug.

◆ Hull the strawberries. Put about 155 g/5 oz in a blender or food processor with the remaining cream and liquidize until smooth. Season with salt and black pepper and put in a jug.

◆ Prepare the garnish. Carefully remove the other half of the avocado from its shell without spoiling the shape. Cut into slices. Sprinkle with lemon juice to stop it going brown. Slice the remaining strawberries. Set aside.

◆ Put the fish steaks in a dish, add the milk and cover with vented plastic wrap. Cook on high for 4 minutes, or until done, turning once.

◆ Put the jugs of sauce in the microwave and cook on medium for 1–2 minutes, until warmed through.

◆ Put the fish on 4 heated serving plates. Spoon the avocado sauce to one side of the fish and the strawberry sauce to the other.

◆ Garnish with the avocado and strawberry slices and serve at once.

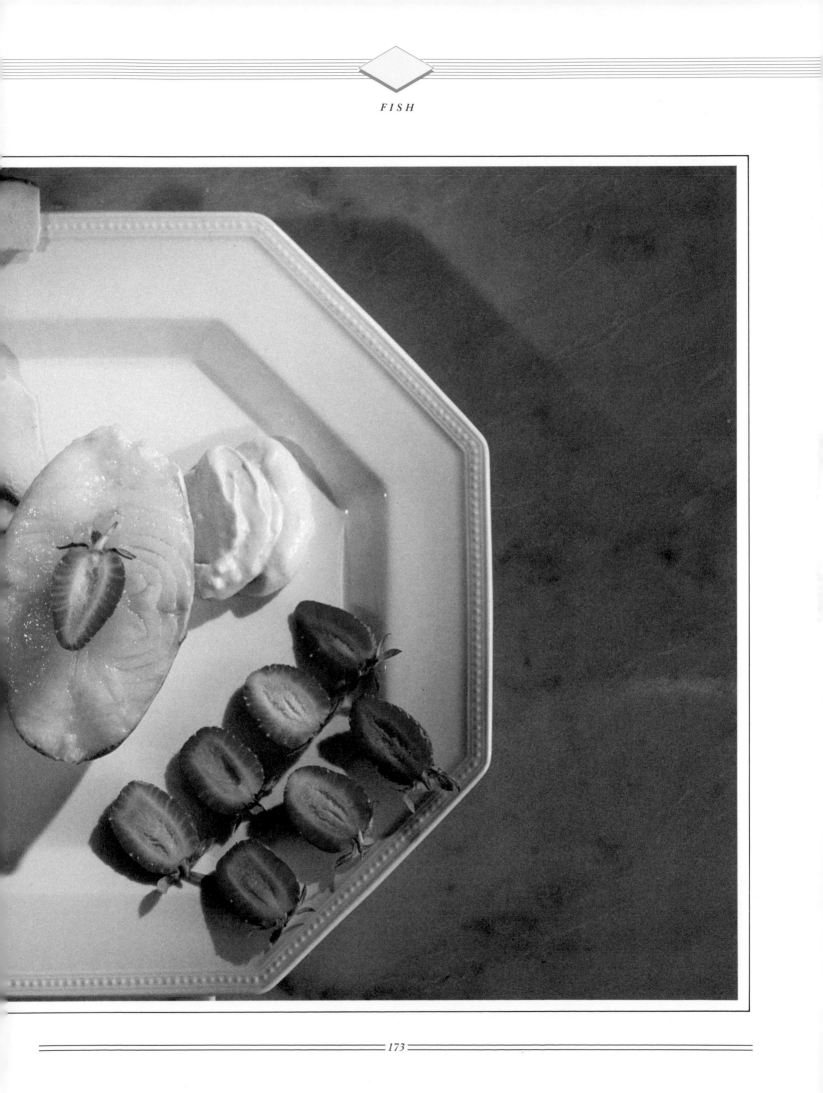

SMOKED FISH AND POACHED EGG

S E R V E S   2   /   S E T :   H I G H   A N D   M E D I U M

Ingredients

2 pieces smoked fish, about 185 g/6 oz each
45 g/1½ oz butter
2 tbsp milk
salt and freshly ground black pepper
2 eggs
sprigs of fennel or parsley

This dish of smoked fish and egg makes a very good brunch or late breakfast.

◆ Put the smoked fish in a buttered dish, dot with two-thirds of the butter and add the milk. Cover with vented plastic wrap and cook on high for 3–4 minutes, turning once. Season and keep warm.

◆ Break the eggs into 2 buttered individual dishes and pierce the yolks carefully with a toothpick to prevent bursting. Cook on medium for 1½–2 minutes.

◆ Put the fish on 2 heated plates, add the remaining butter and the poached eggs.

◆ Garnish with sprigs of fennel or parsley and serve with wholemeal bread and butter.

CRISPY FISH FILLETS

SERVES 4 / SET: HIGH

Ingredients

8 white fish fillets
salt and freshly ground black pepper
2 eggs, beaten
dried breadcrumbs
1 tbsp oil
30 g/1 oz butter
lemon slices

◆ Sprinkle the fish with salt and pepper. Dip in beaten egg and then in dried breadcrumbs, pressing them on well to cover the fish.

◆ Heat a browning dish to maximum, according to the manufacturer's instructions. Add the oil and butter. Cook for 30 seconds. Protecting your hands with oven gloves, tilt the dish so that it is well oiled.

◆ Lay the fish fillets in the dish (cook them in 2 batches if necessary) and cook for 4 minutes, turning once.

◆ Serve with lemon slices and wholemeal bread and butter and a salad if liked.

EELS WITH PEAS AND PARSLEY SAUCE

SERVES 4 / SET: HIGH

Ingredients

750 g/1½ lb eels, skinned, boned and cut into 5 cm/2 in pieces (try to buy it ready prepared)
150 ml/¼ pt boiling fish stock (or see method)
2 slivers of lemon
45 g/1½ oz butter
45 g/1½ oz flour
150 ml/¼ pt milk
salt and freshly ground black pepper
2 tbsp chopped parsley
220 g/7 oz canned large peas, drained

◆ Put the eels in a deep oblong dish and add the boiling fish stock. Alternatively, use the liquid from the canned peas. Add the lemon slivers, cover with vented plastic wrap and cook for 5 minutes, until tender. Discard the lemon.

◆ Put the butter in a jug and cook for 45 seconds. Stir in the flour. Pour on the milk and the cooking liquor from the eels and cook for 3 minutes, whisking after each minute. Season and stir in the parsley.

◆ Add the peas to the dish of eels and pour over the sauce. Reheat for 1 minute, then serve with mashed potatoes.

Crispy Fish Fillets

FLATFISH FILLETS IN BEETROOT SAUCE

SERVES 4 / SET: DEFROST AND HIGH

Ingredients

1 beetroot, cooked
150 ml/5 fl oz light cream
salt and white pepper
4 flatfish fillets, about 185 g/6 oz each, skinned
a little butter
spring onion (scallion) tassels

Spring onion (scallion) tassels are made by cutting 2 slits through the top of each trimmed and washed onion, at right angles to one another, and leaving them in ice water until the tops curl back.

◆ Peel and chop the beetroot. Put it in a blender or food processor, with the cream and reduce to a smooth sauce. Season to taste with salt and pepper. Cook for 1–2 minutes on defrost to heat through. Keep warm.

◆ Trim the fillets to an even size, lay in a buttered dish and dot with butter. Cover with vented plastic wrap and cook for 3–4 minutes, turning once, until cooked through.

◆ Spoon the sauce onto 4 heated plates, lay the fish on top and garnish with spring onion (scallion) tassels.

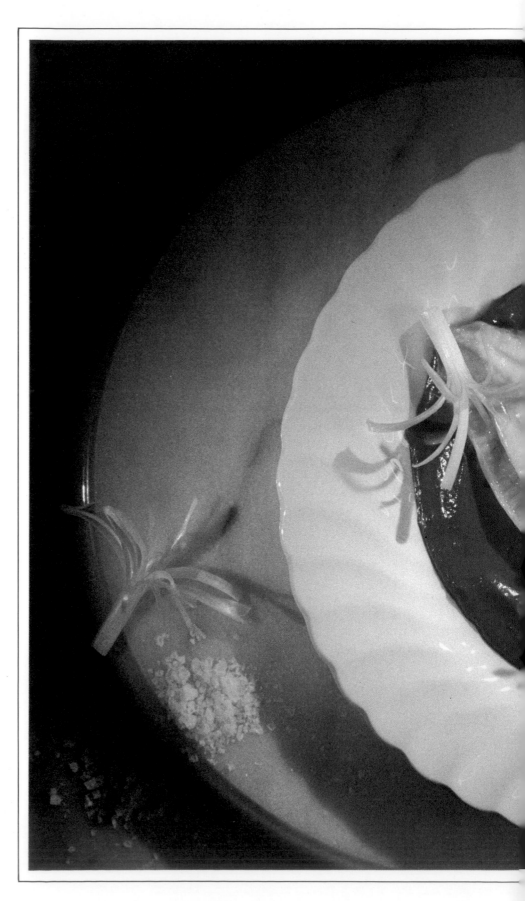

Flatfish Fillets in Beetroot Sauce

FISH KORMA

*SERVES 4 / SET: HIGH
AND MEDIUM*

Ingredients

750 g/1½ lb firm, white fish, skinned and cubed
150 ml/¼ pt yoghurt
1 tsp turmeric
1 clove garlic, crushed
45 g/1½ oz butter
1 large onion, finely sliced
5 cardamons
3 cloves

◆ Put the fish pieces in a dish. Mix together the yoghurt, turmeric and garlic and stir into the fish. Leave to marinate for an hour.

◆ Put the butter in a large dish and cook on high for 45 seconds. Add the onions and spices, cover and cook on high for 3 minutes.

◆ Stir in the fish and marinade, cover and cook on medium power for 10 minutes, stirring once.

◆ Serve with rice.

SPICY FISH CASSEROLE WITH RICE

SERVES 4 / SET: HIGH

Ingredients

750 g/1½ lb white fish fillets, skinned and cut into chunks

salt and freshly ground black pepper

1 tbsp turmeric

2 tbsp olive oil

1 large onion, finely sliced

2 cloves garlic, crushed

1 green pepper, cut into julienne strips

1 red pepper, cut into julienne strips

250 g/8 oz long-grain rice

440 g/14 oz canned tomatoes, drained and juice reserved

boiling water or fish stock

◆ Sprinkle the fish with salt and dust with turmeric. Set aside.

◆ Put the olive oil into a large dish and cook for 30 seconds. Add the onion, garlic and peppers. Cover and cook for 3 minutes.

◆ Stir in the rice. Make the reserved tomato juice up to 625 ml/1 pt with boiling water or fish stock, pour over the rice, cover and cook for 8 minutes.

◆ Stir in the drained tomatoes and the fish. Cover and cook for 4–6 minutes, until the fish and rice are done.

◆ Let the dish stand for 5 minutes, check the seasoning and serve.

ANCHOVY AND POTATO BAKE

SERVES 4 / SET: HIGH AND MEDIUM

Ingredients

45 g/1½ oz butter
1 large onion, finely sliced
1 kg/2 lb potatoes, peeled and coarsely grated
60 g/2 oz canned anchovies, drained, soaked in milk for 30 minutes, then dried and chopped
1½ tbsp capers
cayenne pepper
150 ml/¼ pt light cream
3 tbsp grated Parmesan cheese

◆ Put the butter in a dish and cook on high for 45 seconds. Add the onion, cover and cook on full for 3 minutes.

◆ Mix in the potatoes, cover and cook on high for 8 minutes, until soft.

◆ Stir in the anchovies and capers and season with cayenne pepper. Pour on the cream and top with grated Parmesan.

◆ Cook on medium power for 4 minutes, until hot through.

FISH FILLETS IN MUSTARD SAUCE

SERVES 4 / SET: HIGH AND DEFROST

Ingredients

diamonds of red and green pepper
1 tbsp water
4 firm, white fish fillets, weighing about 185 g/6 oz each
a squeeze of lemon juice
150 ml/5 fl oz light cream
1 tsp English mustard powder

◆ First make the garnish. Cut out the pepper diamonds and put them in a dish with the water. Cook, covered with vented plastic wrap, on high for 2 minutes.

◆ Trim the fillets so that they are of even size and square in shape. Lay them in a dish, sprinkle with lemon juice and cover with vented plastic wrap. Cook on high for 4 minutes, turning once, until cooked.

◆ Mix the cream with the mustard powder to give it a delicate yellow hue and a pleasantly pungent taste. Heat through on defrost power for 1–2 minutes.

◆ Pour a pool of sauce onto each of 4 heated plates.

◆ Lay the fish fillets on the sauce and garnish with the pepper shapes.

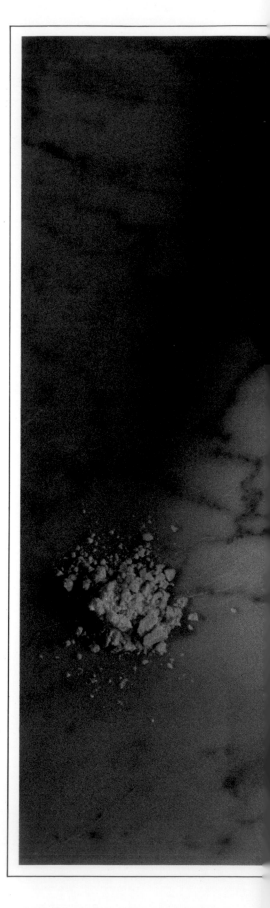

Fish Fillets in Mustard Sauce

CHINESE PRAWNS WITH VEGETABLES

SERVES 4 / SET: HIGH

Ingredients

500 g/1 lb unpeeled prawns
2 tbsp soy sauce
1 tbsp sherry
1 clove garlic, crushed
1 tbsp chopped onion
220 g/7 oz canned water chestnuts, drained
220 g/7 oz button mushrooms
220 g/7 oz canned whole baby corn, drained
125 g/4 oz canned green beans, drained
125 g/4 oz mung bean sprouts
strips of red and yellow pepper

Serve this dish with rice. The prawns look much nicer unpeeled, but peel them if you wish.

◆ Slit the prawns down the back and remove the blackish veins. Put them in a bowl and stir in the soy sauce, sherry, garlic and onion. Leave to marinate for an hour, stirring occasionally.
◆ Stir in the remaining ingredients, cover with vented plastic wrap and cook for 3–4 minutes, stirring once.
◆ Garnish with pepper strips and serve hot with rice.

SQUID IN TOMATO AND WINE SAUCE

SERVES 4 / SET: HIGH

Ingredients

4 small squid
1 tbsp olive oil
2 shallots, chopped
1 clove garlic, crushed
440 g/14 oz canned tomatoes, drained and sieved
1 glass dry white wine
chopped fresh herbs (thyme, parsley and basil)
salt and freshly ground black pepper

◆ Clean the squid. Cut away the eyes and mouth and discard, together with the ink sac and the "nib". Wash the squid thoroughly and pull off the outer membrane. Cut the body and tentacles into rings.
◆ Put the oil in a dish and cook for 30 seconds. Add the shallots and garlic and cook for 2 minutes.
◆ Stir in the sieved tomatoes, wine and squid. Sprinkle on the herbs. Cover with vented plastic wrap and cook for 6–8 minutes, until the squid is tender. Season to taste with salt and pepper.
◆ Serve with rice.

Chinese Prawns with Vegetables

COOKING WITH

Meat

VERONICA BULL

MEAT

MEAT forms a major part of the household budget. By using the correct cooking methods your microwave oven will enable you to produce moist, tender dishes representing good value for money.

For the housewife who is concerned with healthy eating, the microwave cooking method both preserves nutrients and helps to cut down the use of fats.

As with conventional cooking, prime quality meat will produce the best result. However, the less tender cuts of meat can also be cooked successfully. You will achieve excellent results with curries, casseroles and stews cooked at low temperatures over a longer period. These dishes reheat in minutes, losing none of the original freshness, they remain moist and succulent with a flavour that develops and improves. For this reason they are an excellent choice when entertaining, allowing you to spend more time with your guests while producing the perfect meal.

Large roasts of meat brown naturally in a microwave cooker; smaller cuts can be browned in a special browning dish, or by conventional means, in the oven or under the grill, before or after the cooking period. If a crisp finish is not essential, a sauce or glaze will make the dish appear even more appetizing.

The recipes featured in this book include exotic dishes such as Chinese Pancakes and Tandoori Chicken, together with a selection of more traditional fare. Microwaved meat offers a tasty and attractive selection of dishes that will make every meal a special occasion.

CONTENTS

SAVOURY HAMBURGER MIXTURE

SERVES 4 / SET: HIGH

Ingredients

500 g/1 lb minced beef
2 tbsp tomato ketchup
3 tbsp soy sauce
2 tbsp chopped fresh herbs
1/2 tsp celery salt
1 tbsp horseradish sauce
1 tbsp French mustard

◆ Combine all the ingredients in a large bowl and mix well. Place 1 tbsp on a plate and cook on high for 2 minutes. Taste to test for flavour.

◆ This is the basic, uncooked recipe to which sauces and liquids may be added for 'wet' dishes or eggs and breadcrumbs for 'dry' dishes such as hamburgers, meatballs etc.

◆ To cook this dish on its own, place the mixture in a casserole dish, cover and cook for 7–9 minutes, stirring twice during the cooking time. Add sauce or gravy as required.

HAMBURGERS

SERVES 4—6 / SET: HIGH

Ingredients

1 onion, finely chopped

60 g/2 oz fresh breadcrumbs

1 egg, beaten

500 g/1 lb Savoury Hamburger Mixture (see recipe)

4—6 hamburger buns

GARNISH

sliced tomatoes

onion

lettuce leaves

relish of your choice

◆ Add the onions, breadcrumbs and egg to the Savoury Hamburger Mixture and combine well.

◆ Divide into 4 or 6 even portions and shape into patties.

◆ Heat a browning dish to the maximum recommended by the manufacturer and press the hamburgers onto the bottom. Cook for 7½–9 minutes, turning the hamburgers over after 4 minutes.

◆ If you prefer, cook for only half the above time and finish off under the grill or on a barbecue.

◆ Serve with onion, tomato, lettuce and relish in a hot or cold bun.

Hamburgers

LEEKS AU GRATIN

SERVES 2—4 / SET: HIGH AND MEDIUM

Ingredients

375 g/12 oz Savoury Hamburger Mixture (see recipe)
90 ml/3 fl oz hot, thick gravy
4 large leeks
60 g/2 fl oz water
125 g/4 oz grated cheese

◆ Place the Savoury Hamburger Mixture in a dish, cover and cook on high for 6–7 minutes. Stir after 3 minutes. Drain off any fat, then add the gravy and stir well. Keep to one side.

◆ Trim the leeks, and with a sharp knife slice down the length, cutting only as deep as the centre. Spread the leaves apart and wash. Select the widest leaves and place in a dish with the water, cover and cook on high for 1½–2 minutes until softened. Pour over cold water, drain and pat dry with absorbent kitchen paper.

◆ Lay the leeks flat and place 1 tbsp of mince mixture at the narrow end of each leaf. Roll up to enclose the meat. Place in a dish, cover and cook on high for 4–5 minutes or until heated through. Sprinkle over the grated cheese and cook, uncovered, on high for 2 minutes.

STUFFED CANNELLONI IN TOMATO SAUCE

SERVES 2 / SET: HIGH

Ingredients

8 cannelloni tubes
1 tsp dried oregano
1 clove of garlic, crushed
2 tbsp tomato paste
500 g/1 lb Savoury Hamburger Mixture (see recipe)

SAUCE

1 small onion, finely chopped
1 clove garlic, crushed
1 tsp dried oregano
30 g/1 oz butter, diced
30 g/1 oz plain flour
440 g/14 oz canned tomatoes, chopped
60 ml/4 tbsp tomato paste
3 tbsp garlic vinegar
1 tbsp sugar
salt and pepper
4 slices of mozzarella cheese

◆ Stir the garlic, oregano and 2 tbsp of tomato paste into the meat mixture. Place in a shallow dish and cook for 3 minutes, stirring halfway through the cooking time. At this stage the meat will not be completely cooked.

◆ For the sauce, place the onion, garlic, oregano and butter in a bowl, cover and cook for 3 minutes. Stir in the flour, tomatoes, vinegar, sugar and remaining tomato paste with the salt and pepper (to taste). Cook uncovered for 4–5 minutes. Dilute with a little water or red wine if the sauce is too thick.

◆ Stuff the cannelloni tubes with the meat mixture. Place them in an oblong dish, pour on the sauce, cover and cook for 12–15 minutes. Place the cheese slices on top of the cannelloni and melt for 2 minutes or brown under a conventional grill.

Stuffed Cannelloni in Tomato Sauce

LASAGNE

SERVES 4 – 6 / SET: HIGH

Ingredients

185 g/6 oz lasagne
½ tbsp oil
940 ml/1½ pts boiling water
salt to taste
500 g/1 lb Savoury Hamburger Mixture (see recipe)
440 g/14 oz canned tomatoes, chopped
250 g/8 oz button mushrooms, sliced
1 clove garlic, crushed
185 g/6 oz blue cheese
155 ml/5 fl oz light cream
mushroom slices to garnish

◆ Place the lasagne in a deep dish, cover with the boiling water, add oil and salt. Cover and cook for 9–11 minutes. Set aside covered. Alternatively cook on a conventional burner according to the instructions on the package while you prepare the remainder of the dish.

◆ Place the beef mixture in a large shallow dish, cover and cook for 5 minutes. Drain, add the tomatoes, garlic and mushrooms, stir well and cook for 5 minutes, stirring occasionally.

◆ Drain the pasta and, in a shallow oblong dish, place alternative layers of meat and lasagne, finishing with a layer of lasagne.

◆ Place the blue cheese in a bowl and cook for 1 minute. Mash it and blend in the cream. Replace in the oven and cook for a further minute. Blend to a smooth sauce and add it to the dish. Brown under a conventional grill.

◆ Cook the mushroom slices with a little butter for 1 minute and use as a garnish.

MEAT LOAF

SERVES 4–6 / SET: HIGH

Ingredients

250 g/8 oz Savoury Hamburger Mixture (see recipe)
250 g/8 oz ground pork
1 medium onion, finely chopped
1 clove garlic, crushed
125 g/4 oz fresh breadcrumbs
1 egg, beaten
salt and pepper to taste

◆ Place the butter, onion and garlic in a bowl. Cover and cook for 2 minutes.

◆ Mix together the beef, pork, breadcrumbs and seasoning to taste. Stir in the onion, garlic and beaten egg. Combine well and cook uncovered for 5 minutes. Stir and break up with a fork.

◆ Transfer to a microwave loaf dish or any other suitable container, press down and smooth the top. Cook for 5–7 minutes.

◆ Chill and turn out. Slice and serve with salad.

BRAISED BEEF

SERVES 4 / SET: HIGH AND LOW

Ingredients

750 g/1½ lb braising steak (chuck, skirt, flank), cubed
1 large onion, chopped
3 medium sized carrots, sliced
250 g/8 oz button mushrooms
1 celery stick, sliced
2 tbsp tomato paste
1 tsp mixed dried herbs
30 g/1 oz butter, diced
30 g/1 oz plain flour
465 ml/¾ pint hot beef stock

◆ Place the onions, carrots and celery in a large dish with 2 tbsp of stock. Cover and cook on high for 5–6 minutes.

◆ Stir in the meat and butter, cover and cook on high for 4 minutes. Add the flour, mushrooms, herbs, tomato paste and the rest of the beef stock. Stir, cover and cook on high for 6–7 minutes.

◆ Cook for a further 40 minutes on low. Stir several times during the cooking period.

◆ Let it stand covered for 10 minutes. Garnish with parsley and serve.

Braised Beef

CREOLE STEAK

SERVES 4 / SET: HIGH

Ingredients

4 fillet steaks, approx 200 g/6–7 oz each

60 g/2 oz butter, diced

2 onions, finely chopped

4 celery sticks, sliced

125 g/4 oz button mushrooms, chopped

440 g/14 oz canned tomatoes, finely chopped

2 tbsp tomato paste

1 tbsp soy sauce

salt and pepper to taste

◆ Place the steaks in a casserole dish. Cook uncovered for 3–4 minutes, depending on how rare you like your steak. Turn over and rearrange halfway through the cooking time.

◆ Place the butter, onions, celery and mushrooms in a dish, cover and cook for 6 minutes, stirring after 3 minutes.

◆ Stir in the remaining ingredients, season to taste, cover and cook for 4 minutes.

◆ Arrange the steaks on a serving dish, pour over the sauce and sprinkle with parsley.

Creole Steak

BEEF GOULASH

SERVES 4 / SET: HIGH AND MEDIUM

Ingredients

1 kg/2 lb lean braising steak
60 g/2 oz flour
½ tbsp paprika
2 tbsp oil
2 cloves garlic, crushed
1 tbsp tomato paste
2 onions sliced
625 ml/1 pint hot beef stock
1 bay leaf
220 g/7 oz canned tomatoes, mashed
4 tbsp yoghurt
2 tbsp parsley, chopped

◆ Cut the meat into bite-sized cubes. Mix the flour and paprika together and toss the meat in the mixture.

◆ Heat a browning dish on high according to manufacturer's instructions. Pour the oil into the dish and cook on high for 1 minute. Add the beef and cook for 5 minutes on high, turning frequently to brown all sides.

◆ Place the meat in a casserole with garlic, tomato paste, onion, stock, bay leaf and tomatoes. Cover and cook on high for 45 minutes until the beef is tender. Leave to stand for 5 minutes.

◆ Spoon the yoghurt over the casserole and serve garnished with parsley. The dish goes well with noodles or mashed potatoes.

SAUSAGE CASSEROLE WITH DUMPLINGS

SERVES 4 / SET: HIGH AND MEDIUM

Ingredients

1 tbsp cooking oil

1 medium onion, chopped

2 rashers lean bacon, diced

8 sausages

625 ml/1 pt hot gravy

125 g/4 oz button mushrooms

125 g/4 oz mixed frozen vegetables, defrosted

DUMPLINGS

60 g/2 oz self-raising flour

30 g/1 oz beef suet or shortening

pinch dried sage

salt and pepper to taste

water

◆ For the dumplings, mix together all the ingredients, add enough water to make a soft dough, then on a floured board form the dough into four dumplings. Set to one side.

◆ Preheat a browning dish to maximum as recommended by the manufacturer. Add the butter, onions, sausages and bacon. Cover and cook on high for 7 minutes, stirring once. Add the gravy, mushrooms and vegetables, cover and cook on medium for 6–7 minutes.

◆ Then add the dumplings, cook on high for 2 minutes and serve.

Sausage Casserole with Dumplings

BRAISED TOPSIDE

S E R V E S   6 — 8 / S E T :   M E D I U M   A N D   L O W

Ingredients

1.5–2 kg/3–4 lb beef topside
1 beef stock cube
125 ml/4 fl oz hot water
1 tbsp Worcestershire sauce
2 bay leaves
1 large carrot, sliced
2 celery sticks, sliced
1 onion, quartered

◆ Trim off excess fat, pierce the meat all over with a skewer and place in a casserole dish.

◆ Dissolve the stock cube in the hot water and Worcestershire sauce and add to the dish. Cover and cook on medium for 35 minutes.

◆ Turn the meat and add the vegetables and bay leaves, cover and cook on low for 70 minutes. Leave it standing, covered, for 10 minutes. If using a microwave thermometer, remove it from the oven when the temperature reaches 65°C/150°F.

BEEF AND BACON CASSEROLE

SERVES 4 / SET: HIGH AND MEDIUM

Ingredients

30 g/1 oz butter
375 g/12 oz beef, cut into strips
3 rashers of bacon, chopped
1 large onion, quartered and finely sliced
3 medium carrots, thinly sliced
465 ml/15 fl oz hot chicken stock
1/2 tsp dried basil
30 g/1 oz flour for coating

◆ Toss the beef in flour to coat. Preheat a browning dish to maximum, according to the manufacturer's instructions. Add the butter, beef, bacon, onions and carrots. Cover and cook on high for 8 minutes, stirring once.

◆ Add the stock and herbs. Cook on medium for 8–10 minutes.

LAMB HOTPOT

SERVES 4 / SET: HIGH AND LOW

Ingredients

625 g/1 1/4 lb lamb steaks, cut from the leg
30 g/1 oz flour
60 g/2 oz butter, diced
1 onion, finely sliced
1 clove garlic, crushed
1 leek, trimmed and sliced
2 large carrots, finely sliced
4 celery sticks, sliced
1 bay leaf
1 chicken stock cube, crumbled
30 ml/2 tbsp tomato paste
440 g/14 oz canned tomatoes
125 g/4 oz button mushrooms
salt and pepper to taste
2 large cooked potatoes, sliced

◆ Place 30 g/1 oz butter in a large deep casserole dish. Cook on high for 1 minute then add the onion, garlic and leek. Cover and cook on high for 3 minutes. Add the carrots, celery and 2 tbsp of juice from the tomatoes. Cover and cook on high for 6 minutes.

◆ Trim the fat from the lamb and cut it into cubes. Toss the cubes in the flour and add to the vegetables together with the tomatoes, stock cube, tomato paste and bay leaf. Cover and cook on high for 6 minutes, stirring halfway through the cooking time.

◆ Add the mushrooms, reduce to low and cook for a further 30 minutes, stirring every 5 minutes.

◆ Taste and season the stew, then layer the potatoes over the meat, dot with butter and brown in a conventional oven.

Lamb Hotpot

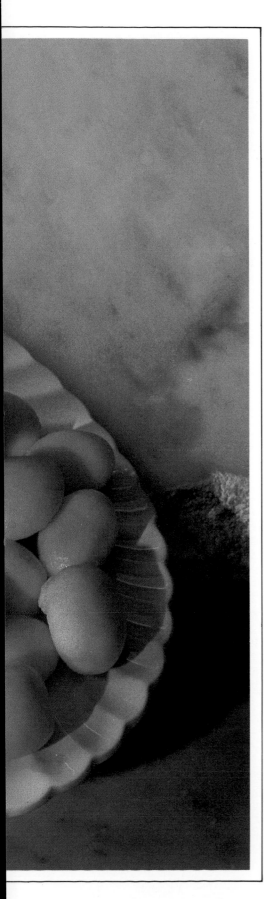

GUARD OF HONOUR

SERVES 4 / SET: HIGH AND MEDIUM

Ingredients

2 racks of lamb, 5–6 cutlets (approx 1 kg/ 2 lb) each
2 tbsp cranberry sauce
1 tbsp mint jelly
cutlet frills (optional)

◆ Weigh the meat and calculate cooking time at 2 minutes per 500 g/ 1 lb on high initially, plus 7–9 minutes per 500 g/1 lb on medium.
◆ Score the fatty side of each piece of meat, interlock the trimmed bone ends to form a 'guard of honour', meaty side inwards. Wrap a piece of foil around each bone end to prevent burning.
◆ Place the cranberry and mint jelly in a bowl and melt them for 1–2 minutes on high. Paint the fatty sides of the lamb mixture. Place the lamb on a roasting rack, cover and cook on high for 4 minutes. Reduce to medium and cook for 15–16 minutes. Remove the lid for the last 8 minutes. Paint on more cranberry mixture. Loosely wrap with foil and leave it to stand for 10 minutes.
◆ Replace the foil on the bone ends with the paper frills (if used) and set on a serving dish with vegetables.

VARIATION Stuff the lamb with your favourite stuffing mix (as you would a crown roast) and allow an extra 3 minutes on the cooking time.

Guard of Honour

SAGE AND MOZZARELLA-STUFFED CHICKEN

SERVES 4 / SET: HIGH

Ingredients

1.75–2 kg/3½–4 lb oven-ready chicken
6 sage leaves
30–60 g/1–2 oz mozzarella cheese, sliced
30 g/1 oz butter
1 onion, chopped
60 g/2 oz fresh white breadcrumbs
2 tsp fresh sage, chopped
salt and freshly ground black pepper
150 ml/¼ pint hot chicken stock
GLAZE
30 g/1 oz butter
1 tbsp brown sugar
1 tbsp sherry

◆ Grasp the flap of skin at the end of the bird and with the other hand, pull the skin away from the flesh as far as you can. Slide in the sage leaves and cheese slices.
◆ Place the butter and onion in a bowl, cover and cook for 3 minutes. Mix in the breadcrumbs, sage, seasoning and stock to form a moist, doughy consistency. Stuff the chicken and cook 8–10 minutes per 500 g/1 lb.
◆ Halfway through the cooking time, place the butter, sugar and sherry in a small jug. Cook for 1 minute. Remove the bird from the oven and brush with the glaze. Return bird to oven, giving the dish a half turn, and complete cooking. Check to see if the chicken is done by sticking a skewer into it where the leg joins with the breast. The juices should run out clear.
◆ Allow to stand for 15 minutes before serving.

LAMB CHOPS AND CRANBERRY JELLY

SERVES 2 / SET: HIGH AND MEDIUM

Ingredients

4 noisettes of lamb, each 90 g/3 oz, 2.5 cm/1 inch thick

440 g/14 oz canned consommé

1 tbsp gelatine

5 tbsp cranberry jelly

1 tsp fresh or ½ tsp dried mint

mint sprigs to garnish

◆ Arrange the chops in a shallow dish. Cook on high for 2 minutes, rearrange, and cook for a further 2 minutes. Cover and set aside.

◆ Place the consommé, cranberry jelly and herbs in a bowl and cook on high for 3 minutes. Do not allow it to boil. Sprinkle on the gelatine and stir until dissolved.

◆ Remove chops from the dish and arrange on a serving plate. Brush with the consommé mixture to glaze and chill.

◆ Pour the consommé mixture into a shallow dish and chill until jellied. Chop roughly and arrange around the chops. Garnish with sprigs of mint and serve with salad.

Lamb Chops and Cranberry Jelly

LAMB AND MUSHROOM RISOTTO

SERVES 2 / SET: HIGH

Ingredients

250 g/8 oz cooked lamb, cubed

30 g/1 oz butter

125 g/4 oz long grain rice

1 tsp garam masala (available at Indian grocery stores

1 tsp curry powder

475 ml/15 fl oz chicken stock

125 g/4 oz button mushrooms

1 small onion, finely chopped

125 g/4 oz mixed frozen vegetables

◆ Place the butter in a large deep dish, cook for 1 minute, add the onion, cover and cook for 1½ minutes.

◆ Stir in the rice, garam masala and curry powder. Pour on the stock and cook, covered, for 10 minutes.

◆ Stir in the remaining ingredients. Cook for 5 minutes or until the rice is tender but firm. Allow the dish to stand for 5 minutes.

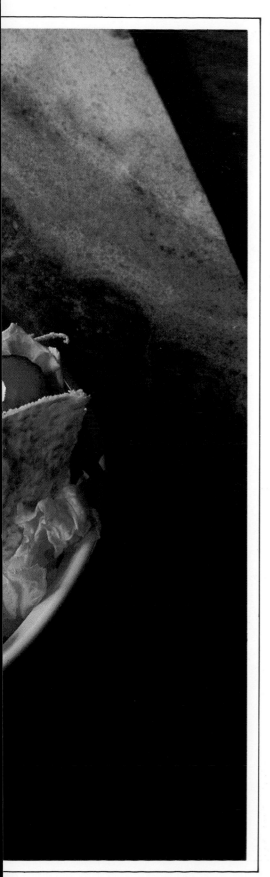

PITA POCKETS

SERVES 4 / SET: LOW, MEDIUM AND HIGH

Ingredients

500 g/1 lb lamb fillet, cubed
15 g/½ oz butter
2 tbsp soy sauce
2 tbsp lemon juice
1 tbsp honey
4 pita breads
2 tbsp mayonnaise
12 cucumber slices
12 tomato slices
1 lettuce heart
1 small onion, cut into rings

◆ Mix together the soy sauce, lemon juice and honey. Add the meat cubes and marinate for at least 2 hours.

◆ Heat a browning dish to maximum, according to the manufacturer's instructions. Remove the meat from the marinade, add butter to the browning dish and stir in the meat. Cook on high for 2 minutes, reduce to medium and cook for a further 9 minutes. Cover and reserve.

◆ Place the pita breads on 2 layers of kitchen paper and warm on low for 2 minutes. Remove from the oven, cut in half, open up the 'pocket' and spread the inside with mayonnaise. Shred the lettuce and add a little to each pocket with a few slices of tomato, cucumber and onion. Pile in the lamb. Alternatively, thread meat and vegetables onto wooden kebab sticks and serve with the pita bread and rice.

LAMB CASSEROLE

SERVES 4 / SET: HIGH AND MEDIUM

Ingredients

750 g/1½ lb boned shoulder of lamb, cubed
15 g/½ oz flour
15 g/½ oz butter
2 medium onions, sliced
1 large apple, sliced
125 g/4 oz stoned prunes
150 ml/5 fl oz chicken stock
150 ml/5 fl oz red wine
salt and pepper to taste

◆ Toss the lamb in the flour to coat. Place the butter in a casserole dish and cook on high for 1 minute. Add the onions, cover and cook on high for 2 minutes. Add the lamb and cook on high for 5 minutes.

◆ Stir in the apple, prunes, chicken stock and red wine. Cover and cook on medium for 25–30 minutes. Stir twice during the cooking period. Season to taste and serve.

Pita Pockets

ARMENIAN LAMB WITH PILAFF

SERVES 4 / SET: HIGH

Ingredients

1 kg/2 lb fillet end leg of lamb
1 tbsp oil
30 g/1 oz butter
2 onions, chopped
1 clove garlic, chopped
30 g/1 oz flour
1 tsp ground cumin
½ tsp ground allspice
2 tbsp tomato paste
315 ml/½ pint hot chicken stock
salt and freshly ground black pepper

PILAFF

45 g/1½ oz butter
1 small onion, chopped
250 g/8 oz long-grain rice
465 ml/¾ pint hot chicken stock
salt and freshly ground black pepper
90 g/3 oz currants
90 g/3 oz almonds, blanched and chopped

◆ Remove meat from bone and cut into bite-sized cubes.

◆ Pour oil into a bowl, add butter and cook for 1 minute. Stir in onion and garlic and cook for 3 minutes. Add the meat and cook, covered, for 3 minutes.

◆ Stir in the flour and add remaining ingredients. Cook, covered, for 10 minutes. Allow to stand for 15 minutes then cook for a further 6 minutes.

◆ To make the pilaff, place the butter in a large shallow dish and cook for 1 minute. Stir in onion and rice and cook for 4 minutes.

◆ Add stock and seasoning and cook for 15 minutes or until rice is fluffy, adding extra liquid if necessary. Check seasoning and stir in currants and almonds before serving with the lamb.

Armenian Lamb with Pilaff

KOFTA MEAT BALLS

SERVES 2 / SET: HIGH

Ingredients

500 g/1 lb minced lamb

½ tsp garam masala (available at Indian grocery stores)

½ tsp ground ginger

2 cloves garlic, crushed

½ tsp ground cumin

1 egg

salt to taste

1 tbsp vegetable oil

◆ Mix together all the ingredients except the oil and roll into small balls.

◆ Meanwhile, preheat a browning dish to maximum as recommended by the manufacturer. Add the oil 30 seconds before the end of this time.

◆ Quickly add the meatballs and cook for 5 minutes, turning once during the cooking time.

MOUSSAKA

SERVES 4 / SET: HIGH

Ingredients

500 g/1 lb minced lamb
30 g/1 oz butter
1 large onion, finely sliced
4 medium eggplants
1 beef stock cube dissolved in 3 tbsp water
4 tbsp tomato paste
salt and pepper to taste
S A U C E
30 g/1 oz butter
30 g/1 oz flour
315 ml/10 fl oz milk
185 g/6 oz cheese, grated

◆ Thinly slice the eggplants, sprinkle with salt and leave for 15 minutes. Pour off the bitter juices, rinse and drain.

◆ Meanwhile, place the butter in a dish, cook for 1 minute. Stir in the onions and eggplants when they are ready and cook covered for 5–6 minutes. Add the meat, stock and tomato paste. Cook covered for 5 minutes.

◆ To make the sauce, cook the butter for 1 minute, add the flour and cook for 2 minutes. Stir in the milk and cook for 3 minutes, stirring every minute until thickened. Add the cheese, stir and keep to one side.

◆ Place half of the meat mixture in a deep casserole, top with half the sauce, then the remaining meat and finally the remainder of the sauce.

◆ Place the dish in the oven and cook for 10 minutes.

◆ Brown under a preheated conventional grill and serve.

LAMB CURRY

SERVES 4 / SET: HIGH AND LOW

Ingredients

1 kg/2 lb shoulder of lamb, cubed
30 g/1 oz butter
4 cloves garlic, crushed
1 medium onion, finely sliced
1/2 oz freshly grated root ginger
1/2 tsp ground mustard seed
1/2 tsp ground fenugreek
1/2 tsp ground cumin
1/2 tsp turmeric
1 tsp chilli powder
440 g/14 oz canned tomatoes, finely chopped
4 tbsp white wine vinegar
1 tbsp sugar

◆ Place half the butter in a dish and cook on high for 1 minute. Add the garlic and onion, cook on high, covered, for 1½ minutes. Add the grated ginger, ground mustard seed, fenugreek, cumin, turmeric and chilli powder and cook for a further 1½ minutes on high. Stir in the tomatoes, vinegar and sugar. Place to one side.

◆ Preheat a browning dish to maximum, according to the manufacturer's instructions. Add the remaining butter and meat and cook on high for 4 minutes, stirring once halfway through the cooking time. Add the curry sauce, cover and cook on low for 25 minutes. Stir every 10 minutes. Let it stand for 5 minutes.

◆ Serve with plain boiled rice.

Lamb Curry

PORK SPARE RIBS IN BARBECUE SAUCE

SERVES 2 / SET: HIGH AND LOW

Ingredients

6 meaty pork spare ribs, total weight 750 g/1 1/2 lb
1 small onion, finely sliced
30 g/1/2 oz butter
S A U C E
2 tbsp honey
2 tbsp soy sauce
4 tbsp tomato ketchup
1 tbsp white wine vinegar
spring onions (scallions) to garnish

◆ Place the butter and onion in a shallow casserole. Cover and cook on high for 3 minutes.

◆ Add the ribs to the casserole dish and pour over the sauce, turning the ribs to coat. Cook on high for 4 minutes.

◆ Spoon over the sauce again, cover and cook on low for 25 minutes, rearranging and turning the ribs every 5 minutes. Drain the sauce into a saucepan and boil on the stove top until reduced and of a syrupy consistency, about 10 minutes.

◆ Place the ribs on a serving dish, coat with the sauce and garnish with spring onions (scallions).

◆ Serve with rice or baked potatoes and salad.

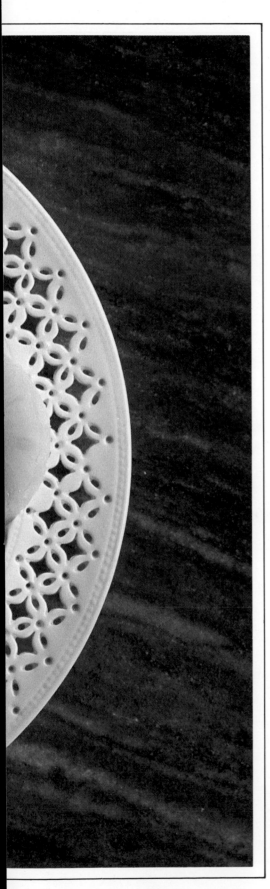

SWEET AND SOUR PORK

SERVES 4 / SET: HIGH AND MEDIUM

Ingredients

500 g/1 lb pork fillet, cut into strips
4 tbsp soy sauce
4 tbsp dry sherry
1 tbsp sesame oil
1/2 small yellow pepper
1/2 small red chilli
1 medium carrot
2 tsp cornflour, dissolved in a little water
2 pineapple rings to garnish
2 spring onions (scallions)
SAUCE
2 tbsp vinegar
4 tbsp tomato ketchup
4 tbsp honey
8 tbsp pineapple juice

◆ Marinate the pork strips in the soy sauce and sherry for 1 hour. Cut the pepper, chilli and carrots into julienne strips.

◆ Drain the meat and heat a browning dish to the maximum recommended by the manufacturer. Add the oil and quickly toss the pork strips in the oil. Cover and cook on high for 3 minutes, stirring after 2 minutes. Drain.

◆ Add the vegetables and sauce ingredients, cover and cook on medium for 2 minutes. The vegetables should be crisp. Add the cornflour and water to the dish and cook on high for 1 minute. Stir well.

◆ Serve with plain boiled rice and garnish with pineapple rings and spring onions (scallions).

TANDOORI PORK CHIPOLATAS

SERVES 4 / SET: MEDIUM

Ingredients

500 g/1 lb pork chipolata sausages
4 tbsp tandoori or curry paste
2 tbsp cooking oil

◆ Prick the sausages. Combine the tandoori or curry paste and cooking oil and marinate the sausages in the mixture for 1 hour.

◆ Preheat a browning dish to the maximum recommended by the manufacturer. Remove the chipolatas from the marinade and place them in the browning dish. Cook for 3 minutes then turn and cook for a further 4 minutes.

◆ Serve hot or cold as a snack.

Sweet and Sour Pork

PORK KEBABS WITH PEANUT SAUCE

SERVES 4 / SET: HIGH

Ingredients

*750 g/1½ lb pork fillet, cut into
2.5 cm/1 inch cubes*

1 red pepper, coarsely chopped

1 yellow pepper, coarsely chopped

*1 small onion, quartered and layers
separated*

30 g/1 oz butter

SAUCE

125 g/4 oz roasted peanuts, ground

2 tbsp soy sauce

1 tbsp sesame oil

◆ Combine the sauce ingredients
and cook covered for 1½ minutes.

◆ Skewer the meat and vegetables
onto wooden kebab sticks and brush
with the peanut sauce.

◆ Place the kebabs on a plate in a
single layer, dot with butter, cover and
cook for 4 minutes. Turn and cook for
a further 4 minutes.

◆ Serve with extra sauce, plain
boiled rice and salad.

CHINESE PANCAKES

SERVES 4 / SET: HIGH

Ingredients

PANCAKES / MAKES 8

125 g/4 oz plain flour

1 egg

315 ml/½ pint milk

pinch salt

shortening to grease pan

FILLING

185 g/6 oz pork fillet, thinly sliced into strips

15 g/½ oz butter

1 bunch spring onions (scallions), sliced

250 g/8 oz can of water chestnuts, thinly sliced

4 tbsp soy sauce

2 tbsp dry sherry

125 g/4 oz roasted salted cashew nuts

2 spring onions (scallions), to garnish

½ red pepper – thinly sliced, to garnish

◆ To make the pancakes, sift the flour and salt into a bowl. Make a well in the centre. Beat the egg and add it to the flour. Pour in half the milk and mix to a smooth batter. Add the remaining milk and allow to stand for 1 hour.

◆ Melt a little fat in a frying-pan, add sufficient batter to cover the bottom of the pan thinly and cook on a conventional burner for 1 minute. Turn the pancake over and cook until golden brown. Cover and keep warm. Repeat with the remaining batter.

◆ To make the filling, heat a browning dish to maximum according to the manufacturer's instructions. Add the butter and the pork strips and cook, uncovered, for 3 minutes, stirring once. Add all the remaining ingredients and mix. Cover and cook 4 minutes.

◆ Fold the pancakes in half, then in half again. Open out the edges to make a pocket and stuff with the filling.

◆ Garnish with spring onion (scallion) tassels and julienne strips of red pepper.

Chinese Pancakes

CURRIED PORK SLICES

SERVES 4 / SET: HIGH

Ingredients

4 pork slices, 1 cm/½ inch thick

4 tbsp curry paste

2 tbsp sesame oil

◆ Mix the oil and curry paste together, add the pork slices and coat with the paste. Marinate for 30 minutes.

◆ Heat a browning dish to maximum according to the manufacturer's instructions. Add the slices, cover and cook for 4 minutes. Turn the meat over and cook for a further 4 minutes. Let them stand for 3 minutes.

◆ Serve with baked potatoes and salad.

QUICK COOK'S PATE

SERVES 4 / SET: HIGH

Ingredients

3 rashers of bacon

1 small onion, finely chopped

1 clove garlic, crushed

1 tsp dried sage

250 g/8 oz pig's liver, chopped

30 g/1 oz butter

2 tbsp light cream

salt and pepper to taste

◆ Place the bacon, onion, garlic and herbs in a dish and cover with plastic wrap. Cook on high for 6½ minutes.

◆ Stir in the liver and butter, cover and cook on high for 6½ minutes. Let it stand for 5 minutes.

◆ Stir in the cream and purée the mixture in a blender or food processor until smooth. Season to taste.

◆ Turn into a dish, smooth the top and chill until set.

◆ Serve with hot crusty bread or triangles of toast.

STUFFED PORK CHOPS

SERVES 4 / SET: HIGH AND MEDIUM

Ingredients

4 loin pork chops, 2.5 cm/1 inch thick, 185 g/6 oz each

125 g/4 oz Cheddar cheese, grated

STUFFING

45 g/1½ oz butter

1 small onion, finely sliced

60 g/2 oz button mushrooms, finely chopped

60 g/2 oz cooked rice

◆ Slice through the pork chops horizontally from one end, leaving a border on two sides to form a pocket.

◆ Cook the butter on high for 1 minute, add the onion and mushrooms and cook on high for 3 minutes. Stir in the rice.

◆ Spoon the stuffing mixture into the pockets in the pork chops and secure with wooden toothpicks.

◆ Arrange the chops in a dish with the thickest parts to the outer edge. Cover and cook on high for 5 minutes. Rearrange and turn the chops, then continue to cook them for a further 9–10 minutes on medium. One minute before the end of the cooking time sprinkle with the grated cheese or brown under a conventional grill.

◆ Serve with mushrooms and tomatoes.

PORK CHOPS WITH CRANBERRY SAUCE

SERVES 4 / SET: HIGH AND MEDIUM

Ingredients

4 loin pork chops, 185 g/6 oz each
125 g/4 oz cranberry sauce
1 tbsp cooking oil
150 ml/¼ pint dry sherry

◆ Preheat a browning dish to the maximum recommended by the manufacturer. Press the chops onto the dish to sear, turn over and cook on high for 5 minutes.

◆ Combine the remaining ingredients and cook on high for 2 minutes. Blend to a smooth sauce and pour over the chops. Cover and cook on medium for 10–12 minutes, turning once.

QUICK HAM AND BEAN HASH

SERVES 4—6 / SET: HIGH
AND MEDIUM

Ingredients

30 g/1 oz butter
4 rashers bacon, diced
1 onion, chopped
440 g/14 oz canned new potatoes, diced
440 g/14 oz canned kidney beans, drained
375 g/12 oz canned corn kernels, drained
250 g/8 oz cooked ham, sliced
440 g/14 oz canned tomatoes, finely chopped
2 tbsp tomato paste
1 tbsp Worcestershire sauce
1 tbsp soy sauce
Tabasco sauce to taste
salt and pepper to taste

◆ Place the butter, onion and bacon in a casserole, cover and cook on high for 3 minutes. Add all the remaining ingredients, stir well and heat on medium for 10–12 minutes or until piping hot.

◆ Serve with crusty bread.

Quick Ham and Bean Hash

GLAZED HAM ROAST

S E R V E S   6 — 8   /   S E T :   H I G H
A N D   M E D I U M

Ingredients

1½ kg/3 lb ham roast, rind removed, soaked overnight
150 ml/5 fl oz water
150 ml/5 fl oz pineapple juice
90 g/3 oz brown sugar
15 g/½ oz butter

◆ Place the roast in a roasting bag with the water, pierce the bag and close it with a non metallic tie. Stand it in a dish and cook for 6 minutes on high. Reduce to medium and cook for a further 25 minutes, turning over after 12 minutes.

◆ Remove the joint from the bag and wrap it loosely in foil, shiny side inwards. Let it stand for 15 minutes.

◆ Place the pineapple juice, sugar and butter in a bowl. Cook on high for 6 minutes, stirring every 2 minutes, to make a glaze.

◆ Stand the joint in a grill pan, brush with the glaze and brown it under a preheated conventional grill.

HAM RISOTTO

SERVES 4 / SET: HIGH

Ingredients
375 g/12 oz rice
690 ml/23 fl oz hot chicken stock
125 g/4 oz button mushrooms, sliced
1 small red pepper, chopped
125 g/4 oz frozen peas, defrosted
375 g/12 oz canned corn kernels
375 g/12 oz ham steak, diced
1 clove garlic, crushed
salt and pepper to taste

◆ Cook the rice in the stock for 15 minutes. Let it stand, covered, for 7 minutes.

◆ Meanwhile, place all the remaining ingredients in a dish, cover and cook for 7–9 minutes. Stir twice during the cooking time.

◆ Mix into the rice and serve.

Ham Risotto

HAWAIIAN HAM

SERVES 4 / SET: HIGH

Ingredients

4 ham steaks

4 canned pineapple rings, drained

30 g/1 oz butter

2 tbsp sultanas

4 slices of cheese

◆ Remove the rind from the ham and snip the fat with scissors at regular intervals.

◆ Place the butter in a bowl, add the sultanas and cook for 1½ minutes, or until they are plump and juicy.

◆ Place the ham steaks on a large plate, cover with absorbent kitchen paper and cook for 9–10 minutes, turning once.

◆ Remove the paper. Place one pineapple ring on each steak, fill the centre with sultanas and place a cheese slice on top. Return to the oven and cook for 2–3 minutes. Serve with tomatoes and mushrooms.

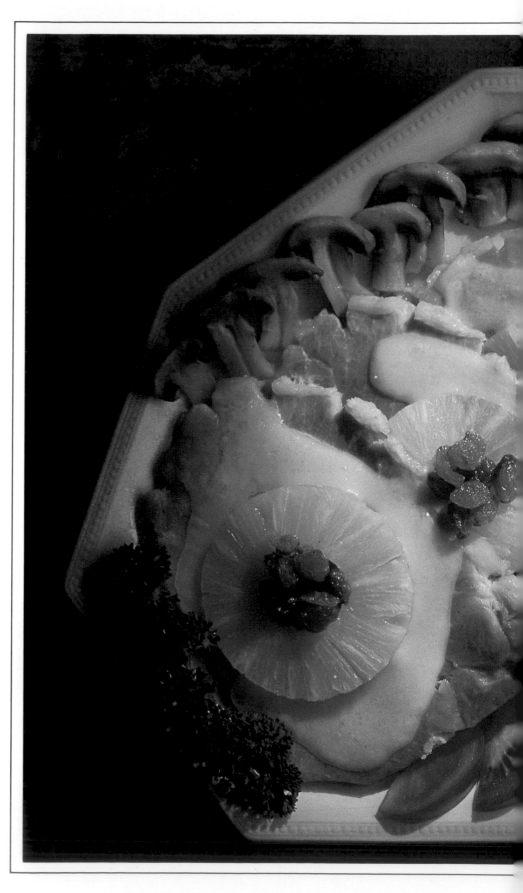

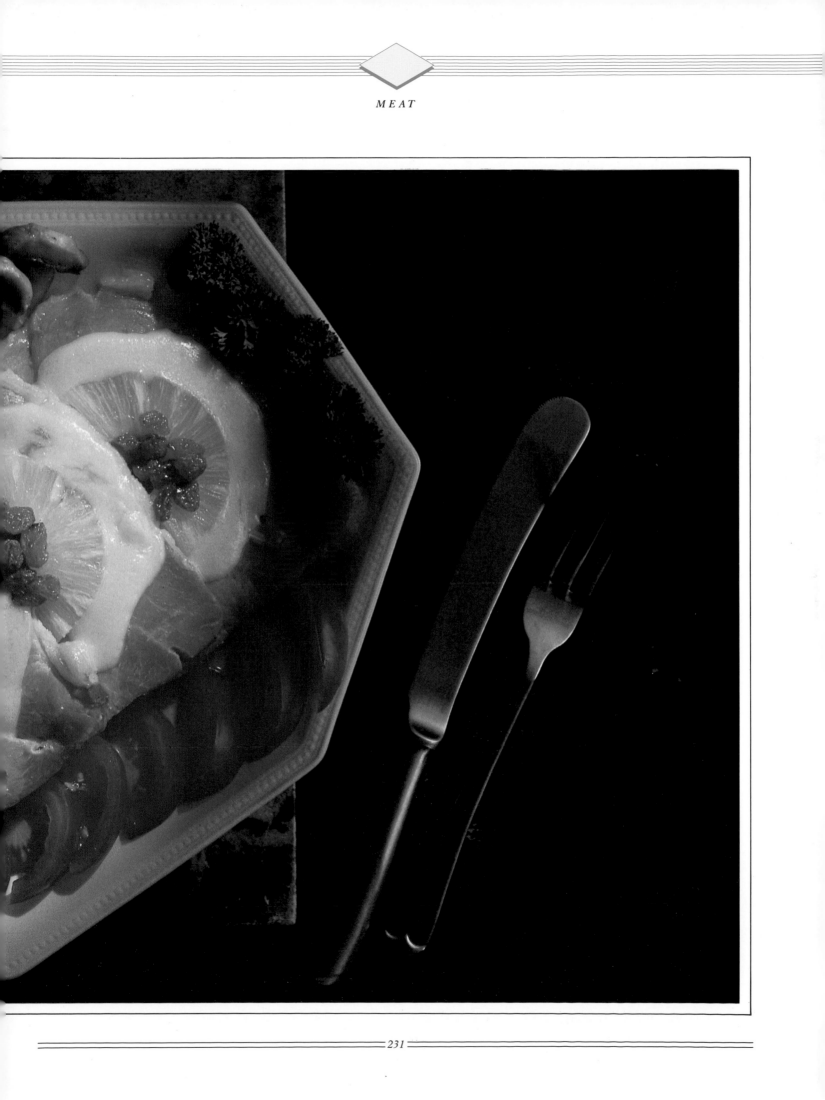

TANDOORI CHICKEN

SERVES 4 / SET: HIGH AND MEDIUM

Ingredients

4 chicken leg portions, 250 g/8 oz each

3 tbsp tandoori or curry paste

150 ml/5 fl oz plain yoghurt

lemon wedges and onion rings to garnish

◆ Skin the chicken portions and make 3–4 deep slashes in the flesh. Place in a dish.

◆ Mix together the tandoori or curry paste and yoghurt, pour the mixture over the chicken and marinate for at least 2 hours.

◆ Remove the chicken from the marinade, place on a roasting rack, cover with the lid and cook on high for 10 minutes, turning halfway through the cooking time. Reset the oven to medium and cook for a further 15–17 minutes, turning and rearranging twice.

◆ Pierce the chicken at the joint and ensure that the juices run clear. If they are pink, return it to the oven and cook a little longer, checking regularly to see if cooked.

◆ Place on a grill rack and char under a preheated conventional grill for 5 minutes.

◆ Garnish and serve with salad and rice.

ROAST TURKEY

SERVES 2 / SET: MEDIUM

Ingredients

2.25 kg/4½ lb turkey

4 sticks of celery, sliced

2 small onions, quartered

2 bay leaves

30 g/1 oz butter

3 rashers bacon

◆ Stuff the turkey with the celery, onion, bay leaves and butter.

◆ Place the turkey, breast down, on a roasting rack and cover with the lid. Cook for 25 minutes.

◆ Turn the bird over, lay the bacon over the breast and cook for a further 25 minutes.

◆ Discard the bacon and wrap the turkey loosely in foil. Let it stand for 10 minutes.

◆ Brown the turkey under a preheated conventional grill.

◆ Serve with roast potatoes and fresh vegetables.

Tandoori Chicken

CHICKEN AND ALMONDS CHINESE-STYLE

SERVES 4 / SET: HIGH

Ingredients

750 g/1½ lb boned chicken breasts, cut into thin strips

1 large onion, quartered and finely sliced

60 g/2 oz blanched almonds

2 tbsp sesame oil

315 ml/½ pint chicken stock

1 tbsp soy sauce

1 tbsp cornflour, mixed with 2 tsp water

185 g/6 oz mung beansprouts

1 small red pepper cut into julienne strips

1 small green pepper cut into julienne strips

◆ Preheat a browning dish to the maximum recommended by the manufacturer.

◆ Add the oil to the dish with the strips of chicken and cook for 3 minutes.

◆ Add the onion and almonds. Cook for 3 minutes, stirring once during the cooking time.

◆ Blend together the chicken stock, soy sauce and cornflour. Stir into the chicken mixture, cover and cook for 4–5 minutes. Let it stand for 5 minutes.

◆ Place the beansprouts and the red and green peppers in a dish with 1 tbsp water, cover with plastic wrap and cook for 1 minute.

◆ Place the vegetables in a dish and pile the chicken and almonds on them. Serve with rice.

Chicken and Almonds Chinese-Style

WHOLE ROAST CHICKEN

SERVES 4—6 / SET: MEDIUM

Ingredients

1.5 kg/3 lb roasting chicken
2 tbsp clear honey
1 tbsp soy sauce
1 tsp paprika
30 g/1 oz melted butter

◆ Mix together the honey, soy sauce and paprika. Brush the chicken with the sauce. Protect the wing tips and drumsticks with foil.

◆ Place the chicken, breast down, on a roasting rack and cover with the lid or a pierced roasting bag closed with a non-metallic tie.

◆ Calculate the cooking time at 9 minutes per pound. Halfway through, turn the chicken, breast up, and brush with butter. Protect the breast bone with a strip of foil. Drain off any accumulated juices from the dish and cook for the remainder of the calculated cooking time.

◆ With a sharp knife, pierce the inside thigh joint and check that the juices run clear. If they are pink, return the chicken to the oven and cook a little longer, checking at regular intervals.

◆ When completely cooked, remove from the roasting rack and cover lightly with foil. Let it stand for 15 minutes.

DUCK IN ORANGE SAUCE

SERVES 4 / SET: MEDIUM AND HIGH

Ingredients

4 duck portions, total weight approx 2.25 kg/4½ lb

SAUCE

1 tbsp clear marmalade

250 ml/8 fl oz orange juice

2 tbsp port wine

2 tbsp lemon juice

2 tbsp honey

2 tsp cornflour, mixed with 1 tsp water

orange slices and watercress to garnish

◆ Arrange the duck portions on a rack in a large deep dish. Cook covered on medium for 45–60 minutes. Reposition and turn the pieces over several times during the cooking period and drain off the surplus fat. Test to see that they are cooked by piercing with a sharp knife at the joint, the juices should run clear. Brown the cooked duck under a conventional grill.

◆ For the sauce, place the marmalade jelly in a dish and cook on high for 1 minute. Add the rest of the sauce ingredients and cook for a further 3 minutes or until bubbling. Cool slightly and stir in the cornflour, cook on high for 1 minute and stir well.

◆ Place the duck on a warm serving dish, pour over the sauce and garnish with orange slices and watercress.

QUICK CHICKEN PASTA

SERVES 4 / SET: HIGH

Ingredients

375 g/12 oz green tagliatelle
l tbsp cooking oil
1 tsp salt
1 small red pepper, diced
1 small green pepper, diced
125 g/4 oz frozen peas, defrosted
315 g/10 oz canned condensed mushroom soup
150 ml/5 fl oz water
500 g/1 lb cooked chicken, diced

◆ Place pasta in a deep dish and pour over enough boiling water to cover. Add the oil and salt, cover and cook for 6 minutes. Let it stand for 6 minutes.

◆ Place the peppers in a dish, cover and cook for 3 minutes. Add the peas and cook for a further 3 minutes.

◆ Combine the mushroom soup and water, and add it with the chicken to the vegetables. Cook uncovered for 6–8 minutes, stirring once halfway through the cooking time.

◆ Drain the pasta and place in a warm serving dish. Arrange the chicken mixture on top and serve.

TURKEY BREASTS CORDON BLEU

SERVES 4 / SET: HIGH AND LOW

Ingredients

4 turkey breasts, approx 185 g/6 oz each
60 g/2 oz butter, diced
4 slices of ham
4 slices of mozzarella cheese
pinch of paprika

◆ Place the turkey breasts in a shallow dish and dot with the butter. Cover and cook on high for 4 minutes. Rearrange and turn the breasts over, cover and cook on low for 5–6 minutes, turning them again halfway through the cooking time.

◆ Transfer the pieces to a microwave proof serving dish. Place a slice of ham and a slice of cheese on top of each breast and cook on high, uncovered, for 3 minutes.

◆ Sprinkle with paprika and serve.

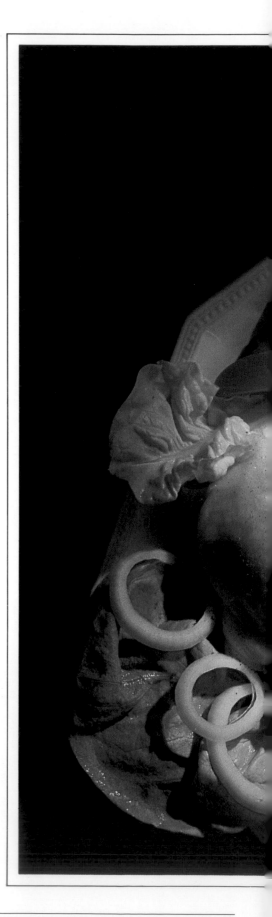

Turkey Breasts Cordon Bleu

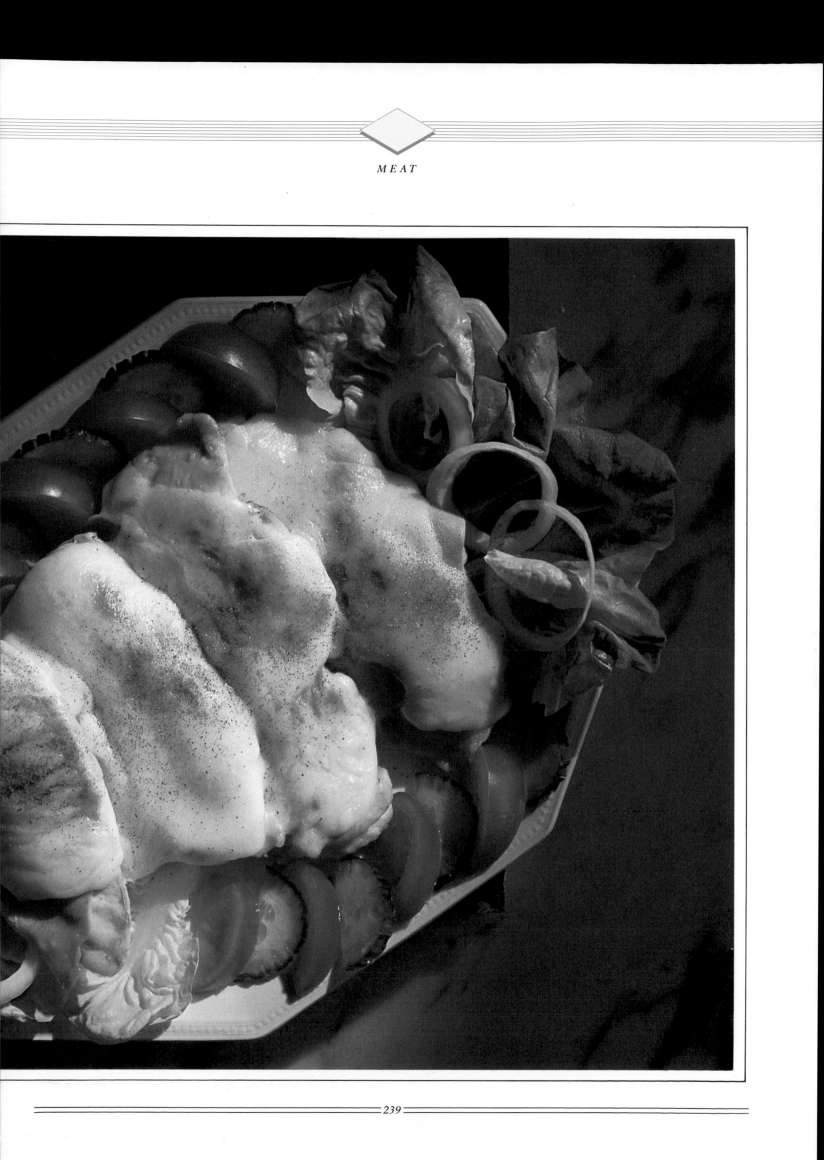

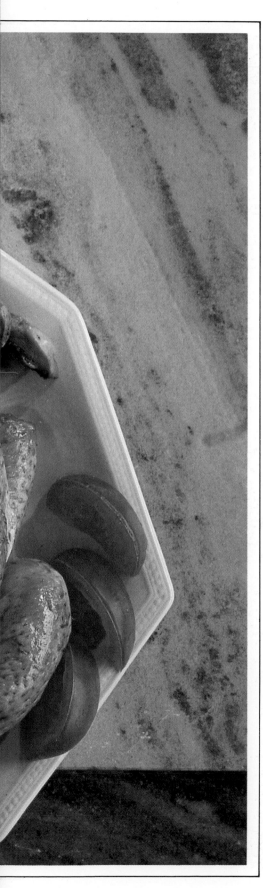

ROAST POUSSINS

SERVES 2 / SET: MEDIUM

Ingredients

2 young chickens, 500 g/1 lb each

STUFFING

155 g/5 oz redcurrant jelly

45 g/1½ oz butter

60 g/2 oz cooked rice

2 tbsp sultanas

salt and pepper to taste

GLAZE

2 tbsp soy sauce

1 tbsp honey

◆ Combine the stuffing ingredients in a bowl, cover and cook for 1½ minutes.
◆ Stuff the chickens and lay them on a roasting rack, breast down.
◆ Mix the soy sauce and honey in a bowl, and cook for 1 minute. Brush the chickens with half the glaze, cover with a lid and cook for 15 minutes.
◆ Drain, then turn the chickens breast up. Coat with the remainder of the glaze, cover and cook for a further 15 minutes. Remove from rack, cover in foil and allow to stand for 10 minutes.

Roast Poussins

LIVER AND BACON KEBABS

SERVES 2 / SET: HIGH

Ingredients

250 g/8 oz chicken livers

8 rashers bacon

125 g/4 oz button mushrooms

Worcestershire sauce to taste

◆ Cut each bacon rasher into 2 or 3 pieces and wrap the pieces around the livers.
◆ Thread onto wooden kebab sticks, alternating with the mushrooms. Sprinkle with Worcestershire sauce to taste.
◆ Place the kebabs on a plate in an even layer. Cover with absorbent kitchen paper and cook for 6–7 minutes, turning once during the cooking time.

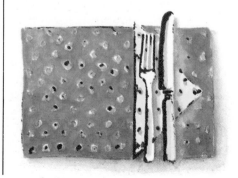

VEAL ITALIENNE

SERVES 4 / SET: HIGH AND MEDIUM

Ingredients

375 g/12 oz tagliatelle
1 tsp oil
1 tsp salt
500 g/1 lb diced fillet of veal
250 g/8 oz diced ham steak
15 g/½ oz butter
1 large onion, thinly sliced
125 g/4 oz button mushrooms, halved
2 gherkins, chopped

SAUCE

30 g/1 oz butter
30 g/1 oz flour
315 ml/½ pint milk
salt and pepper to taste
julienne strips of red pepper to garnish

◆ Place the pasta in a deep dish, pour over enough boiling water to cover, add the salt and oil. Cook on high for 6 minutes. Cover and keep to one side.

◆ Place the veal, ham and butter in a dish. Cover and cook on high for 3 minutes, stirring once. Add the onion and mushrooms. Cook on high for 2 minutes and place to one side.

◆ For the sauce, melt the butter on high for 1 minute then stir in the flour and cook for a further minute. Add the milk and cook on high for 3 minutes, stirring every minute. Add this to the meat mixture and cook on medium for 15 minutes. Stir in the chopped gherkins and season to taste.

◆ Drain the pasta, arrange in a serving dish and top with the meat sauce. Garnish and serve.

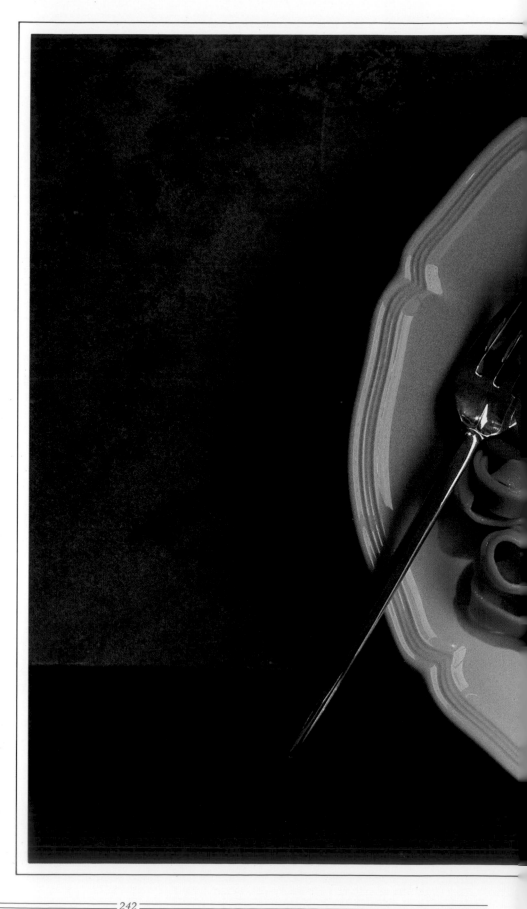

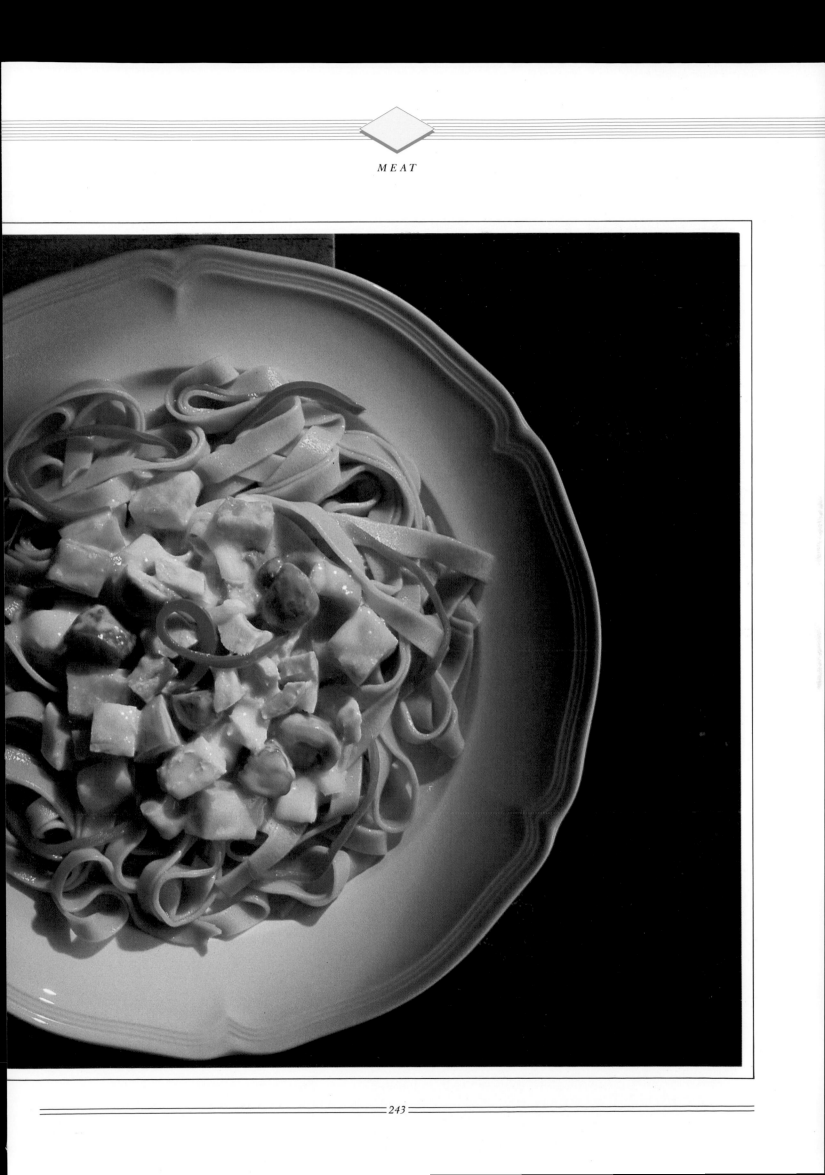

VEAL ROULADE AND MUSHROOM SAUCE

SERVES 4 / SET: HIGH AND MEDIUM

Ingredients

4 veal escalopes beaten thin

2 large carrots cut into long sticks

2 tbsp water

8 frozen French beans

60 g/2 oz butter

SAUCE

315 g/10 oz canned condensed mushroom soup

150 ml/5 fl oz water

salt and pepper to taste

◆ Cook the carrots in 2 tbsp of water in a covered dish for 3 minutes on high. Add the French beans and cook for 1 minute.

◆ Lay the veal escalopes on a board and place a carrot stick and 2 beans at the shortest end. Roll up neatly and secure each roll with a wooden toothpick.

◆ Arrange the veal in a shallow dish, dot with butter, cover and cook for 5 minutes on high. Rearrange and continue to cook for a further 9 minutes on medium. Add salt and pepper to taste, cover and reserve.

◆ Blend the soup with the water and cook on high for 5 minutes or until hot. Transfer to a warm sauceboat.

◆ Remove toothpicks from roulades and slice into even-sized rings. Serve with the sauce, new potatoes, French beans and carrots.

MEAT AND FRUIT PILAFF

*SERVES 4 / SET: HIGH
AND MEDIUM*

Ingredients

375 g/12 oz brown rice
375 ml/12 fl oz hot chicken stock
250 g/8 oz diced cooked meat
1 banana, sliced
1 red apple, diced
1 green apple, diced
1 peach, peeled and diced
1 tbsp lemon juice
125 g/4 oz cashew nuts
60 g/2 oz sultanas
salt and pepper to taste

◆ Place the rice in a deep dish, add the hot stock, cover and cook on high for 30–35 minutes. Let it stand, covered, for 10 minutes.

◆ Toss the apples and banana in the lemon juice. Combine with the rest of the ingredients. Cover and cook on medium for 5 minutes. Mix into the cooked rice and serve.

COOKING WITH

Vegetables

ELIZABETH CORNISH

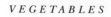

VEGETABLES

V EGETABLES prepared in the microwave are cooked to
perfection. They are both tender and crisp and full of
flavour and freshness. The vegetables look as if they have been
harvested only moments before, because they keep their shape
and their colour. They keep their goodness too – research has
shown that microwave cooking destroys fewer nutrients than
any other method.

These advantages are due to the speed of the microwave, and
to the fact that the moisture content of vegetables is high, so
that they literally cook in their own juices.

Gone are the days of soggy sprouts and cabbage, when their
crisp leaves were boiled until they had collapsed, lost all their
colour and flavour and become virtually worthless as a source
of nutrient. Now you can cook these and other vegetables in
just a few minutes without getting a kitchen full of steam and
unpleasant smells that linger in the house for days. What you
will get is a vegetable looking and tasting like nature intended it
to – delicious.

Microwaved vegetables are good for slimmers as well as the
generally health-conscious, because they retain their fibre
content and even if you are cooking in fat, very little is needed.
For the most part, fat can be avoided altogether.

Bearing in mind that the taste and appearance of the vegetable
will not be altered by microwave cooking, you should select only
the best specimens. Buy fresh vegetables in season, or frozen
vegetables, which are picked and then frozen at their best.

This book will give you plenty of ideas for all kinds of vegetable
dishes. Many are meals in themselves; others can be served as
light suppers, starters, or as part of a vegetarian meal or an
accompaniment to meat and fish.

CONTENTS

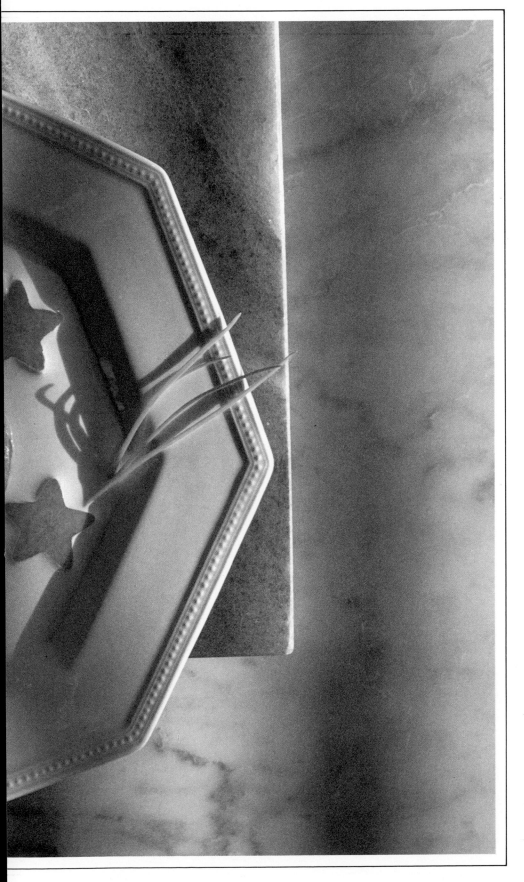

PUREE OF ROOT VEGETABLES

SERVES 4 / SET: HIGH

Ingredients

375 g/12 oz carrots, sliced
375 g/12 oz swede, sliced
2½ tbsp water
butter to taste
salt and freshly ground black pepper
150 ml/5 fl oz light cream
chopped chives

◆ Peel the vegetables and slice them thinly. Reserve some of the carrot slices and cut them into star shapes for the garnish.

◆ Put the vegetables in a dish with the water. Cover with vented plastic wrap and cook for 6–8 minutes, until soft.

◆ Drain the vegetables and purée in a blender or food processor with butter to taste. Season the purée and reheat for 1 minute.

◆ To serve, spoon a thin pool of cream onto each of 4 heated plates. Make a small mound of purée on each plate and garnish the surrounding cream with shooting stars made of carrot and snipped chives.

VARIATION You can make this purée with any of the winter root vegetables, such as turnip, parsnip and sweet potato.

ARTICHOKE HEARTS, KIDNEY BEANS AND MUSHROOMS WITH VEGETABLE PUREE

SERVES 4 / SET: HIGH

Ingredients

1 onion, sliced

1 clove garlic, crushed

1 tbsp sunflower oil

250 g/8 oz mushrooms, wiped and sliced

440 g/14 oz canned kidney beans

220 g/7 oz canned artichoke hearts, drained

salt and freshly ground black pepper

fresh coriander or parsley

185 g/6 oz Puree of Root Vegetables (see recipe)

This delicious and rather unusual mixture of flavours is enhanced even further by the tang of fresh coriander leaves.

◆ Put the onion and garlic in a casserole with the oil, cover and cook for 3 minutes. Stir in the mushrooms, kidney beans – with a little of the liquid from the can – and artichoke hearts and cook, covered, for about 5 minutes, stirring once, until the mushrooms are done and the beans cooked through.

◆ Season to taste with salt and pepper and sprinkle with coriander or parsley leaves.

◆ Serve with vegetable purée.

HOT POTATO SALAD

S E R V E S 4 / S E T : H I G H

Ingredients

750 g/1½ lb new potatoes, washed but not peeled
4 tbsp water
2 tbsp virgin olive oil
1 tbsp lemon juice or white wine vinegar
salt and freshly ground black pepper
1 tsp dry mustard
1 bunch spring onions (scallions)
1 bunch radishes
about 12 black olives, stoned
220 g/7 oz canned green beans, drained (use cooked fresh beans if in season)
chopped chives (optional)

Mix the salad with mayonnaise dressing if you prefer. For less cholesterol, use half and half mayonnaise and yoghurt.

◆ Put the potatoes in a dish with the water, cover and cook for about 8 minutes, shaking twice, until done. Do not overcook the potatoes, or they will be spongy.

◆ Drain the potatoes, slice them and return to the dish.

◆ Make a dressing by combining the olive oil, vinegar or lemon juice, salt, pepper and mustard in a screw-topped jar and shaking well. Pour this over the hot potatoes and keep covered.

◆ Trim the spring onions (scallions) and slice down the stalk, making 2 cuts at right angles to each other. Put the onions in iced water for a couple of minutes. The stalks will curl up to make tassels.

◆ Trim and slice the radishes.

◆ Mix the spring onion (scallion) tassels, radishes, olives, green beans and chives, if liked, into the salad and serve at once.

Hot Potato Salad

GREEN BEAN AND MUSHROOM CURRY

S E R V E S 2 — 4 / S E T : H I G H

Ingredients

60 g/2 oz butter or ghee
1 large onion, chopped
2 cloves garlic, crushed
125 g/4 oz green beans, trimmed and cut into 2 cm/1 in lengths
125 g/4 oz mushrooms, sliced
3 tomatoes, peeled and chopped
1 tbsp lemon juice
2 slices fresh ginger
½ tsp turmeric
½ tsp ground coriander
½ tsp garam masala
fresh coriander or parsley

◆ Place the butter or ghee in a bowl and cook for 1 minute. Add the onion and garlic and cook for 3 minutes.

◆ Stir in the rest of the ingredients except the fresh coriander or parsley. Cover and cook for 8–10 minutes, stirring twice.

◆ Garnish with fresh coriander or parsley and serve with rice.

STUFFED PEPPERS WITH TOMATO SAUCE

SERVES 4
SET: HIGH AND MEDIUM

Ingredients

4 baby peppers, red, green or yellow

3 tbsp water

TOMATO SAUCE

1 tbsp oil

1 large onion, chopped

1 clove garlic, crushed

1 carrot, chopped

1 stick celery, chopped

440 g/14 oz canned tomatoes, with juice

1 tbsp tomato paste

a few sprigs of basil

salt and freshly ground black pepper

STUFFING

185 g/6 oz cooked rice

60 g/2 oz cooked bacon, chopped

60 g/2 oz salami, chopped

2 tbsp chopped parsley

1 tbsp tomato paste, diluted with
1 tbsp water

salt and freshly ground black pepper

Use baby peppers for this dish. They look much more tempting – and less daunting – than the large ones.

◆ Cut the tops off the peppers and reserve. Scoop out the pith and seeds. Put the peppers and their lids in a deep dish with the water, cover and cook on high for about 7 minutes, rearranging twice. Drain and keep warm.

◆ To make the sauce, put the oil in a pot and cook for 30 seconds. Add the onion, garlic, carrot, and celery and cook on high, covered with vented plastic wrap for 4 minutes.

◆ Stir in the tomatoes, tomato paste and basil. Cover and cook on high power for 8 minutes, stirring twice. Put the sauce in a blender or food processor and blend until smooth. Season to taste.

◆ For the stuffing, mix together the rice, bacon, salami and parsley. Stir in the tomato paste, diluted with water, and season to taste with salt and pepper.

◆ Stuff the peppers with this mixture and put on their lids. Stand the peppers upright in a deep dish, cover with vented plastic wrap or a lid and cook on medium power for 8–10 minutes, turning the dish 3 times, until the peppers are cooked through and the filling hot.

◆ Remove the lids and serve each pepper in a pool of the reheated sauce.

PARSNIPS AND MUSHROOMS IN A CHEESE SAUCE

SERVES 4 / SET: HIGH

Ingredients

500 g/1 lb parsnips
3 tbsp water
1 tbsp lemon juice
250 g/8 oz mushrooms, wiped and sliced
SAUCE
45 g/1 1/2 oz butter
45 g/1 1/2 oz flour
315 ml/1/2 pt milk
60 g/2 oz grated cheese
salt and freshly ground black pepper
nutmeg

◆ Peel the parsnips, trim them and cut into eighths. Cut away any very woody cores. Put them in a dish with the water and lemon juice. Cover with vented plastic wrap and cook for 7 minutes, stirring twice.

◆ Stir in the mushrooms. Cover again and cook for a further 3–4 minutes, until the vegetables are done. Keep hot.

◆ Make the sauce. Put the butter in a dish and cook for 30 seconds. Stir in the flour. Pour on the milk and cook for 3 minutes, whisking after each minute. Stir in the cheese. Cook for a further minute, then whisk again. Season to taste with salt, pepper and nutmeg.

◆ Drain the vegetables and pour the sauce over them. Reheat for a minute if necessary.

NEW POTATOES WITH PEAS AND BACON

SERVES 4 / SET: HIGH

Ingredients

500 g/1 lb new potatoes, washed and scrubbed

1 kg/2 lb fresh peas (500 g/1 lb peas shelled weight)

3 tbsp water

2 rashers bacon

150 ml/¼ pt cream

paprika

mint leaves or chopped chives (optional)

◆ Put the potatoes and peas in a dish with the water, cover and cook for about 8 minutes, shaking the dish twice. Test the potatoes before the cooking time is up. You should not overcook them, or they will go spongy.

◆ Put the bacon rashers on a browning dish, cover with a sheet of kitchen paper to stop them splattering and cook for 1½ minutes. Chop up the bacon and mix it with the vegetables.

◆ Heat the cream in a jug for 1–2 minutes, pour over the vegetables and sprinkle with paprika.

◆ Serve garnished with mint leaves, or chopped chives if available.

New Potatoes with Peas and Bacon

BLACK-EYED BEANS WITH MUSHROOMS AND CORIANDER

SERVES 4 / SET: HIGH

Ingredients
30 g/1 oz butter
1 large onion, chopped
2 cloves garlic, crushed
500 g/1 lb cooked black-eyed beans
440 g/14 oz canned tomatoes, drained and mashed
1 slice fresh ginger
salt and freshly ground black pepper
garam masala
fresh coriander

◆ Put the butter in a dish and cook for 45 seconds. Add the onion and garlic and cook, covered, for 3 minutes.
◆ Add the black-eyed beans, tomatoes and ginger and cook, covered, for 4–5 minutes until heated through, stirring once.
◆ Season to taste with salt, pepper and garam masala and stir in plenty of chopped coriander leaves. Eat hot with rice.
◆ This dish is also delicious cold.

BRUSSEL SPROUTS WITH WATER CHESTNUTS, GARLIC AND MUSHROOMS

SERVES 4 / SET: HIGH

Ingredients
15 g/¹/₂ oz butter or margarine
1 clove garlic, crushed
440 g/14 oz baby Brussel sprouts, trimmed
100 g/4 oz mushrooms, sliced
220 g/7 oz canned water chestnuts, drained
soy sauce

◆ Put the butter in a dish and cook for 30 seconds. Add the garlic and cook for 1 minute.
◆ Add the sprouts, mushrooms and water chestnuts, with 1 tbsp of the chestnut liquid. Cover and cook for 3–4 minutes, until hot through.
◆ Season with soy sauce and serve.

VARIATION This recipe can also be cooked as for Mixed Vegetable Sauté (see recipe).

Brussel Sprouts with Water Chestnuts, Garlic and Mushrooms

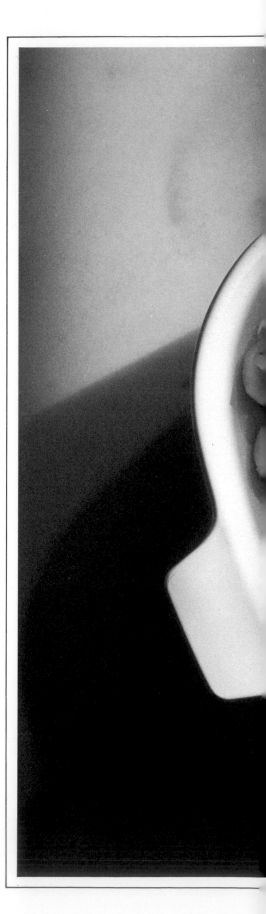

LASAGNE WITH RATATOUILLE

SERVES 4 / SET: HIGH

Ingredients

Ratatouille (see Ratatouille Alla Mozzarella)
6 sheets spinach lasagne
boiling water
salt
oil
250 g/8 oz ricotta
4 tbsp Parmesan cheese

◆ Make the Ratatouille according to the instructions (omitting the mozzarella) and keep warm.

◆ Put the lasagne in a deep dish and cover with boiling water. Add a pinch of salt and a few drops of oil, cover with vented plastic wrap and cook for 15 minutes. Leave to stand for 3 minutes, then drain and rinse thoroughly under cold running water. Lay the lasagne on a tea towel to dry. Do not use kitchen paper – it will stick.

◆ To assemble, put a layer of lasagne in the bottom of an oblong dish, cover with pasta, then spread with ricotta and sprinkle with Parmesan cheese. Continue until all the ingredients are used up, finishing with a sprinkling of Parmesan cheese.

◆ Heat through in the microwave or, if you want the top to brown, under the grill or in a conventional oven.

MIXED VEGETABLE SAUTE

SERVES 4 / SET: HIGH

Ingredients

30 g/1 oz butter or margarine
1 yellow pepper, seeded and chopped
125 g/4 oz broccoli florets
90 g/3 oz snow peas
90 g/3 oz mushrooms, sliced
60 g/2 oz spring onions (scallions)
soy sauce (optional)

The good thing about using the microwave to cook vegetables together is that they retain their individual flavours.

◆ Heat a browning dish to maximum, according to manufacturer's instructions. Add the butter or margarine and, using oven gloves, tilt the dish so that it is coated with the hot fat.

◆ Put the vegetables in the dish and cook for 2 minutes, stirring once.

◆ Serve with soy sauce and rice.

Mixed Vegetable Sauté

CHICORY IN HAM AND CHEESE SAUCE

SERVES 4 / SET: HIGH

Ingredients

4 heads chicory
3 tbsp water
45 g/1½ oz butter
45 g/1½ oz flour
315 ml/½ pt milk
60 g/2 oz Parmesan cheese
60 g/2 oz cooked ham, chopped
salt and freshly ground black pepper

◆ Trim the chicory and cut in half lengthways. Lay in a dish and add the water. Cover with vented plastic wrap and cook for 4–6 minutes, until tender, turning the dish twice.

◆ Make the sauce. Put the butter in a dish and cook for 1 minute. Stir in the flour. Pour on the milk and cook for 3 minutes, whisking after each minute. Stir in the cheese, cook for a further minute and whisk again. Stir in the ham and season to taste.

◆ Drain the chicory, pour over the sauce and heat through for 1 minute.

EGGPLANT LASAGNE

SERVES 4 / SET: HIGH

Ingredients

2 medium eggplants

2–3 tbsp water

6 sheets spinach lasagne

salt

oil

Tomato Sauce (see Stuffed Peppers with Tomato Sauce)

CHEESE SAUCE

45 g/1½ oz butter or margarine

45 g/1½ oz flour

315 ml/½ pt milk

60 g/2 oz Edam cheese, grated

salt and freshly ground black pepper

◆ Slice the eggplants. Arrange them in a deep oblong dish, in which you will cook the finished lasagne. Add the water, cover with vented plastic wrap and cook for 7 minutes, rearranging once, until tender. Drain and set aside.

◆ Put the lasagne in a large deep bowl and pour over enough boiling water to cover. Add salt and a few drops of oil to stop the pieces sticking together. Cover and cook for 12–15 minutes, until done.

◆ Drain the lasagne into a colander, rinse thoroughly under running cold water and drain again. If you omit this step you are liable to be left with a soggy mass of unmanageable pasta. Lay the sheets to dry on a tea towel. (Don't use kitchen paper – they will stick.)

◆ To make the cheese sauce, put the butter or margarine in a bowl and cook for 1 minute. Stir in the flour and pour on the milk. Cook for 3 minutes, whisking after each minute. Stir in the cheese. Cook for a further minute and whisk again. Season to taste with salt and pepper.

◆ To assemble the dish start with a layer of eggplant, then cover with tomato sauce, a layer of pasta and a layer of cheese sauce. Continue until all the ingredients are used up, finishing with a layer of cheese sauce.

◆ Heat through in the microwave, or in a conventional oven or under the grill if you want the top to brown.

◆ Serve hot.

VARIATION Omit the pasta for an Eggplant Layer Bake.

Eggplant Lasagne

LEEK PARCELS

SERVES 4 / SET: HIGH

Ingredients

45 g/1½ oz polyunsaturated vegetable margarine or butter

45 g/1½ oz flour

315 ml/½ pt milk

60 g/2 oz Edam cheese, grated

1–2 tsp mustard (optional)

salt and pepper

4 leeks

2 tbsp water

4 slices ham

◆ First make the sauce. Put the margarine or butter in a bowl and cook for 1 minute. Stir in the flour. Pour on the milk. Cook for 3 minutes, whisking after each minute. Stir in the cheese and mustard, if used. Cook for a further minute and whisk again. Season to taste with salt and pepper. Keep the sauce warm while you cook the leeks.

◆ Trim the leeks and wash thoroughly. Put them in a dish with the water, cover with vented plastic wrap and cook for about 8 minutes, rearranging once, until done.

◆ Drain the leeks and cut off a few rings for the garnish. Wrap each in a slice of ham, lay side by side in the dish and pour the sauce over. Cover and cook for 2–3 minutes until hot through.

◆ Garnish with leek rings and serve at once.

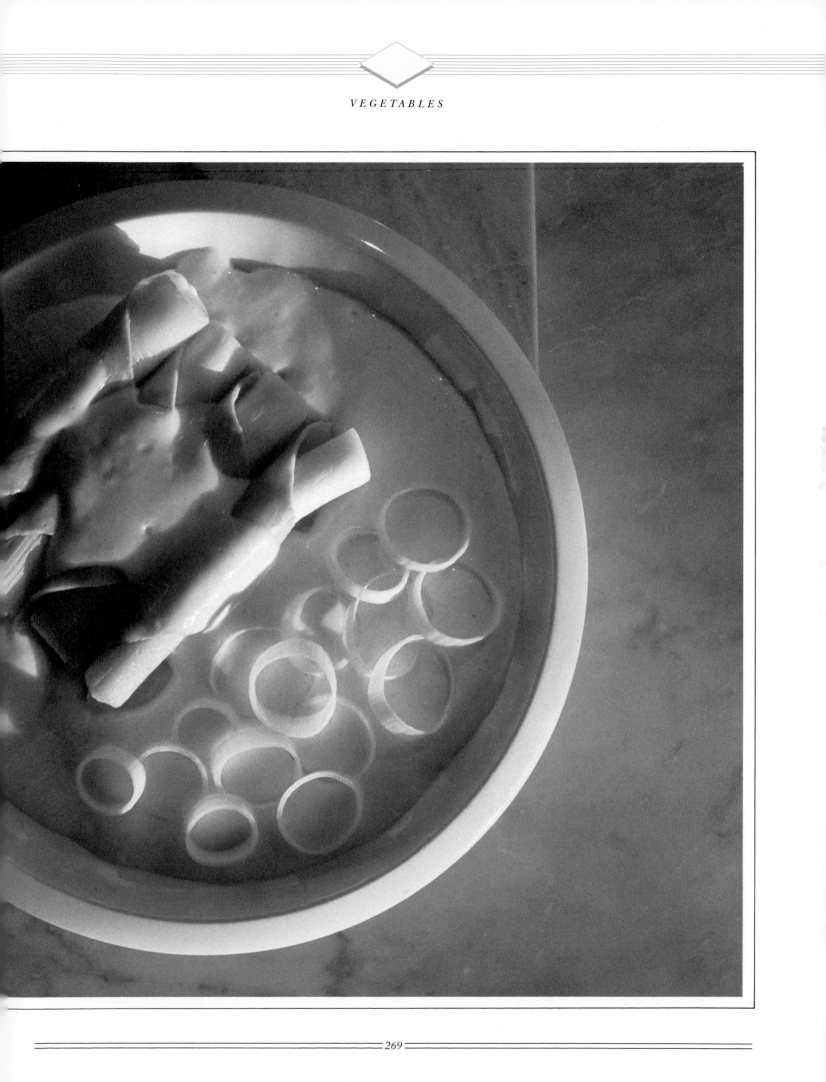

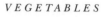

FRENCH BEAN SALAD

SERVES 4 / SET: HIGH

Ingredients

500 g/1 lb French beans, trimmed and left whole

4 tbsp water

500 g/1 lb tomatoes, peeled, seeded and cut into strips

1½ tbsp olive oil

1½ tbsp lemon juice

salt and freshly ground black pepper

2 hardboiled eggs

chives (optional)

◆ Put the beans in a dish, add the water, cover with vented plastic wrap and cook for 6 minutes, rearranging twice. The beans should be done but still crisp. Set aside, covered, while you make the dressing.

◆ Mix the oil, lemon juice and seasoning. (Shake them together in a screw-topped jar if you have one handy.)

◆ Drain the beans, mix them with the tomatoes and toss in the dressing.

◆ Separate the whites from the yolks of the eggs. Chop both. Garnish the salad with the egg.

VARIATION If you are feeling artistic, tie the beans into bundles with the chives instead of mixing them together with the tomatoes.

BROCCOLI WITH ALMONDS AND BLUE CHEESE SAUCE

SERVES 4 / SET: HIGH

Ingredients
500 g/1 lb broccoli
3 tbsp water
150 ml/¼ pt cream
45 g/1½ oz Danish blue cheese
salt and white pepper
45 g/1½ oz flaked toasted almonds
diamonds of red pepper

◆ Wash the broccoli and remove the outer leaves and tough stalks. Make slits up the stalks to speed up cooking.
◆ Put the broccoli in a dish with the water. Cover with vented plastic wrap and cook for 10 minutes, rearranging once, until tender. Drain and keep hot.
◆ Mash the cream into the cheese until smooth. Cook for 1–2 minutes. Season with salt and pepper and pour over the broccoli.
◆ Serve garnished with flaked almonds, or with the broccoli florets in a pool of sauce, as shown, and decorate with diamonds of red pepper.

Broccoli with Almonds and Blue Cheese Sauce

ARTICHOKE HEARTS WITH SPINACH

SERVES 4 / SET: HIGH

Ingredients

1 kg/2 lb fresh spinach

30 g/1 oz butter

1 large onion, chopped

8 artichoke hearts, fresh or canned

90 g/3 oz Parma ham, cut into strips

SAUCE

45 g/1½ oz butter

45 g/1½ oz flour

315 ml/½ pt milk

60 g/2 oz grated Parmesan cheese

nutmeg

salt and freshly ground black pepper

◆ Wash the spinach and discard tough stalks and discoloured leaves. Put it in a boiling or roasting bag and tie loosely. Cook for about 6 minutes, shaking the bag once, until the spinach has collapsed. Let it stand for a while, then chop coarsely.

◆ Put the butter in a dish and cook for 30 seconds. Add the onion and the artichoke hearts and cook for 3 minutes. (If using canned artichoke hearts, however, arrange them on top of the onion when cooked.)

◆ Lay strips of Parma ham in between the artichokes and put the chopped spinach in a layer on top of that.

◆ To make the sauce, put the butter in a bowl and cook for 30 seconds to 1 minute to melt it. Stir in the flour. Pour on the milk and cook for 3 minutes, whisking after each minute. Add the cheese. Cook for a further minute and whisk again. Season to taste with nutmeg, salt and pepper.

◆ Pour the sauce over the vegetables and heat through in the microwave, or brown in a conventional oven or under the grill.

EGGPLANT WITH TWO SAUCES

SERVES 4 / SET: HIGH

Ingredients

2 medium eggplants, sliced

4 tbsp water

flour

beaten egg

fresh breadcrumbs

a little butter

Tomato Sauce (see Stuffed Peppers with Tomato Sauce)

Cheese Sauce (see Eggplant Lasagne)

◆ Put the eggplants in a dish, add the water, cover with vented plastic wrap and cook for 7 minutes, rearranging once, until tender.

◆ Dust the drained eggplant slices with flour, then dip in the beaten egg and breadcrumbs. Push the breadcrumbs on well with your fingers.

◆ Heat a browning dish to maximum, according to the manufacturer's instructions. Add a little butter and, holding the dish with oven gloves, tilt it to cover with the hot fat.

◆ Fry the eggplant slices in batches for 30 seconds on each side, until golden. Keep warm.

◆ Serve with the Tomato Sauce and Cheese Sauce.

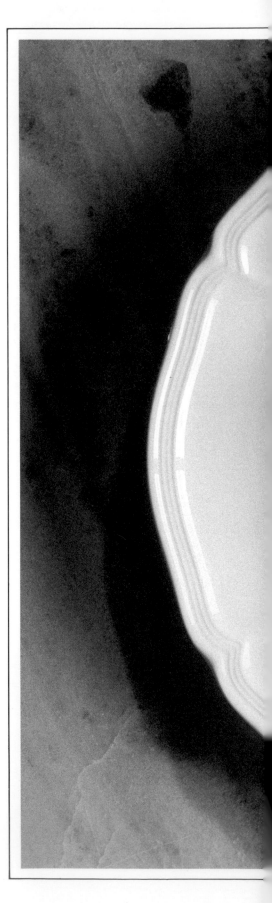

Eggplant with Two Sauces

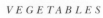
CAULIFLOWER IN ORANGE SAUCE

SERVES 4 / SET: HIGH

Ingredients

1 cauliflower
3 tbsp water
30 g/1 oz butter
30 g/1 oz cornflour
315 ml/½ pt unsweetened orange juice
finely grated rind of ½ orange
orange bows

This makes a welcome change from cauliflower cheese.

◆ Trim the cauliflower and break into florets. Put them in a dish, add the water, cover with vented plastic wrap and cook for 8–10 minutes, depending on size, until tender but not soft. Drain and keep warm.

◆ Put the butter in a jug and cook for 30 seconds. Stir in the cornflour and cook for 1 minute. Stir in the orange juice and cook for 3 minutes, whisking after each minute. Stir in the orange rind.

◆ Serve the cauliflower on pools of sauce, garnished with the orange bows.

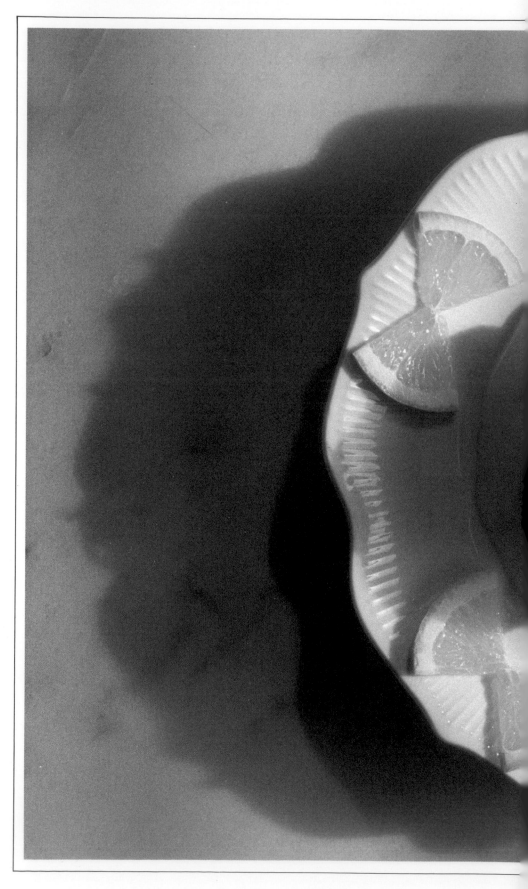

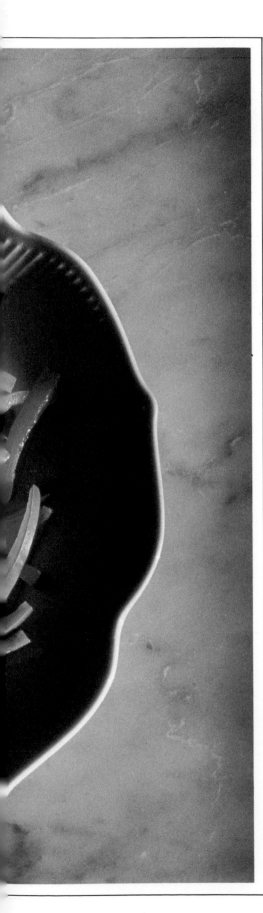

PEPPERS AND FRIED EGGS

SERVES 4 / SET: HIGH

Ingredients

1 red pepper, cut into julienne strips
1 green pepper, cut into julienne strips
1 yellow pepper, cut into julienne strips
2 large tomatoes, peeled, seeded and cut into strips
1 bunch spring onions (scallions), trimmed
3 tbsp water
a knob of butter
4 eggs
salt and pepper

◆ Put the vegetables into a dish with the water, cover with vented plastic wrap and cook for 4–5 minutes, stirring once, until tender but not soft. Keep warm.

◆ Heat a browning dish for 3–4 minutes. Add the butter and, using oven gloves, tilt the dish to coat with the hot fat. Break an egg into each corner of the dish and pierce the yolks with a toothpick. Cook until nearly set (about 2½ minutes, but this will depend on the size of the eggs). Allow to stand for 30 seconds.

◆ Divide the vegetables between 4 heated plates and lay an egg on each.

◆ Offer salt and pepper at the table.

VARIATION You can add garlic to the ingredients if you like and, for a touch of style, make the spring onions (scallions) into tassels.

Peppers and Fried Eggs

PERFECT ASPARAGUS

SERVES 4 / SET: HIGH

Ingredients

375 g/12 oz asparagus spears
3 tbsp water
45 g/1½ oz butter
2 tbsp Parmesan cheese

If you have too little asparagus to go round, serve it with fried eggs, or scrambled eggs and triangles of toast.

◆ Trim the woody ends from the asparagus spears so that they are all the same length. Lay them in a dish arranged top to tail and pour on the water. Cover with vented plastic wrap and cook for 5–7 minutes, depending on the size of the spears.

◆ Drain the asparagus and keep warm.

◆ Put the butter and Parmesan in a jug and cook for 1 minute

◆ Serve the sauce separately.

RED CABBAGE AND APPLE

SERVES 4 / SET: HIGH

Ingredients

500 g/1 lb red cabbage, finely shredded

250 g/8 oz cooking apples, peeled, cored and sliced

3 tbsp red wine vinegar

1 ½ tbsp brown sugar

a pinch of mixed spice

salt and freshly ground black pepper

Cooked conventionally, red cabbage turns blue. Microwave it if you want it to keep its crunch and stay red. This combination is very good with pork chops and baked potatoes.

◆ Mix all the ingredients together in a large dish.

◆ Cover and cook for 15 minutes, stirring twice, until tender but still crunchy.

ITALIAN STYLE ZUCCHINI

SERVES 4 / SET: HIGH

Ingredients

440 g/14 oz zucchini, sliced
1 small onion, chopped
1 clove garlic, crushed
3 tbsp water
440 g/14 oz canned tomatoes, drained and sieved or blended
salt and freshly ground black pepper
3 tbsp grated Parmesan cheese

◆ Put the zucchini in a dish with the onion and garlic. Add the water. Cover with vented plastic wrap and cook for about 7 minutes, until nearly done.

◆ Stir in the sieved tomato and season with salt and pepper. Cover and cook for 2–3 minutes, until hot through.

◆ Sprinkle with grated Parmesan cheese and serve.

VARIATION You can layer the zucchini with sliced mozzarella cheese and tomato sauce instead of serving them with Parmesan.

BAKED POTATOES WITH . . .

SET: HIGH

◆ Wash the potatoes, 1 per person, and prick with a fork to stop the skins bursting. Put them in the oven on a sheet of absorbent kitchen paper. Arrange in a circle if you are cooking several.

◆ Cook for 4 minutes (1 potato weighing about 185 g/6 oz); 6–8 minutes (2 potatoes); or 12–14 minutes (4 potatoes). Turn them over half-way through cooking time.

SUGGESTED FILLINGS

Chilli Beans (see recipe)
Blue cheese mashed with cream
Cottage cheese and chives
Grated Cheddar and crispy bacon pieces
Butter melted with garlic and herbs
Broad beans and corn.

Baked Potatoes with a selection of fillings

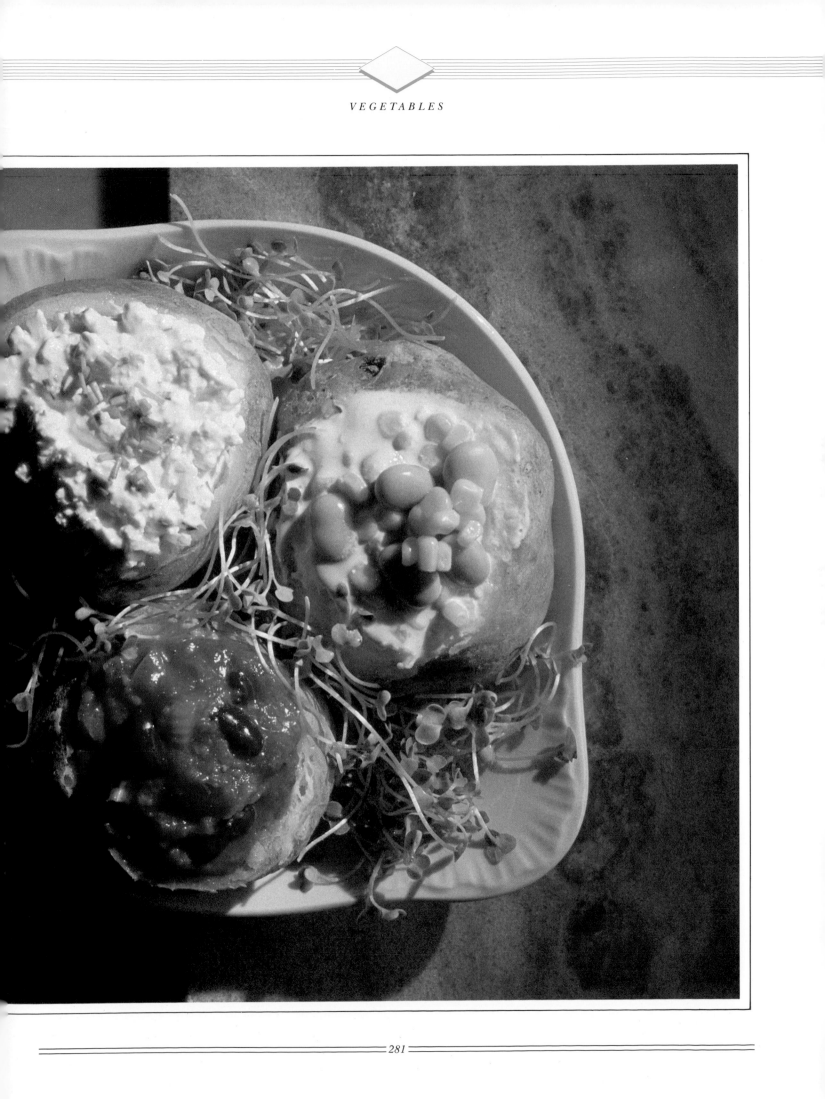

CHILLI BEANS

SERVES 4 / SET: HIGH

Ingredients

1 large onion, chopped
1–2 cloves garlic, crushed
1 tbsp sunflower oil
1 fresh green chilli, chopped and seeded
chilli powder to taste
¹/₂ red pepper, seeded and chopped
¹/₂ green pepper, seeded and chopped
440 g/14 oz canned tomatoes, drained and mashed, juice reserved
880 g/28 oz canned kidney beans, drained
salt
red and green pepper cut into julienne strips
sliced green chillies, (optional)
triangles of toast

Use as much or as little chilli powder as you like.

◆ Put the onion and garlic in a casserole with the oil, cover and cook for 3 minutes. Stir in the chilli, chilli powder, chopped red and green peppers and 4 tbsp reserved tomato juice. Cover and cook for 5 minutes.

◆ Stir in the tomatoes and kidney beans, cover and cook for 5 minutes, or until the mixture is heated through, stirring once. Season with salt to taste.

◆ Garnish with julienne strips of red and green pepper and sliced chillies if liked (remember to warn your guests!).

◆ Serve with triangles of toast. This is also good with rice or baked potatoes.

GLAZED ONIONS

SERVES 4 / SET: HIGH

Ingredients

8 small onions, peeled but left whole
2 tbsp honey
30 g/1 oz butter
2 tbsp hot water

◆ Put the onions in a dish. ·

◆ Cream the honey and butter with the water and pour over the onions. Cover with vented plastic wrap and cook for 8–10 minutes, until the onions are tender, shaking or stirring the dish once.

◆ Serve hot. This is particularly good with pork chops and mashed potatoes.

CRUDITES WITH HOT ANCHOVY DIP

SET: HIGH

Ingredients

A selection of crisp raw vegetables, cut into manageable pieces, such as: carrots, celery, green, red and yellow peppers, cucumber, cauliflower and broccoli florets, radishes, mushrooms.

DIP

125 g/4 oz butter, diced

2 cloves garlic, crushed

8 anchovy fillets, pounded

315 ml/½ pt heavy cream

◆ To make the dip, put the butter in a pot and cook for 1 minute until melted. Add the garlic and cook for 30 seconds.

◆ Put the anchovy fillets with the cream in a blender or food processor and blend until smooth.

◆ Pour the anchovy cream onto the garlic butter, stir well and cook for 1–2 minutes, until hot.

◆ Put the pot with the anchovy dip on a large platter and arrange the crudités around it.

Crudités with Hot Anchovy Dip

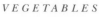

COUSCOUS WITH VEGETABLES

SERVES 4 / SET: HIGH

Ingredients

½ cauliflower, cut into florets
250 g/8 oz carrots, diced
1 large parsnip, diced
3 tbsp water
440 g/14 oz canned chick peas, drained
220 g/7 oz canned peas, drained
Tomato Sauce (see Stuffed Peppers with Tomato Sauce) made with chilli powder to taste instead of basil
375 g/12 oz couscous
465 ml/¾ pt boiling water
salt
30 g/1 oz butter

◆ First prepare the vegetable topping. Put the cauliflower, carrots and parsnip into a dish with the water, cover with vented plastic wrap and cook for 5 minutes, stirring once.

◆ Stir in the chick peas and peas and cook for a further 4 minutes, stirring once. Drain and keep hot.

◆ For the couscous, put the grain in a deep dish, cover with the boiling water, add a pinch of salt and cook for 4 minutes. Stir in the butter.

◆ Reheat the tomato sauce for 3 minutes in a sauce boat.

◆ Serve the couscous topped with the spicy vegetable mixture and allow guests to serve themselves with the sauce.

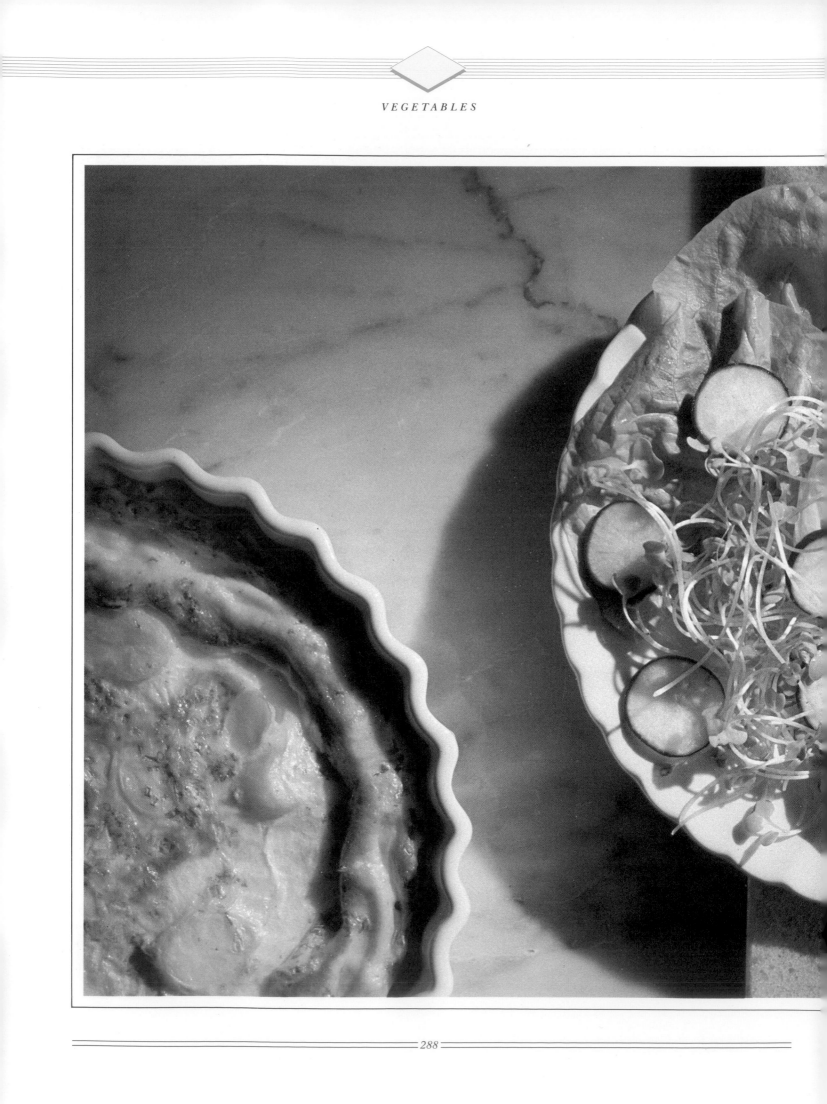

POTATO OMELETTE

SERVES 2
SET: HIGH AND LOW

Ingredients

125 g/4 oz cooked potato, sliced
a little butter
4 eggs
salt and freshly ground black pepper
freshly chopped herbs or chives (optional)

This is a good way of using leftover potatoes. Add other vegetables, if you like.

◆ Put the potato in 1 or 2 layers in a buttered dish. Use a shallow dish. Cover and cook on high for 45 seconds.

◆ Beat together the eggs, seasoning and chives or herbs if used and pour them over the vegetables. Cook on low power for 8 minutes, or until almost set.

◆ Leave to stand for 1–2 minutes before serving, then cut in two.

◆ Left until cold, then cut into wedges, this makes a good picnic dish, especially if served with salad.

NOTE Quite often quiches and omelettes won't cook in the 'cold spot' in the middle of the microwave. To correct this place under a hot grill for 2–3 minutes.

LASAGNE AND LEEK ROLLS

SERVES 4 / SET: HIGH

Ingredients

4 young leeks
boiling water
2 tbsp water
4 sheets spinach lasagne
salt
oil
boiling water
125 g/4 oz ricotta cheese

Use only very young leeks to make this elegant-looking dish.

◆ Trim the leeks and blanch the discarded tops by pouring boiling water over them and leave to stand for 2 minutes. Put to one side. Put the leeks in a dish with 2 tbsp water, cover with vented plastic wrap and cook for 4 minutes, until tender. Drain and allow to cool.

◆ Put the pasta in a deep dish with a pinch of salt and a few drops of oil. Cover with boiling water. Cook for 10 minutes. Let the pasta stand for 2 minutes, then drain and rinse thoroughly under cold running water. Lay the pasta on a tea towel to dry. (Do not use kitchen paper – it will stick.)

◆ When the pasta has cooled, spread each sheet with 30 g/1 oz ricotta cheese. Lay a leek at the end of each sheet and roll up tightly.

◆ Trim away any excess leek, and cut the rolls into slices.

◆ Trim the blanched leek tops and arrange on individual plates as shown. Place the slices in the middle and serve cold.

Lasagne and Leek Rolls

ARTICHOKE RISOTTO

SERVES 4 / SET: HIGH

Ingredients

45 g/1½ oz butter
1 onion, chopped
375 g/12 oz long-grain rice
775 ml/1¼ pt boiling water
1 chicken stock cube
4 very small globe artichokes
salt and freshly ground black pepper
2 tbsp Parmesan cheese

To make this risotto you will need very young, very tender artichokes. If these are not available, use canned artichoke hearts.

◆ Put half the butter in a deep bowl and cook for 30 seconds. Add the onion, cover and cook for 1 minute.

◆ Stir in the rice. Pour over the boiling water and crumble on the stock cube. Cover and cook for 8 minutes.

◆ Meanwhile, prepare the artichokes. Trim off the stalks and remove any tough outer leaves. Slice the artichokes vertically. Stir them into the rice and cook for a further 4 minutes. Let the pot stand, covered, for 7 minutes.

◆ Stir in the remaining butter, season with salt and pepper and stir in the Parmesan cheese.

◆ Serve at once.

TURNIP AND POTATO BAKE

SERVES 4 / SET: HIGH

Ingredients

500 g/1 lb turnips, peeled and thinly sliced
500 g/1 lb potatoes, peeled and thinly sliced
butter
salt and freshly ground black pepper
4 tbsp light cream
chopped chives

◆ Layer the turnips and potatoes in a round dish, dotting each layer with butter and seasoning with salt and pepper. Cover with waxed paper and press well down.

◆ Stand the dish on an inverted plate. Cover and cook for 9 minutes, turning once.

◆ Slowly pour over cream so that it seeps between the layers. Brown slightly under the grill, garnish with chives and serve.

OKRA WITH TOMATOES

SERVES 4 / SET: HIGH

Ingredients

500 g/1 lb okra

vinegar

30 g/1 oz butter

1 tbsp olive oil

1 tbsp lemon juice

1 onion, chopped

1 clove garlic, chopped

500 g/1 lb fresh tomatoes, skinned, seeded and cut into strips

salt and freshly ground black pepper

plenty of chopped flat-leaved parsley or fresh coriander

lemon wedges

Canned okra are a perfectly acceptable alternative to the fresh variety, should these be unavailable. Serve this dish with rice.

◆ Cut off the okra stalks without damaging the seed cavity inside. Soak them for 30 minutes in cold water acidulated with a little vinegar. This is to combat the stickiness of the vegetable. Rinse in fresh water and pat dry.

◆ Put the butter, olive oil and lemon juice in a dish, add the onion and garlic and cook, covered, for 3 minutes. Add the okra and tomatoes, cover and cook for 4–5 minutes, until tender.

◆ Season to taste with salt and freshly ground black pepper and sprinkle with parsley or coriander.

◆ Serve with lemon wedges.

Okra with Tomatoes

ROMAN SPINACH

Ingredients

1 kg/2 lb fresh spinach
½ tbsp oil
½ tbsp butter
60 g/2 oz pine nuts
60 g/2 oz sultanas
2 rashers bacon, derinded and diced
1 clove garlic, crushed
salt and freshly ground black pepper

◆ Wash the spinach and discard tough stalks and discoloured leaves. Put it in a roasting or boiling bag and tie loosely. Cook for about 6 minutes, shaking the bag once, until the spinach has collapsed.

◆ Put the oil and butter in a dish (use more if you want a richer taste), and add the pine nuts, sultanas, diced bacon and garlic. Cook for 1 minute.

◆ Meanwhile, shred the spinach, add it to the dish and toss well. Season with salt and pepper to taste.

◆ Cook for a further minute, covered with vented plastic wrap, to heat through.

DAL

Ingredients

250 g/8 oz red lentils
465 ml/¾ pt boiling water (approx)
2 slices fresh ginger
a pinch of turmeric
a pinch of salt
1–2 tbsp sunflower oil
1 tsp mustard seeds
1 clove garlic, crushed
1 green chilli, chopped
a pinch of garam masala
pita bread

◆ Put the lentils in a dish and pour on the boiling water. Add the ginger, turmeric and salt, cover and cook for 12–15 minutes, stirring twice, and adding more boiling water if it becomes dry. (Cooking time and the amount of water needed depend on age of lentils.)

◆ Leave the dish to stand, covered, while you prepare the dressing.

◆ Put the oil in a jug and cook for 1 minute. Add the mustard seeds, garlic and chilli, cover with vented plastic wrap (the seeds might shoot out, as they start to pop when very hot), and cook for 2 minutes. Stir into the dal. Stir in the garam masala and serve hot with pita bread.

◆ If you have any left over, add a little water to thin it down before reheating.

Dal

BEETROOT WITH CREAM AND MUSHROOMS

SERVES 4 / SET: HIGH

Ingredients

30 g/1 oz butter
1 clove garlic, crushed
250 g/8 oz mushrooms, sliced (or whole button mushrooms)
500 g/1 lb beetroot, cooked and chopped
150 ml/¼ pt cream
2 tbsp grated Parmesan cheese
2 tbsp breadcrumbs

◆ Put the butter in a dish and cook for 1 minute to melt it. Add the garlic and mushrooms, cover with vented plastic wrap and cook for 3–4 minutes, stirring once.

◆ Mix in the beetroot.

◆ Stir the cream and cheese together and pour over the vegetables.

◆ Sprinkle on the breadcrumbs and cover and cook for 4–5 minutes, until hot through.

MARINATED MUSHROOMS

SERVES 4 / SET: HIGH

Ingredients

500 g/1 lb button mushrooms, wiped

3 tbsp olive oil

3 tbsp lemon juice

1 tbsp coriander seeds

salt and freshly ground black pepper

parsley or coriander leaves

chopped chives (optional)

toast

◆ Put the mushrooms in a dish with the oil, lemon juice and coriander seeds. Let them marinate for an hour or two or in the fridge overnight.

◆ Remove the mushrooms from the marinade with a slotted spoon and place in a shallow dish. Brush with the marinade and cook for 3 minutes, stirring every minute.

◆ Season to taste, sprinkle with parsley or coriander, and chives, if liked, and serve with triangles of toast.

Marinated Mushrooms

RUSSIAN BEETROOT

SERVES 4 / SET: HIGH

Ingredients
90 g/3 oz butter
5 medium uncooked beetroots, diced
2 tbsp red wine vinegar
1/2 tsp dried dill
1/2 tsp dried fennel
salt and freshly ground black pepper
30 g/1 oz cornflour
2 tbsp milk
fresh dill or fennel
sour cream

◆ Place butter in a bowl and cook for 1 minute. Stir in beetroot, vinegar, herbs and seasoning. Cover and cook for 8 minutes or until beetroots are tender.

◆ Place cornflour and milk in a small bowl and mix until smooth. Stir mixture into beetroot and cook, covered, for about 4 minutes until thickened.

◆ Allow to stand, covered, for 2 minutes. Garnish with fresh dill or fennel and serve hot or cold, with sour cream, to accompany cold meats.

CABBAGE WITH BACON AND POTATOES

SERVES 4 / SET: HIGH

Ingredients
1 curly cabbage, shredded
2 rashers bacon, chopped
90 g/3 oz spicy sausage, diced
250 g/8 oz baby onions, peeled but left whole
150 ml/1/4 pt chicken stock
500 g/1 lb potatoes, cooked and mashed
2 egg yolks
butter
milk
salt and freshly ground black pepper

◆ Put the cabbage, bacon, sausage and onions in a dish and pour over the stock. Cover with vented plastic wrap and cook for about 8 minutes, stirring once, until done.

◆ Purée the potatoes with the egg yolks in a blender or food processor, adding enough butter and milk to make them smooth and creamy. Season to taste with salt and pepper.

◆ Put the potato purée on top of the cabbage, cover and cook for 3 minutes, or until hot through. If preferred, brown in a conventional oven or under the grill.

Cabbage with Bacon and Potatoes

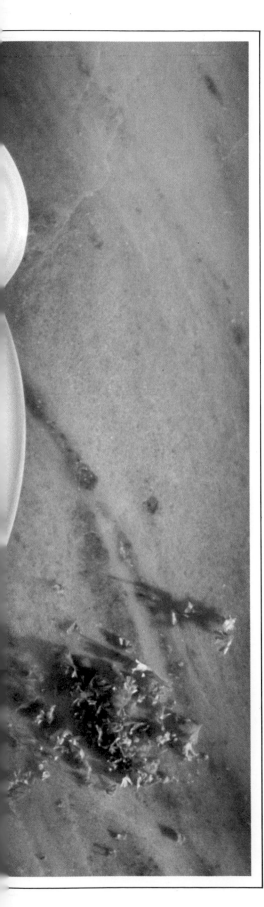

Rice with Peppers and Cheese

RICE WITH PEPPERS AND CHEESE

SERVES 4 / SET: HIGH

Ingredients

375 g/12 oz rice
775 ml/1¼ pt boiling water
1 beef stock cube
1 small red pepper, seeded and chopped
1 small yellow pepper, seeded and chopped
1 small green pepper, seeded and chopped
125 g/4 oz Edam cheese, grated
salt and freshly ground black pepper
1 bunch parsley, chopped

◆ Put the rice in a deep dish, pour over the boiling water and crumble on the stock cube. Cover and cook for 8 minutes.
◆ Stir in the green, yellow and red peppers. Cover and cook for 4 minutes.
◆ Stir in the cheese. Check the seasoning and add salt and pepper if necessary (depending on the saltiness of the stock cube). Cover and leave to stand for 5 minutes.
◆ If the cheese has not melted heat through again for 2 minutes.
◆ Stir in the parsley and serve.

ARTICHOKES WITH HOLLANDAISE SAUCE

SERVES 2 / SET: HIGH AND MEDIUM OR DEFROST

Ingredients

2 globe artichokes
2 tbsp lemon juice
6 tbsp water
HOLLANDAISE SAUCE
60 g/2 oz butter, diced
1 tbsp lemon juice
2 small egg yolks
salt and white pepper

◆ Soak the artichokes for an hour or so in a bowl of water, acidulated with half of the lemon juice, to loosen any soil or grit that may be stuck between the leaves. Rinse thoroughly in clean water and set upside down to drain. Trim off the stalk close to the vegetable so that it stands upright. Remove any damaged outer leaves and rub the cut surfaces with lemon juice. Do not bother to cut the points off the leaves – this is unnecessary and ruins the look of the vegetable.
◆ Put the artichokes upright in a dish, add the water and the remaining lemon juice, cover and cook for 7–8 minutes on high. Tug at one of the lower leaves to see if done. If it promises to come away in your fingers, the artichokes are ready. Leave them to stand for 3 minutes while you make the sauce.
◆ Put the butter in a bowl and cook on medium or defrost for 2 minutes until melted. Add the lemon juice and egg yolks and whisk lightly.
◆ Cook on medium or defrost for 1 minute, whisk again and season.
◆ Drain and serve with the sauce.
◆ To eat the artichoke, pull away the leaves and suck off the tender fleshy part, dipped in the sauce. When you come to the "choke", cut it away and discard it. Eat the heart with a knife and fork – and more sauce.

RATATOUILLE ALLA MOZZARELLA

SERVES 4 / SET: HIGH

Ingredients
1 large eggplant, sliced
3 zucchini, sliced
3 tbsp olive oil
1 large onion, sliced
2 cloves garlic, chopped
1 small red pepper, seeded and chopped
1 small green pepper, seeded and chopped
125 g/4 oz mushrooms, sliced
440 g/14 oz canned tomatoes, mashed
1 tbsp tomato paste
2 tsp fresh mixed herbs, chopped
1 bay leaf
salt and freshly ground black pepper
125 g/4 oz mozzarella cheese, cubed

◆ Place eggplant and zucchini on a plate, sprinkle with salt and allow to stand for 30 minutes. Rinse in cold water and pat dry. Cut the eggplant into bite-sized pieces.

◆ Pour the oil into a casserole and cook for 1 minute. Add onion and garlic and cook for 1 minute. Stir in peppers, eggplant and zucchini and cook for 5 minutes, stirring once.

◆ Stir in remaining ingredients, cover and cook for 15 minutes, stirring twice. Stir in mozzarella. Cover and cook for 5 minutes until cheese has melted or brown under the grill if preferred. Serve with crusty French bread to mop up the juices.

BABY ONIONS ESCOFFIER

SERVES 4 / SET: HIGH

Ingredients

500 g/1 lb baby onions
1 tbsp oil
1 bay leaf
a sprig of thyme
1 tsp fennel seeds
60 g/2 oz sultanas, soaked
3 tbsp dry white wine
1 tbsp brandy

◆ Peel the onions, but leave them whole. Put them in a dish with the remaining ingredients, cover with vented plastic wrap and cook for about 10 minutes, shaking the dish twice.

◆ Serve with lamb, beef or game.

FENNEL WITH PARMESAN

SERVES 4 / SET: HIGH

Ingredients

2 bulbs fennel
60 g/2 oz butter
1 tbsp lemon juice
salt and freshly ground black pepper
2 tbsp Parmesan cheese
2 tbsp chopped fresh herbs (optional)

◆ Remove the tough outer leaves of the fennel. Trim and slice the bulbs, reserving the feathery fronds.

◆ Put the butter in a dish and cook for 1 minute. Add the fennel and turn in the butter to coat. Cover with vented plastic wrap and cook for about 10 minutes, stirring the dish a couple of times, until the fennel is tender.

◆ Sprinkle on the lemon juice, season with salt and pepper and spoon over the Parmesan cheese.

◆ Garnish with the chopped fennel fronds or fresh herbs.

Fennel with Parmesan

BROAD BEANS WITH CORN IN A SPICY CREAM SAUCE

SERVES 4 / SET: HIGH

Ingredients

30 g/1 oz butter

440 g/14 oz broad beans, shelled

440 g/14 oz corn kernels

2 tbsp water

150 ml/¼ pt cream

a pinch of ginger

a pinch of cayenne pepper

◆ Put the butter in a dish and cook for 1 minute. Add the broad beans and corn with the water, stir, cover with vented plastic wrap and cook for 3–4 minutes, until nearly done, stirring once.

◆ Mix in the cream, with ginger and cayenne pepper to taste. Cover and cook for 1 minute.

◆ Serve hot.

NOTE If you want to make an attractive starter of this dish, arrange on individual dishes as shown and pour on the butter. Cover with plastic wrap and cook for 1½ minutes. Serve the sauce separately.

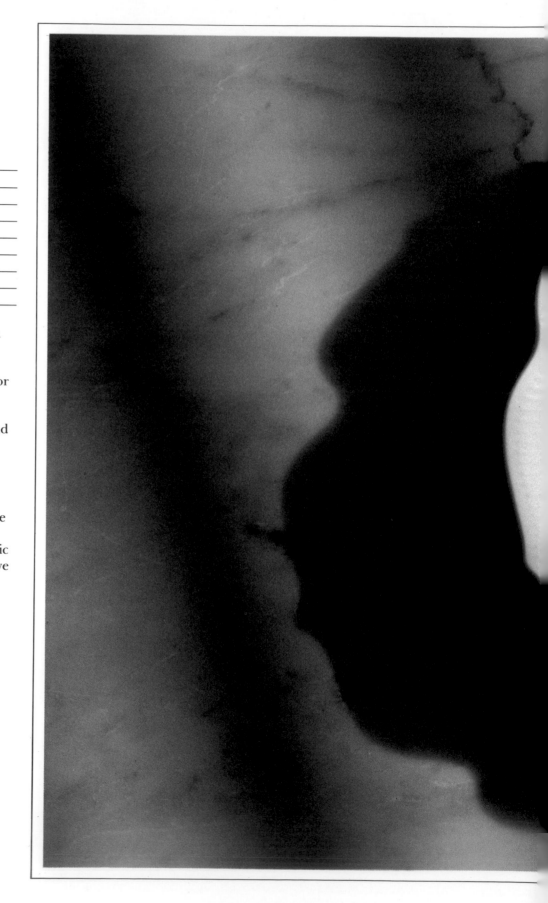

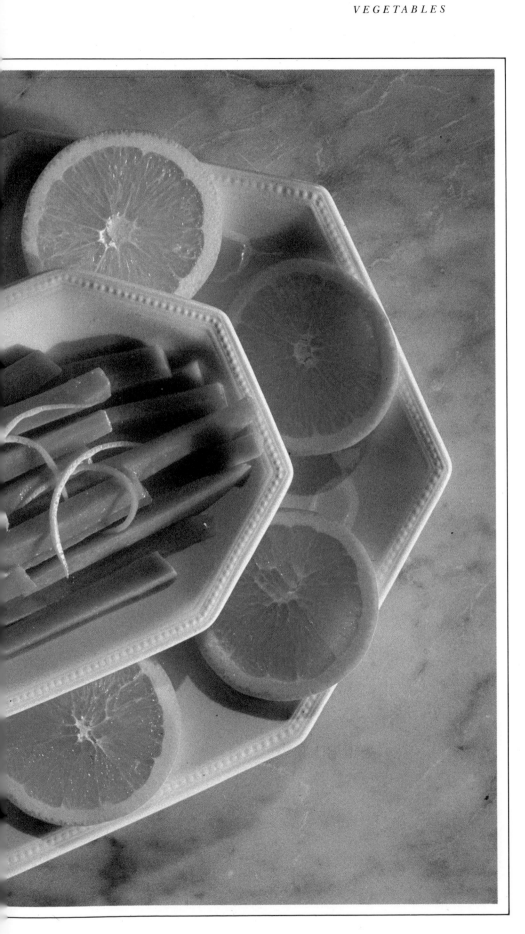

BUTTERED CARROTS WITH ORANGE

SERVES 4 / SET: HIGH

Ingredients

440 g/14 oz baby carrots, scrubbed, with a little bit of leaf, if possible

45 g/1½ oz butter

2 tbsp orange juice

salt and white pepper

orange peel, cut into julienne strips and blanched in water for 1 minute

orange slices

Tiny carrots look and taste much nicer than their large relations, but if you can only get the bigger ones, trim them, peel them and cut into slices. If you manage to find small ones, wash them well, but leave on a few fronds, as they look very pretty.

◆ Put the carrots in a dish with the butter and orange juice, cover and cook for about 10 minutes, until tender. Stir or shake a couple of times during cooking.

◆ Season the carrots lightly with salt and white pepper to taste.

◆ Serve decorated with the orange peel and slices.

CELERY IN STILTON SAUCE

SERVES 4 / SET: HIGH

Ingredients

1 head celery, trimmed and cut into pieces about 5 cm/2 in long (reserve the leaves)
4 tbsp water
125 g/4 oz ripe Stilton
150 ml/¼ pt heavy cream
salt and white pepper
hot toast

◆ Put the celery in a dish and add the water. Cover with vented plastic wrap and cook for about 10 minutes, until tender. Drain and keep hot.

◆ Crumble the Stilton into the cream. Mash with a fork or blend until smooth in a food processor or blender. Season with salt and white pepper. Pour over the celery. Reheat for 1–2 minutes, covered.

◆ Garnish with the celery leaves and serve with hot toast.

Celery in Stilton Sauce

CURRIED RICE

SERVES 4 / SET: HIGH

Ingredients

30 g/1 oz butter

1 onion, chopped

250 g/8 oz long-grain rice

625 ml/1 pt boiling water

a pinch of salt

1 tsp turmeric

2 slices pineapple, chopped

60 g/2 oz sultanas

60 g/2 oz dry-roasted peanuts

a pinch of garam masala

2 tbsp desiccated coconut

◆ Put the butter in a dish and cook for 30 seconds. Add the onion, cover and cook for 3 minutes.

◆ Stir in the rice, pour over the boiling water and add the salt and turmeric. Cover and cook for 10 minutes.

◆ Stir in the pineapple, sultanas and peanuts. Stir in the garam masala and leave, covered, for 5 minutes.

◆ Stir in the desiccated coconut and serve.

COOKING WIT

Desserts

VERONICA BULL

DESSERTS

WHETHER cooking for one or planning a special dinner party, a delicious dessert completes the meal perfectly. There are limitless desserts based upon the enormous variety of fruit grown throughout the world. Fruit cooked in the microwave oven retains its shape, colour and natural fresh flavour. Fruit can be poached or made into delicious sauces, jellies and jams to accompany a dessert.

The microwave oven can also help in many ways in the preparation of a dessert, offering you a quick, foolproof method of dissolving gelatine, melting chocolate, making caramel, sauces and small amounts of jam. Indeed, it is unlikely that you will ever return to conventional methods once you have used your microwave in this way.

The microwave oven offers the best method of reheating, which is a big advantage for the busy housewife. Many desserts can be prepared ahead of time and reheated without losing their fresh flavour and appearance.

A mouthwatering selection of cakes, flans, pastry, cheesecakes and confectionery are featured in the following recipes to serve for all occasions.

CONTENTS

FRUIT FONDUE

SERVES 4 / SET: MEDIUM

Ingredients

500 g/1 lb fresh raspberries or other berries

315 ml/10 fl oz heavy cream, whipped

2 tbsp sugar

4 tbsp brandy

selection of fresh fruit

◆ Mash the raspberries in a glass bowl. Stir in the sugar and fold in the cream.

◆ Place in the oven and cook for 3–4 minutes until warm. Do not let the mixture boil.

◆ Stir in the brandy, fill 4 individual dishes with the sauce and serve with the fruit.

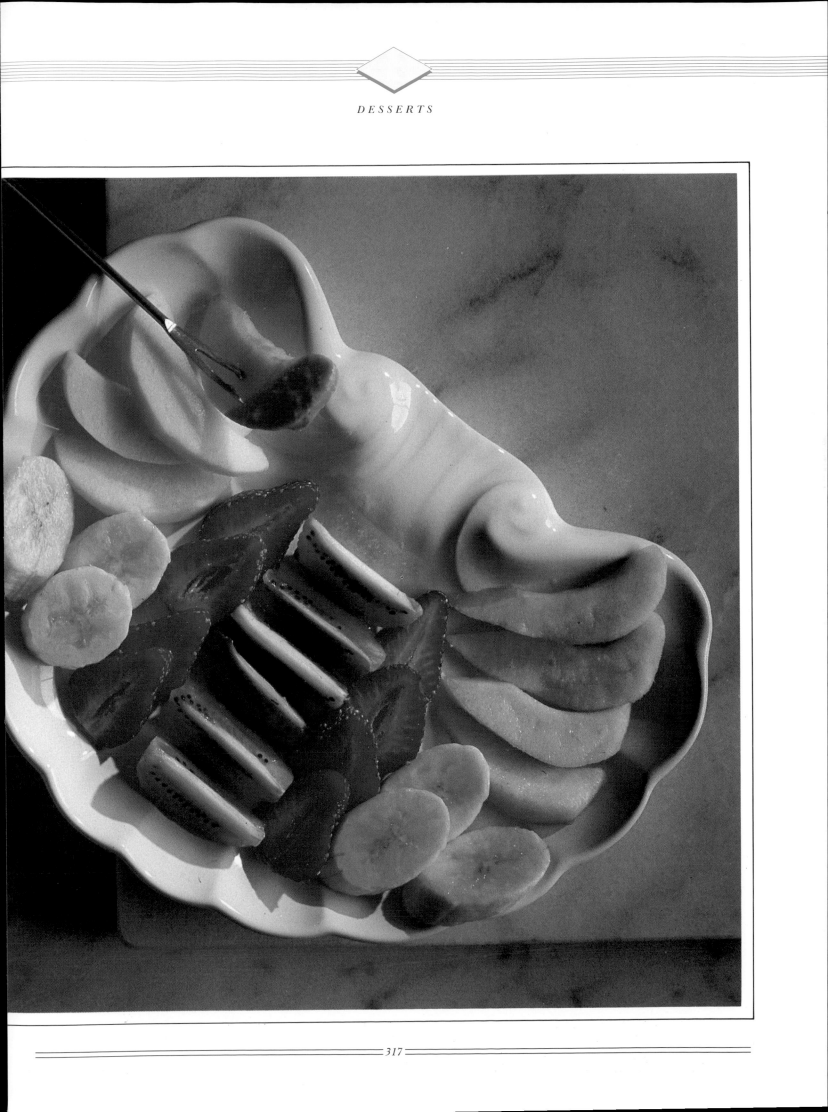

BLACKBERRY SURPRISE

SERVES 4 / SET: HIGH AND LOW

Ingredients

625 ml/1 pt milk

60 g/2 oz ground rice

2 tbsp sugar

2 eggs, separated

880 g/1 lb 12 oz canned blackberries, drained

30 g/1 oz castor sugar

◆ Pour the milk into a bowl, add the rice and 2 tbsp of sugar. Cook on high for 8 minutes.

◆ Beat the egg yolks and stir them in. Smooth out any lumps and then cook on low for 9 minutes until all the milk is absorbed. Fold in half the drained blackberries. Layer the rice and the remaining blackberries in 4 individual dishes.

◆ Whisk the egg whites until stiff, fold in the castor sugar and spoon them on top of the dessert. Cook on high for 2–3 minutes and serve.

LEMON MERINGUE PIE

SERVES 4–6 / SET: HIGH AND MEDIUM

Ingredients

1 Basic Shortcrust Pastry Case (see recipe)

LEMON CURD

grated rind and juice of 2 lemons

2 tbsp cornflour

90 g/3 oz castor sugar

60 g/2 oz butter

3 egg yolks

MERINGUE

3 egg whites

60 g/2 oz castor sugar

◆ Make the Basic Shortcrust Pastry Case as shown in recipe.

◆ For the lemon curd, add to the lemon juice enough water to make 315 ml/½ pt. Blend in the cornflour. Add the sugar, grated rind and butter. Cook for 3 minutes on high. Stir and return to the oven for 2 minutes.

◆ Remove from the oven, stir well and cool slightly. Add the egg yolks, mix well and cook on medium for 1–1½ minutes. Pour into the pastry case.

◆ For the meringue beat the egg whites until stiff, fold in the sugar and pile it on the lemon mix. Cook on high for 1 minute.

◆ Place under a conventional grill to brown. Serve hot or cold.

MANGO MERINGUE DESSERT

SERVES 4 / SET: HIGH

Ingredients

1 can of sliced mangoes, chopped

2 egg whites

125 g/4 oz sifted icing sugar

30 g/1 oz chopped nuts

◆ Divide the mangoes between 4 glasses or bowls.

◆ Beat the egg whites until stiff, beat in the sugar until the mixture becomes stiff again.

◆ Pile the meringue mixture on the mangoes to 2 cm/¾ in below the rim of the glass or bowl.

◆ Place the 4 dishes in a circle in the oven and cook for 2 minutes. Turn the glasses and cook for a further 1 minute or until the meringue puffs up.

◆ Sprinkle with the chopped nuts and serve immediately.

Blackberry Surprise

CARAMEL ORANGES

SERVES 4 / SET: HIGH

Ingredients
4 large oranges, seedless if available
90 g/3 oz sugar
315 ml/¹/₂ pint water
1 pinch ground ginger
orange zest and ginger snaps to decorate

◆ Peel away the rind and pith from the oranges and cut the fruit into horizontal slices. Arrange them in 4 individual dishes either in slices or reshape the orange, and secure it with a toothpick through the centre.

◆ Place the sugar in a bowl with 60 ml/3 tbsp water and cook for approx 4¹/₂ minutes until the colour is pale caramel. Add the ground ginger and the remaining water, stir and heat for 2 minutes.

◆ Pour the mixture over the oranges and decorate with ginger snaps and orange zest, or Caramel Cotton (see recipe).

POACHED BRANDIED PEACHES

SERVES 4 / SET: HIGH

Ingredients

4 fresh peaches
4 tbsp brandy
2 tbsp orange juice
1 tbsp castor sugar
3 tbsp fruit mince
brandy butter or whipped cream

◆ Skin the peaches by placing them in boiling water for a few seconds, then into cold. Peel away the skins.

◆ Cut the peaches in half and remove the stones. Cut a thin slice from the round side of the peach so that it will stand, hollow side up, when served.

◆ Place the peaches hollow side down, in a large round shallow dish. The peaches in the centre must be moved to the outside halfway through the cooking time.

◆ Mix together the brandy, orange juice and sugar and pour the mixture over the peaches. Cover and poach for 3 minutes. Remove from the oven and turn peaches hollow side up. Add 1 tsp of fruit mince to each peach. Return to the oven and cook for 1½ minutes.

◆ Arrange the peaches on individual plates with some of the syrup and serve with brandy butter or whipped cream.

APRICOT LAYER DESSERT

SERVES 4 / SET: HIGH AND MEDIUM

Ingredients

250 g/8 oz self-raising flour
125 g/4 oz shortening
milk to mix
880 g/1 lb 12 oz unsweetened canned apricots, juice reserved
155 g/5 oz sugar
APRICOT SAUCE
155 g/5 oz apricot jam
150 ml/5 fl oz apricot juice
juice of ½ lemon
1 tbsp sherry

◆ Sift the flour and mix in the shortening. Sprinkle the milk on gradually and mix until you have a soft but not sticky dough. Grease a 1.1 lt/2 pt pudding (flat-bottom) bowl.

◆ Reserve one apricot half for decoration and roughly chop the remainder.

◆ Roll out the dough to 5 mm/¼ in thickness. Cut it into 4 circles to fit your bowl. Place one pastry circle in the bottom of the bowl, top with ⅓ of the apricots, sprinkle with sugar to taste and continue to layer the pastry, fruit and sugar, ending with a circle of pastry. Seal the top layer and cover with plastic wrap. Cook on high for 8 minutes. Let it stand for 5 minutes.

◆ For the apricot sauce, place the jam with some of the apricot juice and lemon juice in a bowl and cook on medium for 3 minutes. Work the mixture through a sieve or purée it in a blender or food processor. Add sufficient apricot juice to bring the sauce to the correct consistency. Cook on high for 3 minutes and stir in the sherry.

◆ Turn out the apricot layer dessert. Top with the reserved apricot and serve with the hot sauce.

Apricot Layer Dessert

CHRISTMAS PUDDING

SERVES 10–12 / SET: HIGH AND MEDIUM

Ingredients

185 g/6 oz currants
125 g/4 oz sultanas
315 g/10 oz raisins
125 g/4 oz mixed dried fruit peel
4 tbsp brandy or rum
1 tbsp black treacle
3 large eggs
150 ml/5 fl oz beer
1 tsp gravy browning or brown colouring
125 g/4 oz moist brown sugar
185 g/6 oz shredded suet
90 g/3 oz fresh brown breadcrumbs
90 g/3 oz chopped mixed nuts
1/2 tsp each ground allspice, ginger, nutmeg and cinnamon
grated rind of half a lemon
grated rind of half an orange
185 g/6 oz self-raising flour

◆ The mixture will fill two 1.1 l/2 pt basins (flat-bottom bowls).

◆ Place the dried peel, sultanas, raisins and currants in a large bowl and cover with boiling water. Cook on high for 4 minutes. Let it stand for 1 hour.

◆ Strain and replace the fruit in the bowl, then add brandy or rum. Let it stand overnight.

◆ Stir in all the other liquids and mix in the remaining ingredients. The flavour is improved if you can leave it to stand overnight.

◆ Line the two basins (bowls) with plastic wrap. Divide the mixture between the basins (bowls) and cover with plastic wrap.

◆ Cook the Christmas pudding on medium for 7 minutes. Let it stand for 4 minutes. Cook for a further 6 minutes. Repeat with the second pudding.

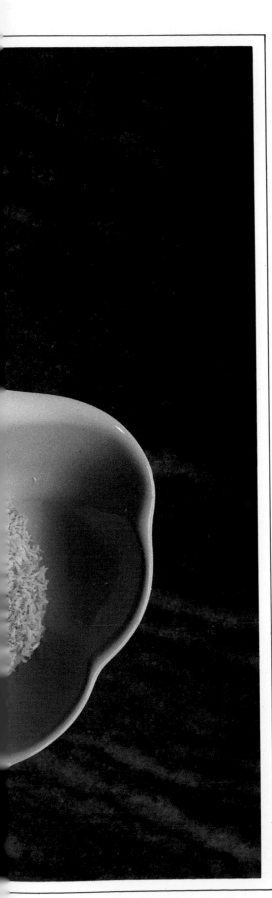

APPLE AND COCONUT RINGS

SERVES 4 / SET: HIGH

Ingredients

6 dessert apples, approx 185 g/6 oz each
2 tbsp lemon juice
4 tbsp brown sugar
185 g/6 oz desiccated coconut
2 tbsp blackberry jam
150 ml/5 fl oz heavy cream, whipped
glacé cherries, to decorate

◆ Peel the apples and cut them horizontally into 0.6 cm/¼ in thick slices. Cut out a circle removing the core, to make the apple rings. Sprinkle with lemon juice.

◆ Mix together the brown sugar and coconut.

◆ Place the jam and 1 tbsp of water in a bowl and heat for 2 minutes. Stir.

◆ Brush the hot jam over the apple rings. Transfer them to a plate and cook for 2–3 minutes. Do not overcook the apples; they should stay firm.

◆ Sprinkle the apples with the coconut mixture, transfer them to 4 individual plates, decorate with glacé cherries. Serve with the whipped cream.

Apple and Coconut Rings

BAKED SHERRY APPLES

SERVES 4 / SET: MEDIUM

Ingredients

4 dessert apples
1 tbsp lemon juice
125 g/4 oz sultanas
2 tbsp honey
4 tbsp sweet sherry
150 ml/5 fl oz heavy cream, whipped

◆ Peel and slice the apples and arrange them attractively in 4 individual dishes. Sprinkle with lemon juice.

◆ Mix together the sultanas, honey and sherry and spoon them over the apples. Cover and cook for 3 minutes (1 dish), 4½ minutes (2 dishes) or 6–7 minutes (4 dishes) or until the apples are tender and the sultanas plump. Cooking time will vary depending on the type of apple.

◆ Serve with whipped cream.

ORANGE ICE CREAM CRUNCH

SERVES 4–6 / SET: MEDIUM

Ingredients

1 Chocolate Crunch Flan Case (see recipe)

FILLING

½ lt/1 pt vanilla ice cream

2 tbsp orange liqueur

5 mandarin orange segments – to decorate

◆ Make the Chocolate Crunch Flan Case as shown in the recipe.

◆ Allow the ice cream to soften slightly. Place it in a bowl, add the liqueur and blend together. Spoon it into the flan case.

◆ Cover the case with foil and place in the freezer until solid.

◆ Just before serving decorate it with the mandarin segments.

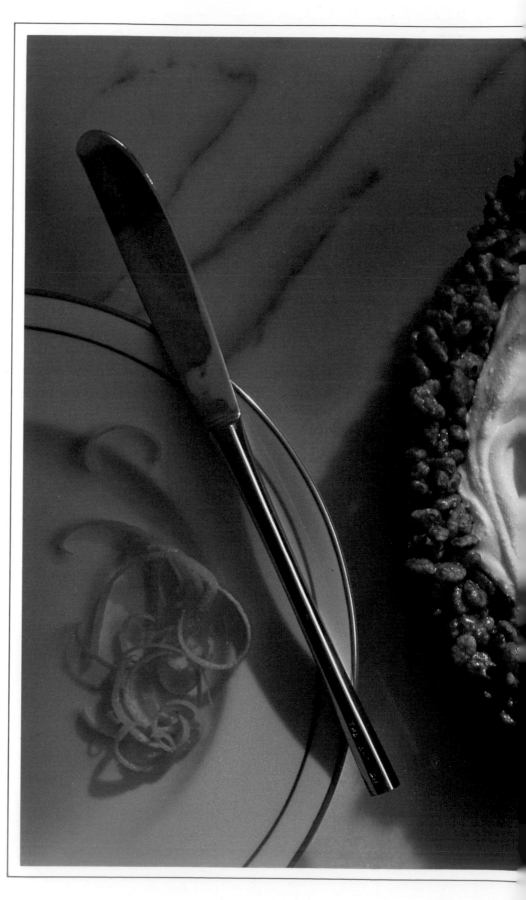

FRUIT SOUFFLE

SERVES 4 / SET: HIGH

Ingredients

2 tbsp orange liqueur

4 tbsp water

2 tbsp powdered gelatine

315 ml/10 fl oz liquidized orange pulp
(puréed in a blender or food processor)

125 g/4 oz sugar

315 ml/10 fl oz heavy cream, whipped

6 egg whites, stiffly beaten

mandarin orange segments to decorate

◆ Place the liqueur and water in a bowl and sprinkle on the gelatine. Cook for 30 seconds or until gelatine has dissolved. Stir well.

◆ Stir in the orange purée and sugar, then cool. Stir occasionally. Fold in the cream and then the egg whites.

◆ Place a collar of greaseproof paper around the outside of a soufflé dish to extend 2.5 cm/1 inch above the rim. Secure it with tape.

◆ Spoon the mixture into the soufflé dish to reach the edge of the paper. Chill until set.

◆ Decorate with mandarin orange segments.

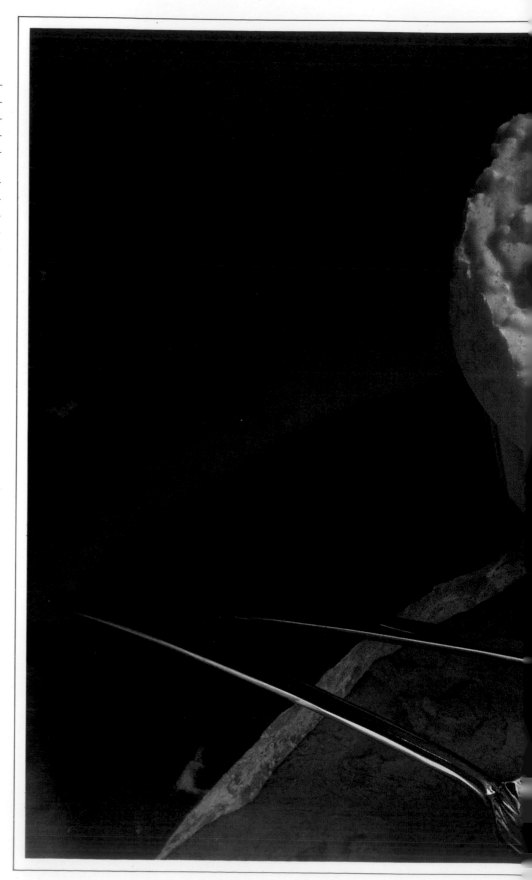

Fruit Soufflé

JAMAICAN DESSERT

SERVES 4–5 / SET: HIGH

Ingredients

125 g/4 oz self-raising flour
125 g/4 oz semolina
60 g/2 oz brown sugar
60 g/2 oz shortening
½ tsp bicarbonate of soda
1 tbsp milk
1 tbsp golden syrup
1 tbsp rum
S A U C E
4 tbsp golden syrup
100 ml/3 fl oz water
125 g/4 oz sultanas
3 tbsp rum
cream

◆ Mix together the flour, semolina, sugar and fat.

◆ Dissolve the bicarbonate of soda in the milk and stir in the syrup and rum. Add this to the dry ingredients. The mixture should be soft enough to drop off a spoon easily. Add more milk if necessary to obtain the correct consistency.

◆ Grease a 1 1/2 pt pudding basin (flat-bottom bowl) and pour in the mixture. Cover and cook for 6 minutes. Let it stand for 3 minutes.

◆ To make the sauce, place all the sauce ingredients in a bowl and cook, covered, for 4 minutes until the sultanas plump up.

◆ Turn the pudding out onto a serving plate and serve with the sauce and cream.

BASIC CRUMB CASE

SERVES 4 / SET: HIGH

Ingredients
90 g/3 oz butter
250 g/8 oz Marie biscuits, crushed
45 g/1½ oz brown sugar
30 g/1 oz chopped nuts

◆ Melt the butter in a 23 cm/9 in pie dish and cook for 40–45 seconds. Add the crumbs, sugar, and nuts and mix well. Press the mixture firmly against the base and sides of the dish, using a spoon.

◆ Stand the dish on an inverted plate and cook for 30 seconds, rotate the dish and cook for a further 45 seconds. Cool before filling.

VARIATIONS
1. Use ginger biscuits.
2. Add chopped raisins to the crumb mix.
3. Add mixed spice to the mix.

JAMAICAN BANANAS

SERVES 4 / SET: MEDIUM

Ingredients
4 large firm bananas
1 tbsp lemon juice
30 g/1 oz butter
2 tbsp orange juice
4 tbsp rum
1 tbsp clear honey
½ tsp cinnamon
8 ginger biscuits, crushed into crumbs
150 ml/5 fl oz heavy cream, whipped

◆ Peel the bananas, cut them in half lengthways and then in half again. Sprinkle them with the lemon juice and dot with the butter.

◆ Stir all the remaining ingredients together and add them to the dish. Cover and cook for 5–6 minutes. Arrange the bananas in 4 individual dishes and sprinkle with the biscuit crumbs.

◆ Serve with whipped cream.

CHOCOLATE BLANCMANGE

SERVES 4 / SET: HIGH

Ingredients
4 tbsp cornflour
2 tbsp cocoa
2 tsp castor sugar
625 ml/1 pt milk
1 tsp vanilla essence
125 g/4 oz butter
12 mini chocolate Swiss rolls or devil's food cake, sliced
440 g/14 oz canned pears, drained
150 ml/5 fl oz heavy cream, whipped

◆ In a large bowl blend together the cornflour, cocoa and sugar. Gradually stir in the milk with the vanilla essence. Cook uncovered for 3 minutes, then stir and cook for a further 3 minutes or until thickened. Stir in the butter. Cool slightly.

◆ Press the sliced Swiss roll or devil's food cake against the sides of four individual glass dishes. Chop the drained pears and spoon them into the centre. Pour on the blancmange and cover with plastic wrap to prevent a skin forming.

◆ Place the dish in the refrigerator to set. Remove the plastic wrap and decorate with the whipped cream.

Chocolate Blancmange

CHERRY CHEESECAKE

SERVES 4 / SET: HIGH

Ingredients

1 Basic Crumb Case (see recipe)
500 g/1 lb cream cheese
2 eggs
125 g/4 oz castor sugar
2 tbsp lemon juice
315 ml/½ pint sour cream
½ tsp vanilla essence
440 g/14 oz can of cherry pie filling
150 ml/5 fl oz heavy cream, whipped

◆ Make the Basic Crumb Case (see recipe).

◆ Beat the cheese until smooth. Whisk the eggs and 90 g/3 oz of sugar together until thick. Add to the cheese with the lemon juice. Pour the mixture into the crumb case and cook for 6 minutes.

◆ Mix together the sour cream, remaining sugar and vanilla essence and pour it over the cheese mixture.

◆ Cook for a further 6 minutes. Gently spread the topping after 3 minutes to ensure that it cooks evenly.

◆ Cool the cake in the refrigerator. Remove it 1 hour before serving, top it with the cherry pie filling and decorate it with whipped cream.

COCONUT ICE

MAKES 1LB / SET: HIGH

Ingredients

500 g/1 lb sugar
150 ml/¼ pt milk
125 g/4 oz desiccated coconut
1 tbsp heavy cream
few drops red colouring

◆ Stir together the sugar and milk in a large bowl until the sugar has dissolved. Cook for 6–8 minutes. The mixture should reach the soft ball stage. To test, drop a little of the mixture in cold water, it should form a soft ball when rolled between the fingers. Check for this stage after 5 minutes and then every minute until ready. Stir occasionally.

◆ Stir in the coconut and cream, beat briskly until the mixture is thick and creamy. Pour half of it into a buttered 20 cm/8 in square tin.

◆ Colour the remaining half pink with the red colouring and spread it over the white layer. Cool until firm and set. Mark into squares and cut into pieces when cold.

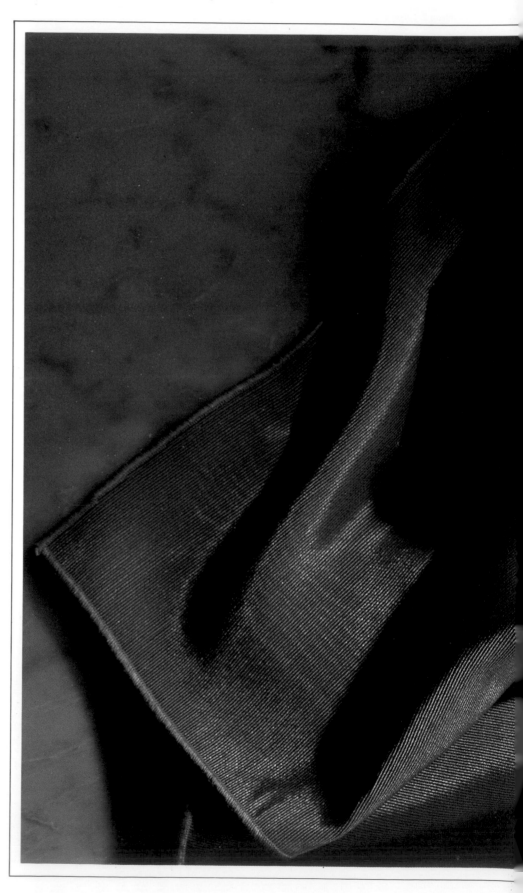

GINGERED PEARS

SERVES 4 / SET: HIGH

Ingredients

4 pears, peeled, halved and cored
150 ml/5 fl oz lemonade
100 ml/3 fl oz ginger wine or ginger ale
1 tbsp brown sugar
whipped cream (optional)

◆ Place all the ingredients in a dish, cover and cook for 3–4 minutes or until tender.

◆ Serve with whipped cream if desired.

VARIATION Leave the pears whole with the stalk intact.

PEACH CRUMBLE

SERVES 4 / SET: HIGH

Ingredients

5 fresh peaches

1 tbsp sweet sherry

2 tbsp orange juice

2 tbsp sugar

TOPPING

185 g/6 oz Marie biscuits, crushed

30 g/1 oz butter

30 g/1 oz sultanas

60 g/2 oz chopped almonds

30 g/1 oz brown sugar

◆ Skin the peaches by placing them in boiling water for a few seconds, then plunge them into cold. Peel away the skins, cut them in half and remove the stones. Chop them roughly.

◆ Place the peaches, sherry, orange juice and sugar in a shallow dish. Cover and cook for 3 minutes. Keep to one side.

◆ Place the butter and sultanas in a dish, cook for 1½ minutes, add the biscuit crumbs, almonds and sugar. Mix well.

◆ Pile the topping on the peaches, cook for 2 minutes and then brown under a conventional grill. Serve with cream or custard.

VARIATION Replace the peaches with any fruit of your choice.

Peach Crumble

GINGER UPSIDE DOWN PUDDING

SERVES 4 / SET: HIGH

Ingredients

90 g/3 oz butter

90 g/3 oz black treacle

90 g/3 oz golden syrup

150 ml/¼ pt milk

1 large egg

250 g/8 oz self-raising flour, sifted

1 tsp ground ginger

30 g/1 oz brown sugar

440 g/14 oz canned pineapple rings, juice
reserved

4 glacé cherries, halved

SAUCE

reserved pineapple juice

lemon juice

2 tsp cornflour mixed with a little water

syrup to taste

◆ Heat the butter, treacle and syrup
in a bowl for 3 minutes. Add the milk,
stir and cool.

◆ Add the egg and beat well. Pour
the mixture onto the sieved flour. Add
the remaining ingredients, with the
exception of the pineapple rings, and
continue to beat.

◆ Line a 1.1 lt/2 pt bowl with the
pineapple slices and glacé cherries,
pour the gingerbread mixture into the
bowl, cover and cook for 7–8 minutes
or until it is firm to the touch. Let it
stand for 5 minutes, then turn it out
onto a dish.

◆ Decorate with extra pineapple
slices and glacé cherries if desired.

◆ To make the sauce, add the lemon
juice to the reserved pineapple juice to
make 150 ml/5 fl oz. Cook for 2
minutes, stir in the cornflour and cook
for 1 minute or until thickened and
clear. Taste and add syrup if required.
Stir well. Pour the sauce over the
pudding and serve.

PINEAPPLE CUSTARD

SERVES 4 / SET: HIGH
AND MEDIUM

Ingredients

4 tbsp castor sugar
4 eggs, beaten
2 tsp cornflour
465 ml/15 fl oz milk
2 drops vanilla essence
ground cinnamon for dusting
440 g/14 oz canned pineapple rings, drained
1 kiwi fruit, sliced

◆ Beat the sugar and eggs together in a 1.7 l/3 pt bowl. Blend the cornflour with 3 tbsp of milk and stir it into the egg mixture.

◆ Place the remaining milk in a bowl and cook it on high for 2 minutes. The milk must not boil. Pour the egg mixture into the milk and add the vanilla essence. Cook on medium for 4–5 minutes, whisking every minute. Do not allow the mixture to boil as the eggs will scramble.

◆ Arrange the pineapple rings in a dish and pour the custard over them. Do not overfill the dish. Place the dish on an inverted saucer and cook on medium for 10–12 minutes. Turn the dish 4 or 5 times during the cooking period.

◆ The filling should be almost firm in the centre. Let it stand for 10 minutes to cool and set.

◆ Serve the custard cold, dusted with cinnamon and decorated with the kiwi fruit.

Pineapple Custard

CHOCOLATE SEMOLINA PUDDING

SERVES 2–3 / SET: HIGH AND LOW

Ingredients
625 ml/1 pint milk

45 g/1½ oz semolina

30 g/1 oz sugar

30 g/1 oz cooking chocolate, grated

◆ Place all the ingredients in a 2 l/3½ pt glass bowl. Cook on high for 3 minutes. Stir well, and continue to cook on high for a further 3–4 minutes or until the milk boils. Stir.

◆ Cover and cook on high to return to the boil. Reduce to and cook for 10–15 minutes. Stir every 5 minutes. Let the pudding stand, covered, for 5 minutes. Stir before serving.

COFFEE AND WALNUT DESSERT

SERVES 4—6 / SET: MEDIUM

Ingredients
150 ml/5 fl oz strong black coffee
185 g/6 oz marshmallows
4 bananas, 2 chopped, 2 sliced
125 g/4 oz walnut halves, whole or chopped, to decorate
425 g/4 oz walnut halves, whole or chopped, to decorate

◆ Place the coffee and marshmallows in a bowl. Cook for 1–1½ minutes or until dissolved. Let it stand until cold. Stir the chopped bananas and the whipped cream into the coffee mixture.

◆ Spoon half the mixture into 4 glasses. Press the banana slices and walnut halves down the sides of the glasses. Add the remaining coffee mixture and serve.

GRAPEFRUIT AND CAMPARI SORBET

SERVES 4 / SET: HIGH

Ingredients
60 g/2 oz sugar
100 ml/3 fl oz Campari
530 ml/17 fl oz grapefruit juice
1 tbsp gelatine
2 egg whites
mint leaves to decorate

◆ In a medium size bowl, stir the sugar into the Campari. Heat for 2 minutes. Stir halfway through the cooking time.

◆ Add the gelatine to a few tbsp of grapefruit juice. Stir into the Campari and sugar mixture and continue stirring until dissolved. Cool and add the remainder of the grapefruit juice.

◆ Place the mixture in the freezer until lightly frozen.

◆ Whisk the egg whites until stiff and beat them into the lightly frozen grapefruit mixture. Spoon into a container and freeze until required.

◆ To serve, let the sorbet stand at room temperature for approx 30 minutes. Decorate with mint leaves.

BLACKBERRY MALLOW

SERVES 4 / SET: HIGH

Ingredients
500 g/1 lb blackberries
125 g/4 oz marshmallows
125 g/4 oz sugar

◆ Place the blackberries and sugar in a bowl, cover and cook for 2–3 minutes. Stir and mash lightly.

◆ Top with the marshmallows and cook for a further 1½–2 minutes until they have melted. Mix thoroughly into the blackberries.

◆ Let it cool a little, then pour into 4 sundae glasses. Cool for several hours or overnight. Serve with whipped cream.

Coffee and Walnut Dessert

CHOCOLATE RUM TRUFFLES

SERVES 12—16./SET: HIGH

Ingredients

155 g/5 oz cooking chocolate
15 g/½ oz butter
1 tsp rum
1 egg yolk
30 g/1 oz ground almonds
chocolate vermicelli, chopped walnuts and cocoa to decorate

◆ Break the chocolate into pieces in a bowl and cook them for 2 minutes or until the chocolate has melted.
◆ Beat in the butter, egg yolk and rum. Mix in and add the ground almonds.
◆ Set the mixture aside in the refrigerator to thicken. Shape it into small balls and roll half in the chocolate vermicelli and the remainder in the chopped nuts and cocoa.
◆ Place in paper cases and serve as petits fours with coffee.

RASPBERRY PINWHEELS

SERVES 4 / SET: HIGH

Ingredients

250 g/8 oz Swiss roll, sliced

1 package raspberry jelly

500 g/1 lb fresh raspberries

water

◆ Place the raspberries in a bowl. Cover and cook for 2–3 minutes. Drain off any juice and add water to make 625 ml/1 pt.

◆ Place the jelly in 315 ml/½ pt of the liquid and cook for 4–5 minutes or until melted. Stir halfway through the cooking time. Allow to cool slightly, then add the remaining liquid stirring vigorously as you pour.

◆ Press the Swiss roll slices onto the base and sides of a 940 ml/1½ pt pudding (flat bottom) bowl.

◆ Stir the raspberries into the liquid and pour the mixture into the lined bowl.

◆ Leave the bowl in the refrigerator to set, then turn out the pinwheels and serve with cream or custard.

TOFFEE APPLE TREAT

SERVES 4 / SET: HIGH

Ingredients

4 dessert apples

500 g/1 lb treacle toffee

1 tbsp water

60 g/2 oz chopped nuts

◆ Peel and core the apples, cut into approx 8 pieces each, keep to one side.

◆ Place the treacle toffee and water in a large bowl and cook for 3–4 minutes or until melted. Stir after 2 minutes.

◆ Spear the apple pieces on wooden toothpicks, dip and coat them in the toffee. Sprinkle them with the chopped nuts, stand them on greaseproof paper and refrigerate for 1 hour.

Toffee Apple Treat

SNOWDEN PUDDING

SERVES 4 / SET: HIGH

Ingredients
30 g/1 oz glacé cherries, halved
125 g/4 oz raisins
125 g/4 oz shortening
125 g/4 oz fresh breadcrumbs
30 g/1 oz ground rice
finely grated rind of 1 lemon
6 tbsp lemon marmalade
2 eggs, beaten
2 tbsp milk
SAUCE
4 tbsp lemon marmalade
150 ml/¹/₄ pt hot water
1 tsp cornflour
2 tbsp cold water

◆ Butter a 1.1 l/2 pt bowl, press half the raisins and cherries, cut side down, against the bottom and sides of the bowl.

◆ Place the remaining raisins, shortening, breadcrumbs, ground rice, lemon rind and marmalade in a mixing bowl. Mix well. Add the eggs and sufficient milk to make a soft dropping consistency.

◆ Spoon the mixture into the bowl and press it down firmly. Cover and cook for 9 minutes. Let it stand for 5 minutes.

◆ For the sauce, place the marmalade and hot water in a bowl and cook for 3 minutes. Mix the cornflour with the cold water, blend into the marmalade mixture and cook for 2 minutes.

◆ Turn out the pudding and serve with the sauce.

Snowden Pudding

SUMMER FRUITS DESSERT

SERVES 4—6 / SET: HIGH

Ingredients

250 g/8 oz peaches, peeled, stoned and chopped

250 g/8 oz apricots, peeled, stoned and chopped

125 g/4 oz rhubarb, sliced

3 tbsp apricot brandy

1 tsp ground ginger

1 tbsp arrowroot

125 g/4 oz sugar

2 tbsp water

ice cream and brandy snaps

◆ Place the fruit in a deep bowl together with the apricot brandy and ground ginger. Cover and cook for 6 minutes or until mushy. Rub through a sieve or purée in a blender or food processor.

◆ Measure the puréed fruit and allow 1 tbsp arrowroot per 625 ml/1 pint of purée. Mix the arrowroot to a smooth paste with 2 tbsp of water. Place to one side.

◆ Add the sugar to the fruit. The dish should be deep enough so that the mixture fills it only one third. Cover and cook for 7–8 minutes or until boiling, stirring every 2 minutes. The sugar should be completely dissolved. Stir in the arrowroot and return it to the boil for 2–3 minutes until clear.

◆ Allow the fruit to cool and pour it into sundae glasses. Chill and serve with the ice cream and brandy snaps.

QUICK LEMON PUFFS

SERVES 6—8 / SET: HIGH

Ingredients

400 g/13 oz frozen puff pastry

8 tbsp Lemon Curd (see Lemon Meringue Pie)

150 ml/5 fl oz whipping cream

icing sugar for dusting

◆ Defrost the pastry at room temperature.

◆ Sprinkle a board with icing sugar and roll out the pastry as thinly as possible. Cut into 10 cm/4 in squares.

◆ Preheat a microwave griddle for 4 minutes. Place three squares of pastry at a time on the griddle and cook for approx 5–7 minutes, turning once. The pastry is ready when it no longer deflates when the oven door is opened.

◆ Slice horizontally through the puffs and spread the bottom layer with lemon curd and whipped cream. Replace the top layer of pastry and dust with icing sugar.

RASPBERRY AND PEACH FLAN

SERVES 4–6 / SET: HIGH

Ingredients

1 Basic Crumb Case (see recipe)

875g/1 lb 12 oz fresh or
canned peach slices, drained

375g/12 oz fresh or thawed frozen
raspberries

60 g/2 oz sugar

15 g/½ oz cornflour

150 ml/5 fl oz heavy cream, whipped

◆ Make the Basic Crumb Case as shown in the recipe.

◆ If using fresh peaches, peel and slice them. Place them in a dish, cover and cook for 3 minutes.

◆ Reserve 125 g/4 oz well-shaped raspberries for decoration and place the remainder and their juice in a small basin (bowl) with the sugar and cornflour. Stir, cover and cook for 3–4 minutes or until thickened and clear. Stir once every minute during the cooking period.

◆ Spoon the pulp over the base of the flan case, arrange the peaches on top with the reserved raspberries in the centre. Spoon the remaining juice over the top, cool to set.

◆ Serve with the whipped cream.

Raspberry and Peach Flan

BASIC VICTORIA SANDWICH CAKE

SERVES 4–6 / SET: HIGH

Ingredients

185 g/6 oz butter

185 g/6 oz castor sugar

3 eggs, beaten

185 g/6 oz self-raising flour

2 tbsp milk

½ tsp bicarbonate of soda

150 ml/5 fl oz heavy cream, whipped

2 tbsp jam

◆ Grease a round 19-cm/7½-in soufflé dish and line the base with greased greaseproof paper.

◆ Cream the butter until soft, add the sugar and beat well until light and fluffy. Add the eggs gradually, beating all the time. Sift the flour and bicarbonate of soda and fold into the mixture. Add the milk and fold in carefully. Add more milk if necessary to obtain a soft dropping consistency.

◆ Place the mixture in the prepared dish and cook for 4–5 minutes. Let it stand for 5 minutes.

◆ Turn it out onto a cooling rack. When cold, cut it in half horizontally and sandwich it back together with whipped cream and jam of your choice.

◆ Omit the whipped cream and jam if using the Basic Sandwich for another recipe in this book.

CHOCOLATE GATEAU

SERVES 4—6 / SET: MEDIUM

Ingredients

1 Basic Victoria Sandwich (see recipe)
replacing 30 g/1 oz self-raising flour with
30 g/1 oz cocoa
185 g/6 oz butter, softened
315 g/10 oz icing sugar
1 tbsp rum
60 g/2 oz cooking chocolate
440 g/14 oz canned sliced peaches, drained
150 ml/5 fl oz heavy cream, whipped
90 g/3 oz chocolate, grated

◆ Make the Basic Victoria Sandwich
Cake (see recipe), replacing some of
the self-raising flour with the cocoa.

◆ Place the 60 g/2 oz chocolate in a
bowl. Cook for 3 minutes and cool.

◆ Cream the butter until soft, add
the sugar and rum and beat well. Stir
in the melted chocolate until well
blended.

◆ Cut the chocolate sponge in half
horizontally. Spread the bottom layer
with the whipped cream. Roughly
chop half the drained peaches and put
them on top of the cream. Replace the
top layer and coat the whole cake with
the chocolate butter cream.

◆ Press the grated chocolate onto the
sides of the cake and serve.

STRAWBERRY DELIGHT

SERVES 4—6 / SET: LOW AND HIGH

Ingredients

750 g/1½ lb fresh strawberries, hulled
220 g/7 oz castor sugar
1 tbsp lemon juice
½ tsp butter
1 large meringue nest or 4—6 individual nests

◆ Mix 250 g/8 oz strawberries, the sugar and lemon juice in a large 2.75 l/5 pt mixing bowl.

◆ Three quarters cover the bowl with plastic wrap. Cook on low for 10–12 minutes, stirring every 3 minutes. Mash and stir until the sugar is dissolved.

◆ Cook uncovered on high for 5 minutes, stir in the butter, then add the remaining strawberries and stir gently.

◆ Cool slightly and pile the strawberry mixture into the meringue nest(s) and serve.

◆ Alternatively place a thin layer of the cooled 'jam' mixture in the meringue nests, slice selected strawberries and arrange them as shown. Brush with a little of the 'jam' to glaze.

Strawberry Delight

CHOCOLATE CRUNCH FLAN CASE

SERVES 4–6 / SET: MEDIUM

Ingredients

250 g/8 oz cooking chocolate

60 g/2 oz butter

90 g/3 oz Rice Bubbles, crushed

◆ Place the butter and chocolate in a large bowl. Cook for 3 minutes.

◆ Stir in the Rice Bubbles. Place the mixture in a 20 cm/8 inch flan dish and press the mixture into the base and up the sides. Put it in the freezer until firm.

CHOCOLATE CHEESECAKE CRUNCH

S E R V E S   4 – 6 / S E T :   H I G H

Ingredients

1 Chocolate Crunch Flan Case (see recipe)
F I L L I N G
500 g/1 lb cream cheese
3 eggs, separated
125 g/4 oz sugar
150 ml/¼ pt sour cream
15 g/½ oz gelatine
4 tbsp warm water
185 g/6 oz cooking chocolate, grated

◆ Make the Chocolate Crunch Flan Case (see recipe).

◆ Place the cheese and egg yolks in a bowl, add half the sugar and beat vigorously. Stir in the sour cream.

◆ Place the water and gelatine in a cup, cook for 30 seconds, stir until dissolved and then cool.

◆ Whisk the egg whites until stiff. Whisk in the remaining sugar.

◆ Stir the gelatine into the cheese mixture. Fold in the egg whites and chopped chocolate.

◆ Pour the mixture into the prepared case, swirl the top with a fork and chill it until set.

◆ Decorate with grated chocolate.

APPLE LAYER DESSERT

SERVES 4 / SET: HIGH

Ingredients

1 kg/2 lb dessert apples
2 tbsp lemon juice
90 g/3 oz ginger biscuits
60 g/2 oz moist brown sugar
60 g/2 oz sultanas
1 tsp ground cinnamon
custard or whipped cream

◆ Peel, core and thinly slice the apples. Sprinkle them with lemon juice.

◆ Crush the ginger biscuits in a polythene bag with a rolling pin. Add the crumbs to the sugar, sultanas and ground cinnamon. Mix well.

◆ In a large soufflé dish, alternate layers of apple and biscuit mixture, ending with a biscuit layer on top.

◆ Cook uncovered for 10 minutes. Serve hot or cold with custard or whipped cream.

Apple Layer Dessert

BASIC SHORTCRUST PASTRY CASE

SERVES 6 / SET: HIGH

Ingredients

60 g/2 oz butter
30 g/1 oz lard
185 g/6 oz plain flour
1/2 tsp salt
3 tbsp cold milk

◆ Rub the butter and lard into the flour and salt in a bowl until the mixture resembles fine breadcrumbs. Sprinkle the milk over it, a little at a time, as you may not need it all. Stir lightly until the mixture forms a soft ball.

◆ Roll out the pastry on a lightly floured surface to 3 mm/1/8 in thickness and 5 cm/2 in larger than the top of your dish.

◆ Transfer the pastry to a 20 cm/8 in flan dish. Pat out any air pockets. Do not stretch the pastry as it will shrink during the cooking. Stand the pastry in a cool place for 15 minutes.

◆ Trim the pastry overhang and thoroughly prick the sides and base with a fork to ensure even cooking. Cover the sides with foil as they will cook faster than the base. Cover the base with a double thickness of absorbent kitchen paper. Place the flan dish on an inverted plate in the oven and cook for 3–4 minutes.

◆ Remove the foil and paper and cook for a further 2–3 minutes, then let it stand for 5 minutes.

◆ Fill the case when it is cool and reheat it if necessary. Do not cook the case with a filling in it as it will become soggy.

LEMON SPONGE SANDWICH

SERVES 5 / SET: MEDIUM

Ingredients

1 Basic Victoria Sandwich (see recipe), replacing milk with 2 tbsp lemon juice

LEMON CURD

250 g/8 oz castor sugar

2 eggs, beaten

grated rind and juice of 1 large lemon

60 g/2 oz butter

315 ml/10 fl oz heavy cream, whipped

125 g/4 oz mixed chopped nuts and lemon-shaped sweets to decorate

◆ Make the Basic Victoria Sandwich as shown in the recipe, replacing the milk with the lemon juice.

◆ To make the lemon curd, put the sugar, butter, juice and rind of the lemon in a bowl and cook for 10–12 minutes. The sugar should have dissolved and the mixture come to boiling point. Add the eggs, return it to the oven and cook for 6–8 minutes, until the mixture thickens. Stir frequently. This will make 500 g/1 lb of lemon curd. Bottle it in the usual way.

◆ Cut the Victoria Sandwich in half horizontally. Coat the base of the cake thickly with lemon curd. Pile on whipped cream to the desired thickness.

◆ Coat the sides and top of the sponge with a layer of whipped cream. Press the chopped nuts onto the sides.

◆ Place the remaining whipped cream into an icing bag and decorate the cake as desired.

CHOCOLATE SPONGE DESSERT

SERVES 4 / SET: HIGH

Ingredients

125 g/4 oz butter
125 g/4 oz castor sugar
2 large eggs
90 g/3 oz self-raising flour
30 g/1 oz cocoa
4 tbsp milk
S A U C E
125 g/4 oz cooking chocolate, broken into pieces
2 tbsp golden syrup
1 small can evaporated milk

◆ Cream together the butter and sugar until soft and light. Beat in the eggs. Sift the flour and fold it into the creamed mixture.

◆ Grease a 1.1 l/2 pt basin (flat-bottomed bowl). Put in the sponge mixture. Cover and cook for 5–6 minutes. Allow it to stand for 5 minutes.

◆ Place all the sauce ingredients in a bowl and cook for 4–5 minutes, stirring after 3 minutes. The chocolate should be melted and smooth.

◆ Turn the sponge out onto a plate and serve with the sauce.

COFFEE AND BANANA CREAM

SERVES 6 / SET: HIGH

Ingredients

1 tbsp plain flour
60 g/2 oz brown sugar
60 g/2 tbsp cornflour
560 ml/18 fl oz milk
3–4 egg yolks
30 g/1 oz butter
2 tsp instant coffee
30 g/1 oz chopped walnuts
2 chopped bananas
banana slices and walnuts to serve

◆ Blend together the flour, sugar, cornflour and milk in a 1.7 l/3 pt bowl. Whisk well and cook for 7–7½ minutes until thick. Whisk vigorously every 2 minutes.

◆ Lightly beat the egg yolks and add 6 tbsp of the custard mixture. Blend it well and add it to the remaining custard. Cook it for 1–2 minutes until thick.

◆ Beat in the butter and coffee. Stir in the walnuts and chopped bananas. Cover with plastic wrap and cool.

◆ Serve in individual dishes topped with banana slices and chopped walnuts.

CHOCOLATE MOUSSE

SERVES 6 / SET: HIGH

Ingredients

250 g/8 oz cooking chocolate, in pieces
3 tbsp water
15 g/½ oz butter
4 large eggs, separated
1 tbsp brandy
T O P P I N G
150 ml/5 fl oz heavy cream
30 g/1 oz icing sugar
15 g/½ oz cocoa
1 tsp instant coffee
1 drop vanilla essence
chocolate sticks to decorate

◆ Place the chocolate and water in a 2 l/3½ pt (microwave) bowl. Cook for 1½ minutes or until the chocolate has melted. Beat vigorously until smooth. Return to the oven and cook for 30 seconds. Beat again.

◆ Beat in the butter and the egg yolks, one by one. Stir in the brandy.

◆ Whip the egg whites into stiff peaks, stir one tbsp into the chocolate mixture and fold in the remainder. Pour into 6 individual dishes and set aside in the refrigerator for 3–4 hours.

◆ Just before serving, whisk together all the topping ingredients until thick. Top the mousse with the mixture.

◆ Decorate with the chocolate sticks and serve.

Chocolate Mousse

CARAMEL COTTON

SET: HIGH

Ingredients
90 g/3 oz castor sugar

3 tbsp water

◆ Place the sugar and water in a deep bowl and cook for 4–5 minutes or until golden.

◆ Remove from the oven using gloves as the dish will be very hot.

◆ Let it cool until the liquid thickens slightly.

◆ Scoop a small amount of caramel into a spoon and pour it slowly back into the bowl. The mixture will stiffen and you will be able to draw it into threads to decorate various desserts. See the Photograph of Caramel Oranges.

◆ Decorate just before serving as the sugar dissolves if left standing too long.

ORANGE RICE PUDDING

SERVES 2 / SET: HIGH AND MEDIUM

Ingredients

60 g/2 oz rice
60 g/2 oz sugar
625 ml/1 pt milk
1 tsp grated orange rind
60 g/2 oz sultanas

◆ Place all the ingredients in a 2¼ l/4 pt glass bowl. Cook on high for 7–8 minutes or until the mixture is just boiling. Stir thoroughly.

◆ Reduce to medium and cook for 20–25 minutes. Stir several times during the cooking period to prevent lumps forming.

◆ Remove the pudding from the oven and allow it to stand and thicken for 7–8 minutes before serving.

Orange Rice Pudding

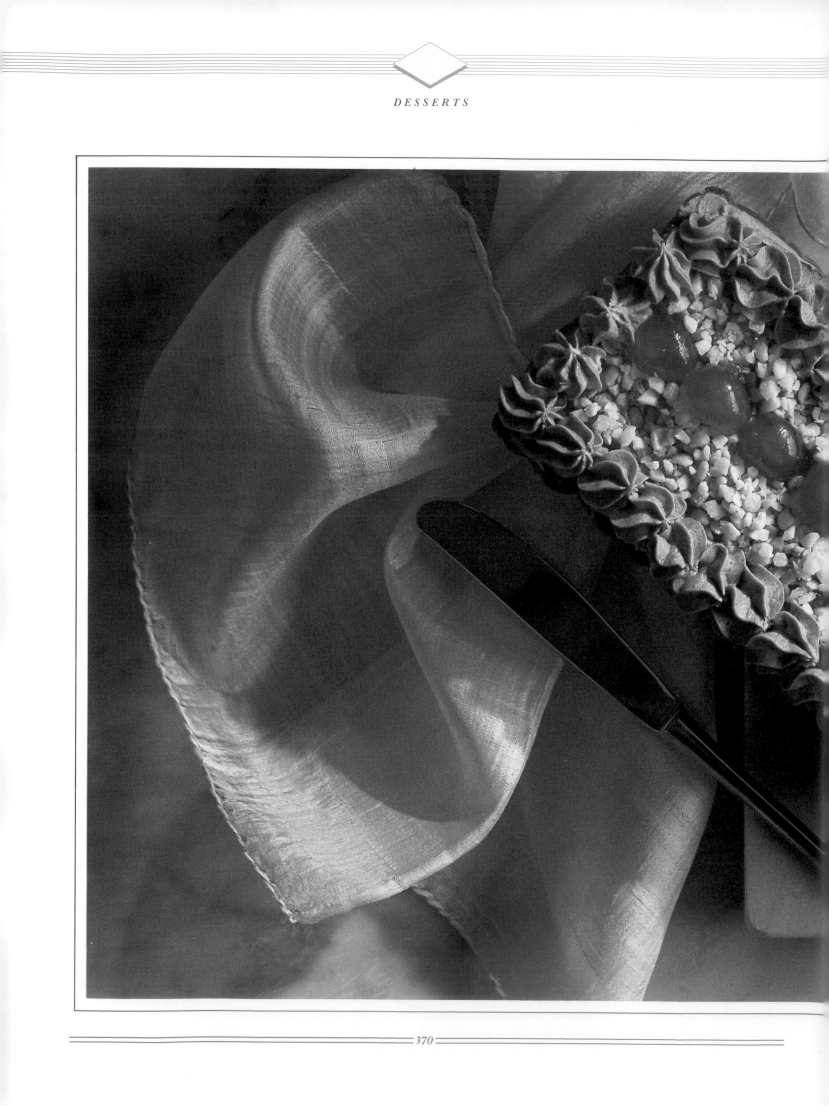

FUDGE CAKE

SERVES 6—8 / SET: MEDIUM

Ingredients

155 g/5 oz butter

2 tbsp golden syrup

155 g/5 oz cooking chocolate, cut into pieces

185 g/6 oz Marie biscuits, crushed

30 g/1 oz sultanas

2 tbsp chopped glacé cherries

60 g/2 oz chopped nuts

TOPPING

60 g/2 oz chocolate in small pieces

90 g/3 oz butter

1 tbsp rum

155 g/5 oz icing sugar

glacé cherries and chopped nuts to decorate

◆ Place the butter, syrup and chocolate in a bowl and cook for 3 minutes. Stir in the biscuit crumbs, sultanas, glacé cherries and chopped nuts. Mix well.

◆ Spoon this into a ½ kg/1 lb springform loaf tin. Chill in the refrigerator for approx 30 minutes until set. Remove the sides of the tin and transfer the cake to a plate.

◆ For the topping, cream together the butter and rum. Add the icing sugar little by little until the mixture is a thick spreading consistency.

◆ Pipe the top of the cake with the topping and decorate it with chopped nuts and glacé cherries.

◆ Serve it sliced, with whipped cream.

FONDANT FANCIES

MAKES 1LB / SET: HIGH

Ingredients

150 ml/¼ pt milk

500 g/1 lb sugar

1 tbsp heavy cream

½ tsp cocoa

◆ Stir the milk and sugar together in a large bowl until the sugar is dissolved. Cook for 6–8 minutes. The mixture should reach the soft ball stage. To test, drop a little of the mixture in cold water, it should form a soft ball when rolled between the fingers. Check for this stage after 5 minutes and then every minute until ready. Stir occasionally.

◆ Stir in the cream and beat until the mixture is thick and creamy. Spoon half the mixture into small paper moulds until they are half full.

◆ Beat the cocoa into the other half of the mixture and spoon it into the moulds.

PINEAPPLE CUPS

SERVES 4 / SET: HIGH

Ingredients

2 medium pineapples, trimmed and halved

4 kiwi fruit, sliced

3 peaches, peeled and sliced

125 g/4 oz black grapes, halved, deseeded

2 tbsp orange liqueur

2 tbsp clear honey

2 tbsp orange juice

◆ Scoop the flesh from the pineapples, leaving the skin intact. Dice the flesh and place in a dish. Add the peaches, kiwi fruit and grapes.

◆ Heat the orange liqueur, honey and orange juice for 2 minutes, stir well and pour it over the mixed fruit. Leave it to marinate until ready to serve.

◆ Cover the fruit mixture and cook it for 4 minutes. Pile it into the pineapple cups with a little of the syrup and serve.

Pineapple Cups

PINEAPPLE DESSERT

SERVES 4 / SET: HIGH

Ingredients

125 g/4 oz pineapple rings, canned or fresh, chopped

125 g/4 oz self-raising flour

pinch of bicarbonate of soda

60 g/2 oz sugar

60 g/2 oz shortening

90 g/3 oz sultanas

1 egg

2 tbsp milk

pineapple rings and glacé cherries to decorate

SAUCE

155 g/5 oz pineapple jam

150 ml/5 fl oz pineapple juice

3 tbsp lemon juice

◆ Mix all the ingredients together in a bowl.

◆ Line an 825 ml–1 l/1½–1¾ pt basin with plastic wrap. Place the mixture in the basin and cover with plastic wrap.

◆ Cook for 7 minutes on high. Let it stand for 3 minutes, then turn out onto a serving dish and decorate with the pineapple rings and cherries.

◆ For the sauce, place the jam with some of the pineapple and lemon juice in a bowl and cook for 1½–2 minutes. Work it through a sieve or pureé it in a blender or food processor. Add sufficient pineapple juice to bring the sauce to the correct consistency. Cook for 2 minutes, pour over the pudding and serve.

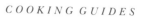
FRESH VEGETABLES COOKING GUIDE

vegetables	quantity	minutes on high
globe artichokes	4	10 – 20
asparagus spears	250 g/8 oz	6 – 7
beans	500 g/1 lb	8 – 10
beetroot, sliced	500 g/1 lb	7 – 8
broccoli florets	500 g/1 lb	4 – 5
Brussel sprouts	500 g/1 lb	8 – 10
cabbage, shredded	500 g/1 lb	7 – 10
carrots, sliced	250 g/8 oz	7 – 10
cauliflower florets	500 g/1 lb	10 – 11
celery	1 head	10 – 13
corn on the cob	1	3 – 5
eggplant, diced	500 g/1 lb	5 – 6
kohlrabi	500 g/1 lb	7 – 8
leeks, sliced	500 g/1 lb	7 – 10
mushrooms, whole	250 g/8 oz	5 – 6
okra	500 g/1 lb	8 – 10
onions, sliced	250 g/8 oz	5 – 7
parsnips, sliced	250 g/8 oz	8 – 10
peas	500 g/1 lb	7
potatoes, new	500 g/1 lb	8 – 10
potatoes, jacket (baked)	2 large	8
potatoes, boiled	500 g/1 lb	6 – 7
pumpkin, chopped	500 g/1 lb	5 – 7
spinach	500 g/1 lb	5
squash, sliced	500 g/1 lb	8 – 10
swedes, sliced	500g/1 lb	6 – 7
tomatoes, sliced	500 g/1 lb	2 – 3
turnips, sliced	250 g/8 oz	6 – 7
zucchini, sliced	4	7 – 10

FROZEN VEGETABLES COOKING GUIDE

vegetables	quantity	minutes on high
asparagus spears	250 g/8 oz	6 – 7
beans	250 g/8 oz	7
broccoli spears	250 g/8 oz	6 – 8
Brussel sprouts	250 g/8 oz	5 – 6
cabbage, chopped	250 g/8 oz	6 – 7
carrots, sliced	250 g/8 oz	6 – 7
cauliflower florets	250 g/8 oz	4 – 6
corn	250 g/8 oz	4 – 6
corn on the cob	1	4 – 5
peas	250 g/8 oz	4
spinach, chopped	250 g/8 oz	5
swedes, cubed	250 g/8 oz	7
vegetables, mixed	250 g/8 oz	4 – 6
zucchini, sliced	250 g/8 oz	4

FRESH MEAT COOKING GUIDE

meat	minutes on high per 500 g/1 lb	standing minutes
bacon, rashers, 4	4½	—
beef, boned roasts, rare	5 – 6	15 – 20
beef, boneless roast, medium	7 – 8	15 – 20
beef, boneless roast, well-done	8 – 9	15 – 20
beef, roasts with bone, rare	5 – 6	15 – 20
beef, roasts with bone, medium	6 – 7	15 – 20
beef, roasts with bone, well-done	8 – 9	15 – 20
beef, ground, 4 hamburgers	10	5
chicken, whole roast	8 – 10	10 – 15
chicken, portions	6 – 8	10
lamb, boned roast	7 – 8	20
lamb, boned and rolled roast	9	20
lamb, roast with bone	6 – 7	20
lamb, crown roast	9 – 10	20
lamb chops	2	10
liver, chicken	5	5
liver, lamb	7	5
pork, boned rolled roast	8 – 10	15
pork, roast with bone	8 – 9	15
poussin, pigeon, pheasant, quail	5 – 7	5
sausages, 4	4	—
turkey, whole roast	11	10 – 15
turkey, portions	15	10

FROZEN MEAT DEFROSTING GUIDE

meat	minutes on low per 500 g/1 lb	standing minutes
beef, boned roasts	8 – 10	30
beef, roasts on bone	8 – 10	30
beef, minced	8 – 10	2
beef steak, cubed	6 – 8	5
hamburgers, 2	2	2
hamburgers, 4	4	2
chicken, whole	6 – 8	30
chicken portions	5	30
duck and duckling	5 – 7	30
kidney, lamb	6 – 9	5
lamb, boned roasts	5 – 6	30 – 45
lamb, with bone	8 – 10	30 – 45
lamb chops	8 – 10	15
liver, lamb	8 – 10	5
pork, boned roasts	7 – 8	30
pork roast with bone	7 – 8	45
poussin, pigeon, pheasant, quail	5 – 7	10
sausages, 4	5 – 6	5
turkey, whole	10 – 12	60
veal, boned rolled roast	5 – 6	30
veal, with bone	8 – 10	45
veal chops	8 – 10	30
veal, minced	8 – 10	5

FISH
Defrost and Cooking Guide

fish	weight	defrost minutes	standing minutes	cooking in minutes on high
bass	250 g/8 oz	5 – 6	15	5 – 6
barramundi	250 g/8 oz	3 – 4	5	4
bream	250 g/8 oz	—	15	10 – 12
cod fillets	250 g/8 oz	4 – 5	5	4 – 6
cod, whole Murray	1 kg/2 lb	13 – 15	5	7 – 10
crab claws	125 g/4 oz	5	5	2 – 3
crabmeat	125 g/4 oz	2	10	3 – 4 (medium – high)
flathead	250 g/8 oz	3 – 4	5	4
flounder fillets	250 g/8 oz	4 – 5	5	4
haddock fillets	125 g/4 oz	4 – 5	5	5 – 7
hake	125 g/4 oz	4 – 5	5	4 – 6
John Dory	250 g/8 oz	3 – 4	5	4
mackerel	250 g/8 oz	6 – 8	8 – 10	4 – 5
mullet	250 g/8 oz	6 – 8	8 – 10	4 – 6
mussels	250 g/8 oz	5	5	4 – 5 (medium high)
oysters	250 g/8 oz	5	5	4 – 5 (medium high)
prawns, raw King	250 g/8 oz	5	5	4 – 6
salmon	250 g/8 oz	5	5	4 – 5
scallops	250 g/8 oz	5	5	5 – 7
schnapper	250 g/8 oz	6 – 8	8 – 10	5 – 7
shrimp	250 g/8 oz	5	5	2 – 3 (medium high)
sole	250 g/8 oz	5 – 6	8 – 10	4
trout	250 g/8 oz	6 – 8	8 – 10	7
tuna steaks	250 g/8 oz	10	15	4 – 5 (medium high)
yellowtail	250 g/8 oz	6 – 8	8 – 10	7
whiting	250 g/8 oz	3 – 4	5	4

PASTA AND GRAINS COOKING GUIDE PER 250 G/8 OZ

food	boiling salted water to add	cooking in minutes on high	standing minutes
long grain rice	770 ml/1¼ pt	14	5
short grain rice	770 ml/1¼ pt	14	5
brown rice	940 ml/1½ pt	30	5
oatmeal	770 ml/1¼ pt	6 – 7	4
egg noodles & tagliatelle	1 litre/1¾ pt with 2 tsp oil	6 – 8	2 – 3
spaghetti	1 litre/1¾ pt with 2 tsp oil	12	5 – 10
pasta shells & shapes	1 litre/1¾ pt with 2 tsp oil	12 – 14	5 – 10
macaroni	1 litre/1¾ pt with 2 tsp oil	12 – 15	2 – 3
lasagne	1 litre/1¾ pt with 2 tsp oil	9	2

CAKES, BREAD AND DESSERTS DEFROSTING GUIDE

product	quantity	minutes on low	standing minutes
bread, whole loaf	1 large	6 – 8	5 – 15
bread, whole loaf	1 small	4 – 6	10
bread, sliced loaf	1 large	6 – 8	10
bread, sliced loaf	1 small	4 – 6	5
bread slice	30 g/1 oz	10 – 15 secs	1 – 2
bread rolls, crumpets,	2	15 – 20 secs	1 – 2
scones, etc	4	25 – 35 secs	1 – 2
cakes, butter	375 g/12 oz	45 – 60 secs	10
cakes, small	2	30 secs	5
cupcakes	4	1 – 1¼	5
cakes, sponge	185 g/6 oz	45 secs	10
cheesecake	23 cm/9 in	3 – 4	20
dough, pizza and bread	500 g/1 lb	4	10
dough, shortcrust and puff	500 g/8 oz	4	20
dough, shortcrust and puff	440 g/14 oz	6	20
mousse, small	1	30 secs	15
pie, fruit	780 g/26 oz	5	10
trifle	1	1	15

TIME AND SETTINGS FOR PASTA AND GRAINS

Although there are no real time savings in cooking rice and pasta in the microwave, it may be a more foolproof way of cooking as there is no risk of sticking to the pan. Standing is usually necessary to complete cooking.

Cooking times will vary according to the type of pasta. Fresh pasta needs microwaving for only 1 minute. It requires no standing time, but should just be drained and served immediately. Times for dried pasta and rice are given below.